WE'RE DEAD, COME ON IN

WE'RE DEAD, COME ON IN

By Bruce Davis

PELICAN PUBLISHING COMPANY
GRETNA 2005

To my father, the Reverend Richard Davis

*The word "Pelican" and the depiction of a pelican are trademarks
of Pelican Publishing Company, Inc., and are registered in the
U.S. Patent and Trademark Office.*

Library of Congress Cataloging-in-Publication Data

Davis, Bruce, 1950 Nov. 16-
We're dead, come on in / by Bruce Davis.
p. cm.
Includes bibliographical references.
ISBN-13—978-1-58980-326-8 (alk. paper)
  1. Law enforcement—Missouri—Case studies. 2. Law enforcement—
Missouri—History—20th century. I. Title.
HV8145.M8D38 2005
364.152'3'0977878—dc22
2005004477

Printed in the United States of America
Published by Pelican Publishing Company, Inc.
1000 Burmaster Street, Gretna, Louisiana 70053

Contents

Preface

Growing up, I knew the names of the famous gangsters who had captured the public imagination in the generation before I was born—"Pretty Boy" Floyd, "Baby Face" Nelson, John Dillinger, Bonnie and Clyde, the Barker Gang, et. al. I would not learn of Harry Young until I was almost fifty years old—and then, only because I stumbled onto a marker outside the Springfield, Missouri, police station and saw the names of all the officers who had died on the same date. I first thought the chiseler must have made a mistake—this can't be right—I would have surely heard of such a catastrophe—but it was and I hadn't.

What came to fascinate me most about massacre of January 2, 1932, is the intersection of place and crime. The infamous killers of the Depression-era were migratory creatures, murder on wheels. And while fast cars certainly play a big part in this story, the localized nature of this crime—Ozarks boys trapped at home—offers a unique opportunity to look at the interplay of culture and criminal.

Furthermore, what has previously been written on the subject (and that's not much) has been so focused on the Young family that the officers themselves are offered as little more than targets in a shooting gallery. One of the images that has driven this telling is that of Sheriff Marcell Hendrix starting the day with a dawn raid on bootleggers, pouring the confiscated liquor onto the street; the day ending with his blood poured out on the linoleum floor of a neighbor's farm house.

What clinched it for me was trying to drive the route Harry and his brother Jennings would have taken the night of January 2, 1932, leaving Springfield about the time they would have, driving through the night. Even on vastly superior roads, in a vastly superior vehicle, I finally got tired enough that I pulled over into a motel in southern Oklahoma. The point had been made, the story 3-D in my head, insisting that I try to tell it.

What follows is a wild ride. Thanks for making it with me.

A lot of folks helped get this book to the publisher. Many thanks to the Local History and Genealogy staff at the Springfield-Greene County Library, including Sharol Neely, Michael Glenn, and, most particularly, John Rutherford. Frances Goodknight, of Frederick, Oklahoma, has been a huge help, as has been Sherry Adams of Houston, Texas. My initial entrée into the story was Owen Brown's son, Mick; Mick's daughter, Linda Carpenter, has been of invaluable assistance in the production of this manuscript. On the "nuts and bolts" side, I also want to thank Misty Brown, Peggy Thomas, Melissa Dodd, and Warren Harris. Officer Kirk Manlove of the Springfield Police Department opened important doors, including one to Gail DeGeorge at the "Calaboose." Other encouragers of particular note have been Jim Simpson, Mary Frances Davis, Kathleen O'Dell, and my literary cousin, Stephen Davis. But the indispensable person—in this and all that I do—is my sweetie, the Reverend Nancy Eunice Groseclose Davis.

BRUCE DAVIS

The Players

The Posse

Marcell Hendrix—sheriff, son of Daniel and Rosella, husband of Maude, father of Glenn, Merle, and Maxine. Killed.

Wiley Mashburn—deputy sheriff, husband of Maude. Killed.

Tony Oliver—chief of detectives, husband of Maude. Killed.

Sidney Meadows—detective, husband of Lilly. Killed.

Charles Houser—patrolman, husband (?) of Augusta, brother of Fred. Killed.

Ollie Crosswhite—Unemployed, husband of Ethel, father of six, including cop-killer Keith. Killed.

Virgil Johnson—detective. Wounded.

Ben Bilyeu—officer/mayoral bagman. Wounded.

Frank Pike—detective, son of G. C. Pike. Wounded.

Owen Brown—Detective. Escaped without injury.

Ralph E. Wegman—Civilian. Just along for the ride.

The Youngs

Archibald Alexander and wife Elender/Eleanor—the first of the Youngs to settle in the Ozarks. Begat John, A. A. II, et. al, and, finally, James Monroe Young.

James Monroe Young and wife Mary Ellen—begat James David (J.D.) Young.

J. D. Young—married Willie Florence Haguewood. Begat Loretta, Mary Ellen, Jarrett, Oscar, Paul, Jennings, Holly Gladys, Florence Willie, Harry, Lorena, and Vinita. On January 2, 1932, they were living in Wichita, Kansas (Loretta/"Rettie"); Frederick, Oklahoma (Mary Ellen and Holly Gladys); Stuttgart, Arkansas (Jarrett); Houston, Texas (Paul and Florence—see "Texans"); Greene County, Missouri (Oscar and Vinita, the latter with her mother on the family farm north

9

of Brookline); and without discernable permanent address (Jennings, Harry and Lorena).

Other Young Family Members

Albert Conley—unemployed, married to Lorena.

Natalie Conley—Lorena and Albert's daughter.

Ettie Smith—Jennings Young's mother-in-law.

Mabel Conn Young—wife of Oscar.

Frances Lee O'Dell—Harry's first wife.

Judd Haguewood—brother of Willie Florence Young, uncle to Harry, Jennings and the brood.

Florence Calvert Young (?)—Harry's second wife. See "Texans."

Rescuers

Sam and Otto Herrick—brothers, auto merchants, among the very first at the scene.

Lon Scott—journalist who heard the voice, "uhmmm."

Lee Jones—officer/barber; went with Lon Scott through the cornfield.

Frank Rhodes—reporter who ventured up the dark farm lane.

Cecil McBride—officer who shot at *somebody* and maybe even hit Harry Young.

Lewis Canady—ambulance driver.

Scott Curtis—constable who mass-deputized the mob.

Springfield City Officials

Thomas H. Gideon—mayor, son of Thomas J., nephew of James J, and grandson of William C., (the latter "bushwhacked" in 1863). Convicted in 1930 of violating Federal prohibition law, but still in office on January 2, 1932.

G. C. Pike—chief of police, father of Frank. Sentenced to Leavenworth Federal Penitentiary in 1930.

Henry Waddle—chief of police, son of Ed. Filled the vacancy left by G. C. Pike.

Hansford L. Teaff—deputy police chief; the first to be rolled by the Feds.

Greene County Officials

Dan Nee—prosecuting attorney. Veteran of the Keet kidnapping case and the Great War.

James Hornbostel—assistant prosecuting attorney.

Murray Stone—coroner.

R. E. Hodge—deputy sheriff who was elsewhere in the county and missed the raid at the Young farm. Although the newspapers referred to him as Deputy R. E. Hodge, in the 1930 census he is Earnest R. Hodge.

Frank Willey—jailer, kind with children, tough on wrongdoers.

Maude Hendrix—succeeded her husband in office of sheriff.

Citizens of Greene County

Edson K. Bisby—editor of the *Springfield Daily News & Leader.*

Beth Campbell—reporter whose coverage of the Young women was up close and personal.

Lewis Milton Hale—pastor of First Baptist in Springfield.

Lillard Hendrix—brother of the sheriff and prominent farmer in his own right.

Arch McGregor—business leader. Organizer of the widows and orphans fund.

E. E. E. McJimsey—newspaperman, defeated by Gideon in the mayoral election of 1928.

Clyde Medley—auto dealer whose tip to the police put wheels in motion.

Harry Rogers—another auto dealer. Was missing a Ford Coupe.

W. L. Starne—undertaker, a deeply troubled man.

Other Law Enforcement Officials

Francis "Ted" DeArmond—officer, Springfield Police Department. Killed by Dob Adams, June 18, 1928.

Carl Gailliher—chief of police, Bowling Green, Ohio. Thought it likely "Pretty Boy" Floyd was among the killers at the Young farm.

Mark Noe—constable, Republic, Missouri. Killed by Harry Young, June 2, 1929.

W. K. Webb—among the heroes of the Dob Adams' fiasco, fired from the Springfield PD in 1929 for opposing Mayor Gideon in the recall election.

Other Missourians of Note

Roscoe Patterson—Senator, who once served as defense attorney for Jennings and Oscar Young.

Tom Pendergast—Kansas City, archetype of machine "boss."

Albert Reeves—Federal Judge.

Harry Truman—Senator, who was no fan of Judge Albert Reeves.

Criminal Types (in order of infamy)

Charles Floyd—"Pretty Boy."

Fred Barker—Who killed Sheriff Kelly in West Plains and was identified by Ben Bilyeu as among the shooters at the Young farm.

Alvin Karpis—Barker's running mate and accomplice in the murder of Sheriff Kelly.

Jake Fleagle—"The Wolf Of The West."

The 1/27/31 Jailbreak Sextet—Tommie Vaughn, Sam Bass, Howard Walker, William Michaels, and the "Jackson Jellies," Tex Hayes and Bert Oglesby.

Dobb Adams—Husband of Meada (herself no picnic), apprehended by Tony Oliver after killing three, including two women and Officer Ted DeArmond.

Johnny Owen—Preacher's kid, who pulled the trigger that got Keith Crosswhite a life-sentence.

Roscoe Tuter—Harry's first partner in crime, who netted $6.41 for his efforts.

Oval LaFollette—Harry Young's companion in the carousel that led to the murder of Mark Noe.

Jesse Moore—Known to run with the Young Brothers and number one suspect in aiding their escape.

Texans

H. H. Carroll—farmer who offered to pull a Model A out of his field with mules.

Mrs. A.E. Gaddy—Telephone operator, Streetman, Texas.

A.E. Gaddy Jr.—Who sent a telegram to Springfield.

E.C. Hogan—Good Samaritan, who picked up two wrecked men.

Isaac Levy—Less enthusiastic Samaritan, who feared he might get kidnapped for his efforts.

Florence Willie Young Mackey—Sister of the killers, a solid churchgoing woman.

Florence Calvert Young (or was it Walker?)—Harry's "million dollar baby."

Lily Calvert Shaw—Harry's sister-in-law.

J. L. Tomlinson—Rented his front room to a man named "Wallace."

A. P. Singleton—Housepainter, in the wrong place at the wrong time.

Percy Heard—Chief, Houston Police Department.

Claude Beverly—Detective Lieutenant, Houston P.D.

Harry McCormick—Reporter, not just on the scene, but *in* the scene.
Paul Young—Older brother of the killers; had an alibi.

Oklahomans
Gordon B. Kinder—Druggist, who was open late.

Important Dates
August 10, 1861—The Battle of Wilson's Creek.

May 10, 1889—Hanging of "Baldknobbers" Dave Walker, Billy Walker and John Mathews outside the Christian County Courthouse in Ozark.

July 10, 1865—James Butler "Wild Bill" Hickok shoots and kills Dave Tutt in downtown Springfield.

April 14, 1906—Fred Coker, Horace Duncan and Will Allen "hanged and roasted" on the Springfield public square.

May 30, 1917—Kidnapping of "Baby" Lloyd Keet.

June 18, 1928—Dob Adams' triple-murder spree.

October 14, 1930—Jake Fleagle, the "Wolf of the West," apprehended in Branson shootout.

December 19, 1932—Fred Barker and Alvin Karpis murder Sheriff C. Roy Kelly in West Plains.

Place Names
Don't confuse Vinita, Oklahoma, and Vinita Young.

Ozark is a town in the Ozarks, the county seat of Christian County.

Part I

"They went to their deaths, their faces to the front, guns in their hands. In all the annals of preservation of the peace there is no story that runs more gallantly than this—the knocking upon the door of a house where they knew death might await them, their carrying on the battle till every man but one was dead or wounded."
—*The Springfield Leader,* January 4, 1932

CHAPTER ONE

Horror Show

"Blazing guns bellowed a savage hymn of hate as manhunters ringed a killer's lair, bent on avenging a comrades's murder.

"But the law, battling to the death, could not stand against the murderous fire.

"Here is a gripping eye-witness account of the sensational affray, climaxed by an unforgettable coup which outrivals fiction."

—"I Survived Missouri's Posse Massacre" by Detective Frank Pike
Startling Detective Adventures Magazine

> The sheriff thought the Youngs had probably escaped. Tony Oliver and Ollie Crosswhite were more cautious.
>
> "Go easy," Crosswhite advised, "This is a bad gang. They will shoot it out, if they are in there."
>
> The sheriff chuckled. Like most of the men of the Ozark hills, he had no idea of fear.
>
> "Then they're going to have some shooting to do," he said. "Toss some gas bombs in those top windows. That should bring them out."
>
> The bombs were tossed. We waited. No results.
>
> "Let's go in boys," the sheriff said."[1]

For the price of a quarter, Ma Young would show you who fell where. Sheriff Hendrix's body was found in her kitchen. Ollie Crosswhite was behind the storm cellar. Tony Oliver managed to drag himself over to the fence line before he died. Sid Meadows and Charlie Houser were in the front yard, both with holes in their foreheads. When relief finally arrived, Wiley Mashburn was sitting up outside the house, his face shot off, but still alive—though not for long.

Two others, Virgil Johnson and Ben Bilyeu, made it to one of the cars parked in the front yard; both were wounded, but ambulatory.

Johnson scrambled behind the wheel, hell bent on getting out of the killing yard. Virgil threw the car in reverse gear, roaring backwards down the dirt lane to the east-west farm road, frantically working the gearshift into drive, pressing the accelerator to the floorboard in the direction of Springfield and reinforcements.

That left two, Frank Pike and Owen Brown, cowering behind soft maple trees, both out of ammunition. They heard a voice from the house say, "Throw down your guns and come in here. We are going to kill you if you don't." Pike and Brown threw down their guns, alright—but lit out in the opposite direction, zigzagging and dodging bullets until reaching the relative safety of Haseltine Road. There they paced anxiously, waiting for help that seemed an eternity in arriving.

Virgil Johnson, "the lone messenger on whose successful mission rested the lives of his companions," had run into problems of his own. Johnson was said to be a very intense fellow, easily startled. He had braved death just getting to the car in the first place—birdshot hitting him in the ankle, windshield glass exploding around him. Unbeknownst to Virgil, Ben Bilyeu had taken refuge behind the driver's seat on the floor. Johnson was having quite enough challenge holding himself together as it was. With some distance between them and the farm, Bilyeu rose up and said, "Boy, we sure had a close call back there, didn't we?"—whereupon Virgil ran the car off the road. That's one version.[2]

When reinforcements finally did come dribbling down Haseltine Road from Springfield, they found Pike and Brown on foot. Frank and Owen were quite sure the others were all dead. The farmhouse was occupied by an army of men, and anyone approaching was sure to be killed, too, which served as disincentive to approaching the farmhouse.

In town that night, *Frankenstein* was opening at the fabulous Fox-Gillioz theatre, Boris Karloff starring in the role of the monster. While Karloff didn't have many lines, it was a talking-picture, still quite the novelty. As reported in the *Springfield Press,* "Springfield apparently likes its evening's gory for after the excitement of the slaying Saturday night, long lines formed at the box office and the audience simply lapped it up."[3]

But nothing on the screen at the Fox-Gillioz could compare to the real life horror six miles east of Springfield, described by "Edward Eddy"[4] in Springfield's *Sunday News & Leader:*

Deep crimson seams bordered the western horizon of the fading gray sky. Knots of silent men clotted the lane leading through the plowed fields to the house and barn that had been the home of Mother Young and her beastly brood. No man stood nearer than a hundred yards of the buildings—the house ahead of them to their left, looming dimly in the twilight, the darker bulk of the barn ahead to their right.

None knew what had happened—but the air was thick with a sense of nameless terror. None knew what lay ahead in the shadows of the lightless buildings. Each man hesitated to venture into those shadows. There was no leader—none to shout a rallying cry for a rush into the graveyard of unburied dead.

And this was before anyone saw what was left of Mashburn.

The first rescuers at the farmhouse must have resembled the villagers in the Karloff film, huddled together at the mouth of the lane leading up to the gloaming castle. It was an ad hoc group of officers and citizens. One of the first to arrive was an auto dealer. There was, in fact, no leader. Given that four of his men were among the rumored dead, Springfield Chief of Police Ed Waddle might have been expected to lead the charge, but the chief chose to remain in town at his desk. With "none to shout a rallying cry," even as their numbers increased into the dozens and then hundreds, the villagers could not bring themselves to go up that pathway where the monster might be waiting.

And in all fairness, if the creature had slain men such as Ollie Crosswhite, Tony Oliver, and Marcell Hendrix, what chance did these others have? Tony Oliver had once bested crazed-killer Dob Adams. Mashburn was a veteran fighter, who that very morning had defeated another set of gangsters. It was said that Crosswhite would "fight a buzz saw."[5] If the buzz saw up at the farmhouse had destroyed Ollie and the rest of the best of local law enforcement, this leaderless collection of merchants, reporters, non-ranking officers, and farmers could hardly be blamed for keeping its distance.

Among the exceptions was Lon Scott, who had been at police headquarters when Johnson and Bilyeu came roaring into town, "exclaiming that they wanted more ammunition and more help because several of the officers had been shot and some killed." Officer Waite Phillips ran for his Chevrolet Sedan, Scott jumped in beside him. Other passengers included Detective Grover White, auto dealer Sam Herrick Jr. and Roscoe Gaylor. "We were nearly killed on the way out," reported Scott, "when [Phillips] vaulted a railroad track."

Lon Scott was well known in the Ozarks. Following his service in the Great War and assorted newspaper gigs, Scott was hired as public relations director for the fledging National U.S. 66 Highway Association. The challenge was formidable: Route 66 went online with "warnings about deep sand traps, soft shoulders, washouts, deep ruts."

In an "era of flag-pole sitting, barnstorming and marathon dances," it was Lon Scott who visioned the "Bunion Derby"—a transcontinental foot-race from one end of his highway, Los Angeles, to the other, Chicago, then on to New York—a total distance of 3,422 miles. Two hundred seventy-five entrants paid $100 a piece to compete for a $25,000 first prize. The race started on March 4, 1928, ending eighty-seven days and 573 hours of actual running time later.[6]

On the evening of January 2, 1932, the creator of the Bunion Derby made a much shorter but vastly more harrowing walk, from the huddled cluster of men at the farm lane to a crest some yards west and north, in the direction of the white, wood-frame fortress. From his war experience, Scott recognized a good place to reconnoiter. Having reached the swell, the journalist/public-relations man dared to stand and take a look.

In front of him was the two-story, wood-frame farmhouse, the length of which ran north to south, the front door facing east. A car was parked at the fence line separating the front yard from the vehicle turn-around area, the auto's unlit headlights staring at the front porch. To the right and some yards north of the house was a barn, much larger than the house itself. The barn door was open and Scott could see another car inside. A few yards south and east of the barn, directly across from the farmhouse, was a smaller outbuilding that would be variously described as a tool shed or machine shed. To Scott's left was "a long low building"—the poultry house.

From this position, Scott was viewing the rear of the farmhouse. The back door was wide open. "Between the house and myself," he wrote, "I could make out plainly a wood pile consisting of poles and small logs."

Scott went back to the mouth of the farm lane. The number of would-be rescuers continued to increase, ambulances were arriving from Springfield, but no one was showing any inclination to advance in the direction of the lair. Lon Scott sought out Officer Lee Jones. "I said, 'Lee, how much guts have you got?' He replied, 'By G— as much as you have.'"

Earlier that afternoon, Lee Jones had assumed he would be in on the raid with Oliver, Hendrix, and the others, but the former barber was assigned instead to the task of cutting hospitalized Officer Oscar Lowe's hair. Perhaps the deployment was Waddle's idea, or maybe Oliver's. Either way, Jones was more than a little miffed, begging Tony Oliver to wait for him. Oliver did not wait. While his friends were dying, Lee Jones had been absent with leave; here was a chance to make amends.[7]

So began the tribulations of Lon Scott and Lee Jones. The two men made a second foray to the crest. Seeing no movement and encouraged that no one was shooting at them, Scott and Jones approached "slowly through the corn stalks." This being January, it is doubtful that the "stalks" provided much if any concealment. Out of the stalks, into the wide open, Scott made a dash toward the pole pile, but tripped on his own overcoat, falling on his face in the open field.

That's when he heard the "Uhmmn!"—as if someone was clearing his throat. "Uhmmn!" Like the monster in the movie. By his own estimate, Scott lay there fifteen or twenty minutes, "Every few seconds it seemed like I could hear this 'Uhmmn!'"

Scott's first person narrative was published in the *Springfield Press:*

> Finally I decided to try and locate Lee Jones or to find out who else was anywhere near but I did not dare stand up so I let out a good old fashioned war whoop.
>
> Lee Jones hollered, "Is that you Scott?"
>
> I hollered, "Where are you Lee?"
>
> He yelled back, "In the cornfield, where are you?"
>
> I answered, "Close to the pole pile."
>
> He yelled, "Can you hear or see anybody?"
>
> I said, "A man has me cornered at the pole pile."
>
> He said, "What will we do?"
>
> I said, "Let's run for the chicken house."
>
> He said, "Is there anybody in it?"
>
> I said, "No."
>
> He said, "All right, let's go," and in a crouched position I made for it as fast as I could go.
>
> When I reached [the poultry house], he was already behind it and was looking through the cracks inside. We stood erect and Lee said, "Lon, what are we going to do?"
>
> I said, "We have to get to that pole pile before we can see anything. There is a man there but he hasn't got anything probably but a shotgun."
>
> We peeked around the end of the chicken house but could see nothing move anywhere between the wood pile and the house. Lee said, "Do you think it's the thing to do to make a cover back of the poles?"

I said, "I'm willing to try it if you are."

He said, "By G— I'll go, how will we make the run?"

I replied, "I know more about the lay than you do. I'll go first and you follow. Let me have your shotgun."

He said, "All right, but there is only one shell and I haven't any more ammunition. Give me your rifle." He took the rifle and examined it and said, "How does this work?"

I said, "Just like any other bolt-action high-powered rifle."

He moved the bolt back to load and then to cock, held the rifle up and pulled the trigger to see that it worked. Nothing happened. He said, "That is a d—- fine gun to have in a place like this."

I said, "Let me have it," and I tried to shoot it off but the trigger was broken, so we were on the spot with one shotgun shell between us.

Lee said, "Now what are we going to do?"

I said, "I don't know, we might as well have a crate of tomatoes," and he said, "Yes, or two ice cream cones."

We decided to make the dash for the pole pile with me in the lead carrying the shotgun with the trigger cocked. When we got ready we both lit out and instead of following me, Jones actually passed me on the way and slid behind the poles ahead. We got our breath on our hands and knees and soon heard this "Uhmmn." We awaited and heard it again, then quietly we crawled to the east end of the pole pile and through some openings we could see a man sitting outside the kitchen door swaying forward and back.

Lee said, "Lon, that is one of our boys."[8]

It was, in fact, Wiley Mashburn, face blown off, passing his left hand in front of sightless eyes. War veteran Scott described it as "the most ghastly wound that has ever been my experience to look upon":

It seemed like someone had taken a long heavy knife and cut Mr. Mashburn's head just below the brow deep in his skin because his eyes and his nose were hanging down over his mouth on his chin and he was running the fingers of his left hand through the open wound.

Having expended all this time and tension stalking a dying officer, Scott and Jones were no longer restrained in shouting for help. The first response from down the lane was, "Go to hell." But there was movement now. "Men leaped upon the [ambulance] running boards, their shotguns dangling dangerously. The driver meshed his gears. Then men on the sides of the car bent their heads to the charge. 'Come on now, all you home town heroes. Let's get in there.'"[9]

As Scott and Jones made their cautious approach through the fields, reporter Frank Rhodes dared the lane itself, in the company of Springfield contractor Ralph Langdon and dairyman E.L. "Bun" Barrett. Langdon carried a borrowed rifle; Bun was armed only with a flashlight. Rhodes would tell his readers that "We stopped a little way from the house. It was dark by now and the moon was coming up. I walked about 15 feet and stumbled over something. It was the body of Oliver."

Fifteen or twenty feet away, "feeble moonlight" revealed Charlie Houser. When Bun Barrett shone the flashlight on Houser, Sid Meadows was illuminated beside him.

A figure walked toward them out of the darkness. Frank Rhodes later said, "The flashlight was put upon him, and he was commanded to put up his hands. It was Lon Scott."[10]

More movement, someone was coming around the corner from the back of the house. Guns pointed in that direction. "Don't shoot!" Young J.T. Hulsman had located Ollie Crosswhite in the brush behind the cellar, the body "doubled up with the arms clasped around the knees." Which left only Hendrix unaccounted for. Could he somehow still be alive?

Lon Scott had seen the back door "wide open," but that was deceptive. This door opened on to a utility room. Between the utility room and kitchen was another door, barricaded shut. By now, the hometown heroes were on the scene in full force. The front door was finally breached, a gas bomb thrown inside. Some were saying they ought to just go ahead and torch the place, but cooler heads prevailed. Hendrix might be inside, and the flames would make silhouette targets of them all.

The gas cleared. "Men went into the littered house. Men's feet slipped in blood. Men's feet stumbled over a crumpled form." The form was Sheriff Marcel Hendrix, whose day had started with a daring raid on bootleggers in nearby Ash Grove, standing in the middle of main street, pouring prohibited beverage onto the pavement, and ended with his own life's blood poured out onto a neighbor's linoleum floor. "Overhead a million million stars gleamed coldly, clearly in the black dome of the shattered night."[11] It had been the single most disastrous episode in the history of American law enforcement and would remain so until September 11, 2001.

But where were the doers of this monstrous deed?

Mary Shelley described the Modern Prometheus of Dr. Frankenstein's creation: "Oh! No mortal could support the horror of that countenance. A mummy again endued with animation could not be so hideous as the wretch. I had gazed on him while unfinished: he was ugly then; but when those muscles and joints were rendered capable of motion, it became a thing such as even Dante could not have conceived."[12]

In this story, the monster is a 5'6" runt of a man, prematurely bald.

The wretch had a brother—four of them, actually—each his elder. One participated in the depravity of this Saturday afternoon—he *more* than participated. The older brother was certainly the more capable of the two; a hardened criminal when the fiend was still being created. But it's as if this family had been an unwitting genetic and behavioral laboratory, producing a graduated series of male progeny, each more dangerous than the one before. It was only with the fifth and final of the line that a taste for human blood was acquired.

What was said in the *Springfield Press* review of the Karloff film is equally appropriate to this story: "If you want hysterics, here it is."

CHAPTER TWO

Stolen Cars

"Automobiles, like knives, are useful and necessary tools of society, but they must not be used either criminally or recklessly. . . . The flood of motor traffic has taken us all unawares. Eighteen million automobiles on our streets and highways today—doubled in the past five years—multiplied by seven in the last ten years—there is nothing like it in history."

—*1932 Souvenir Review of the Department of Police, City of Springfield, Missouri.*

Wednesday night, only twenty-five hours remaining in the hard year of 1931, Jennings and Harry Young drove up the farm lane, the last fraction of an eight-hundred-mile drive from Houston, Texas. The brothers were in separate cars, both stolen. A half-hour later, around 11:30 P.M., yet another car from Houston pulled in, this one bearing their sister, Lorena; her husband, Albert Conley; and their daughter, Natalie.

Albert Conley would later swear it was sheer coincidence. He had lost his job driving an ambulance in Texas and was hoping to find employment in Springfield. But if Albert had known Lorena's brothers were going to be here, he would have gone to Waco to see his mother instead, "and wait a few days until they clear out."

Not that Albert had any information about his brothers-in-law. In fact, he'd only met Harry twice. The first time was two years ago, when Lorena was hospitalized after an operation. Much more recently—the day before the Conleys left Texas, in fact—Albert had seen Harry, Jennings, and their brother Paul in Houston, though the brothers hadn't said anything about coming to Springfield. While aware that Harry had been in trouble with the law, Albert was ignorant as to any of the particulars. "I figured I'd be better off if I didn't know too much about other people's business."[1]

The next morning, having rested and shaved, Jennings and Harry drove their respective stolen automobiles twenty-five miles west to Aurora, Missouri. At the lot of Baldwin Motors, they proposed to trade a 1931 Ford Sedan and cash for a new Model A. C. H. Baldwin didn't like the look of their "references."[2] The brothers drove back to the farm, still needing to unload a hot car.

That afternoon, Thursday, the last day of 1931, Lorena Young Conley drove the same 1931 Ford to Medley Motor Company, 452 E. McDaniel in Springfield. Jennings and sister Vinita trailed in another car, parking a block away, so Lorena would have a ride home, assuming the deal went through.

Clyde Medley had been advertising a year-end sale. The merchandise included:

> 1930 Ford Tudor A-1 condition, a real bargain for only $285.[3]
> 1930 Chevrolet Roadster, only slightly used; see it today; only $250.
> 1929 Whippet Coach, looks like new; perfect. Only $185.

If these were beyond a buyer's means, $75 would put you in a 1924 Flint Roadster.[4]

The 1931 Ford must have been in A-1 condition, as Medley offered Lorena $250—but there was a small problem. The Ford was titled in the name of J.P. Young of Brookline. If Lorena was going to sell this vehicle, her name must be on the title. It was a simple matter of signatures: Lorena should have J.P. Young sign the title over to her, then bring the car back to Medley's, and Clyde would give her the cash.

In fact, there was nothing simple about it. Area auto dealers were under long-standing police alert to report any dealings with the Youngs of Brookline.[5] Nevertheless, Clyde Medley did *not* pick up the phone and call the cops on Thursday. The Youngs were bad news and perhaps Medley was hoping the sister wouldn't come back.

But come back Lorena did, the next day, paperwork in order. Medley said he was sorry, but he didn't have that much cash on hand at the moment. Furthermore, this being New Year's Day, the banks were closed, so the exchange would have to wait until tomorrow. Again, Lorena drove away. This time, Clyde Medley made the call.

For the widowed Mrs. James David Young, January 2, 1932, started as a family outing. Saturday was Willie Florence's shopping day. Mother Young came into Springfield with Lorena, Vinita, Natalie, and Albert in the Conley automobile, perhaps as early as ten o'clock.

The ladies spent what remained of the morning at Etta Smith's home on West Madison, just south of the public square. Etta was something akin to "family" herself. Her daughter, Bessie, had married Jennings, and while the marriage was reported to have gone bad, Etta and Willie Florence remained cordial.

There are conflicting reports as to when Albert Conley separated from the group. While there is general agreement he got his hair cut on Saturday, some put it before lunch, others after. As the gathering at Etta Smith's flat was an otherwise all-female assemblage, with housecleaning on the agenda,[6] perhaps Albert excused himself early on, then hung around the public square through the noon hour, having set a time to meet his lady-folk back at Etta's.

After lunch, Lorena, Vinita, Willie Florence, and little Natalie said goodbye to Mrs. Smith and climbed back into the Conley auto. Ma was dropped off at the public square to do her weekly trading; the girls would be back for her in a little while.

Her shopping finished, Willie Florence waited . . . and waited . . . Finally, the white-haired grandmother trudged back to Etta Smith's house, carrying her shopping bags, and that's where the police found her, around six o'clock.[7] She was in hysterics when they arrived. By six o'clock, practically everyone in Springfield knew something terrible was happening at the Young farmhouse.

It would be alleged that when Willie Florence got back to Etta Smith's, she cranked the call box, phoning the farm to alert Harry and Jennings: "They've arrested the girls. You'd better be prepared."[8] The *Houston Chronicle* reported Mother Young's vehement denial: "That's one thing they told on me that isn't so."[9] Springfield newspaperman J. R. Woodside later determined no calls were put through the Brookline exchange to the farmhouse that afternoon. If Willie Florence had made the call, others on the rural party-line would have known.[10]

Not that Willie Florence would have flinched from doing *anything* to protect her sons. But she'd been through one nervous breakdown already and, by her own admission, was always terribly anxious when Harry was around.[11] She loved her baby boy with all her heart, but he was, after all, wanted for murder. When Vinita and Lorena didn't show, her anxiety likely turned to dread. By the time she got back to Mrs. Smith's, perhaps the sixty-five-year-old white-haired woman was too traumatized to think clearly enough to make the call that would have warned her sons and set them in flight before the officers arrived.

This is not to suggest the brothers were necessarily taken by surprise.

Willie Florence would tell the papers, "You know, they really expected officers to come out to the house and get them for stealing cars."[12] Harry and Jennings, it was later reported, "were evidently prepared for a quick getaway. Three packed grips were found in an upstairs room."[13] But they were not quick enough.

As Saturday's timeline would be reconstructed, after dropping Willie Florence off at the public square to do her shopping, the sisters drove back out to the farm, a distance of about six miles. The ladies were at the farm only a short time, just long enough to say hello to their brother, Oscar, and his wife Mabel, who were seated at the dining room table, talking with Harry.[14] Lorena also mentions the presence of Oscar's children.[15] The girls didn't see Jennings; he and Oscar didn't get along, and Jennings had absented himself upstairs.

Lorena later explained she had neglected to bring the title to the 1931 Ford, necessitating the return trip,[16] but it seems more likely the real point was to hide the transaction from their mother. While details are fuzzy, it seems probable Lorena came back into town driving the 1931 Ford destined for sale to Clyde Medley, with Vinita and Natalie following in the Conley auto, so everyone could ride home in the same car they first arrived in that morning.

There are competing narratives as to events leading up to the January 2, 1932, raid on the Young farmhouse. All agree Lorena approached Clyde Medley on Thursday, December 31, setting an appointment for the following day, at which time the deal was to be sealed. The massacre's first historian, J. R. Woodside, believes Lorena failed to show on Friday, and that Sheriff Hendrix, who'd been in the loop all along, took this as yet another in a long line of dead-ends in the hunt for Harry Young.

In the Woodside account, based on reporting from the *Springfield Press,* Medley was surprised when the girls came in on Saturday; the auto dealer furtively called the police, who hustled officers Lee Jones and Virgil Johnson over for the capture.

According to the timeline posited in the January 10 *Springfield Sunday News & Leader*—a week and a day after the slaughter—the girls were indeed at Medley's on Friday. Told that Clyde didn't have the $250 and the banks were closed, Lorena and Vinita came back on Saturday, at which time officers Johnson and Jones were waiting for them. This would become the official version of the Springfield Police Department, as recorded in the department's *1932 Souvenir Review.*

The *Press/Woodside* chronology seems to have originated with

Lorena; the *Daily News* and *Leader* source appears to have been the police department itself. While the latter certainly sounds more authoritative, in 1932 the Springfield PD was not always the most reliable source of information.

It would be enormously helpful, of course, if there were any testimony from Clyde Medley, but he seems to have been determined to keep a low profile, quoted nowhere in the papers and absent at the subsequent inquest. Reports that several Springfield area car dealers had been in cahoots with the Young brothers only whet the appetite for Medley's story, though that is not to imply that reticence necessarily equates with complicity. Medley certainly had other potential reasons to keep his head down. After all, Paul Young was still out there.

This much is certain: Lorena and Vinita, along with little Natalie, were taken to police headquarters, around three o'clock Saturday afternoon.[17] The sisters had a lot to answer for. Chief of Detectives Tony Oliver served as lead interrogator.

Where are your brothers?

Don't know.

Where'd you get the car?

Brother Paul brought it up from Texas last week—but he turned right around and went back. It's stolen? Who would have guessed? Harry? Haven't seen him in the longest time. Hard telling where he might be. Not at the farm, that's for sure.

In one telling, when asked if their brothers were home, "the sisters bent their heads and had a whispered conversation. Vinita said, 'Go out there and you'll find out.' In this account, Oliver came out of his office grinning and said, "I know where Harry and Jennings Young are."[18]

Hendrix was called. The Young farmstead was on county turf; therefore, the sheriff should rightfully be in the lead. Given that Sheriff Hendrix had, in November of 1929, testified against a Springfield city police chief, contributing to the latter's conviction and subsequent incarceration at Leavenworth Federal Penitentiary, the current occupant of the office, Ed Waddle, was perhaps particularly cautious about infringing on Hendrix's jurisdiction.

The posse assembled at the police station, located at College and Market, a block west of the town square. In 1931, this section of College doubled as Highway 66 through Springfield. Two autos left the station shortly before 4 P.M. Sheriff Hendrix and Deputy Wiley Mashburn were in the lead car, with passengers Ollie Crosswhite and city officers Virgil Johnson and Sid Meadows. Charlie Houser drove the second vehicle, chauffeuring Tony Oliver and mayoral bagman, Ben Bilyeu. In one account, Oliver had wanted Officer Lester Scott to come along, and it was only because the latter was out on motorcycle patrol that Houser was included.[19]

Lee Jones, who along with Virgil Johnson had brought the sisters into the station from Medley Auto, suggested three more be included: himself and the sisters, the latter to be used as a negotiating tool. "Hell," said Oliver, "that would be sissy stuff."[20] Perhaps that's when the chief of detectives decided Jones was better suited to cutting hair than hunting desperadoes.

It gets dark fast this time of year. The sun would officially set at 5:03 P.M.[21] Temperatures had hovered all day just above freezing. As the officers drove out Highway 66, the tourist cabins and eating establishments would have been enveloped in deepening shades of gray.

Five miles west of Springfield, the little caravan crossed a set of railroad tracks, then turned left onto a paved road running north and south through sixteen thousand acres of Haseltine orchard. The orchard business was in decline, but the Haseltines still had their own stop on the Frisco Railroad: Haseltine Station. Side rails made for convenient loading from a stone storage shed situated immediately west of the paved road. The "station" also included apple-related housing and a small store.

Passing over the tracks at Haseltine Station, the officers drove due south, through the heart of the orchard, barren trees on either side of the road, broken by occasional clearings for apple mansions—great houses with names such as Hazelcrest and Ivy Palace.[22]

Where orchard ended and fields began, the two cars pulled off to the side of Haseltine Road. Climbing out, Hendrix and Oliver walked up a small crest to the right of the automobiles. A quarter mile or so to the west was the J.D. Young farmstead—though from this vantage point, the house itself would have been mostly obscured by the much larger barn in the foreground. At this juncture, the officers' primary concern seems to have been cutting off possible escape routes.

There was an old road leading through the orchard (more of a rut than a road, really), offering strategic possibilities raised back at police headquarters by Mayor T. H. Gideon, who regularly hunted this area. Now, Hendrix decided to split his force. Oliver, Houser, and Bilyeu took the unpaved road into the orchard, on a course east to west, stopping their car north of the farmhouse. They walked out of the orchard, across a pasture, toward rendezvous with Hendrix. The sheriff's group continued south along Haseltine Road, turning right at the first inter-section, driving west a quarter mile, where another right put them into the lane leading up to the targeted farmhouse.

It is unlikely that Marcell Hendrix was consciously aware of it, but his strategy mirrored that of Gen. Nathaniel Lyon, who on August 10, 1861, very near this place, initiated the first major battle of Civil War armies west of the Mississippi River.

The Confederates of Ben McCullough and Sterling Price were camped along Wilson's Creek, just a couple of rolling hills south and east of the hamlet of Little York, later to be reborn as Brookline. In the face of superior numbers, Lyon audaciously divided his army, sending Franz Sigel on a looping maneuver around the unsuspecting Confederates. Lyon would attack from the north, Sigel from the south, catching the enemy in the crossfire.[23]

The plan didn't work for Lyon, either. He was carried dead from the field, his army limping back to Springfield in defeat. Hard things had a history of happening in this region.

Chapter Three

Aux Arcs

"He waved his hand toward the glowing sky and the forest clad hills. 'This is good for me; it somehow seems to help me know how big God is. One could find peace here—surely, sir, one could find it here— peace and strength.'

"The mountaineer puffed hard at his pipe for a while, then said gruffly, 'Seems that way, Mister, to them that don't know. But many's the time I've wished to God I'd never seen these here Ozarks.'"
—Harold Bell Wright, *The Shepherd of the Hills*[1]

Before the coming of the European-Americans, the Ozarks were home to the Osage, described as a "tall and handsome people." They were not consulted when Napoleon Bonaparte sold their hills, along with the rest of "Louisiana," to Thomas Jefferson. Great White Father didn't see much value in this part of the purchase, using it as a dumping ground for displaced eastern tribes, most particularly the Delaware and Kickapoo. The tribes did not play well together. At the end of the third decade of what the Anglos counted as the nineteenth century, all the tribes—Osage, Kickapoo, and Delaware alike—were deported further west, opening the region to a new people of pale pigmentation.[2]

Southwest Missouri would be formally blessed with state governance on January 2, 1833, in the form of Greene County, which covered the whole of the region. The frontier village of Springfield was designated the "permanent seat of justice." Marcell Hendrix led his ill-fated raid on what was the county's ninety-ninth birthday.

Among the first Anglo settlers was Archibald Alexander Young, who came from Tennessee with his wife Elender[3] and their eight children: John W., Elizabeth, Sarah Ann, Holly, Archibald Alexander, Emily, Jerome, and James Monroe. James Monroe, the baby of the family, was born November 28, 1836. The Youngs settled in present-day Christian County, south of Springfield, along the Finley River.[4]

When Archibald died in 1843 at the age of forty-five, the eldest son, John, took the helm. The family prospered. In 1856, John Young was taxed on five parcels of land totaling four hundred acres, three horses, eleven cattle, and four slaves—the latter valued at $1,800.[5] Census records did not list slaves by name, only gender, age, and racial designation: B for Black, M for Mulatto.

By 1856, the second Archibald Alexander Young had started a family of his own. His household included an adopted Cherokee girl. According to family narrative, the child was found abandoned at the side of the James River,[6] raised by Archibald II and wife Mary, and given the name Ann. Ann is originally listed in census records as "I" for Indian, but when she married a black man named Al Young, Ann was recategorized "B" herself, and her children would be assigned the same racial designation.

A photo of Ann Young Young in old age shows a small, wizened woman in a huge dress, surrounded by five grown children.[7] Is it Faulknerian imagination or does one of Al and Ann Young's "B" sons resemble Paul and Jennings from the "W" side of the family?

The 1860 census of Christian County suggests that the Young family was in transition. John, who had been listed as head of the family since his father's death in 1843, is nowhere to be found. In 1860, Elender is head of the household and owner of two slaves: a black female, age forty, and a twenty-eight-year-old mulatto male. Listed with Elender are two sons, JW (Jerome), age twenty-six, and JM (James Monroe), twenty-two.

It is unclear what happened to John. A county history published in 1998 offers dates of birth and death for his parents and siblings, but can only tell us that John W. was born about 1815, with no record of his passing. It's as if, somewhere between the taxing of 1856 and the census of 1860, John Young just disappeared.

Southwest Missouri had been a particularly nasty place in the years leading up to Civil War. Pro-slavery guerillas raided into free-soil Kansas, then raced back across the border, taking refuge in the Ozark hills. Jayhawkers launched retaliatory strikes, with little (if any) discrimination as to whether an Ozarks farmer was actually a slaveholder or even so much as a sympathizer. Given the future fate of his great-nephews, it would not be unthinkable to suppose John W. Young rode to Kansas on a raid and never came back.

As slaveholding regions went, Southwest Missouri did not compare to plantation life in the Carolinas, or, for that matter, the Missouri River belt stretching from St. Louis to Kansas City. This was a rugged land of small farms, not conducive to large-scale human bondage. In 1860, no slave owner in Christian County possessed more than eleven human beings.

In his authoritative study, *Border Rebellion,* Elmo Ingenthron, long-time Taney County School superintendent, insists:

> When the Wilson's Creek engagement took place, the majority of the people in southwest Missouri and northwest Arkansas had not yet taken sides in the great national conflict. Slavery had not been an issue with them; and secession, a thing they had thought little about, seemed to be no good reason for war. Even though several of the men in the upper White River region had already committed themselves to one side or the other, relatively few of these saw action at Wilson's Creek.[8]

After the decisive Union victory at Pea Ridge[9] in February of 1862, the battle lines were moved into northern Arkansas, "but," says Ingenthron, "no one could say precisely where the front was. In reality it was an obscure area some two hundred miles wide embracing the whole Missouri-Arkansas state line. The border became a battle zone, boiling with hundreds of miniature engagements, skirmishes, ambuscades, incendiarisms, robberies and plain murders."[10]

Springfield Mayor Thomas H. Gideon's grandfather would be among the casualties. At the outbreak of Civil War, William Gideon was farming four hundred acres in Christian County. But Christian County had become an exceedingly dangerous place, particularly for a man of Unionist sympathy. William Gideon abandoned the farm, relocating his family to the relative safety of Springfield, where there was at least a semblance of law and order.

Federal troops had moved back into Springfield in early 1862. The small city served as general headquarters and supply base for the Army of the Frontier. The Union's 14th Missouri Cavalry Militia was stationed at the village of Ozark, which in 1859 had been designated "permanent seat of justice" for the newly formed Christian County, carved out of Greene and Taney counties by the State Legislature before the legislature itself was run out of Jefferson City.

Outside of town, away from the forts, the climate changed dramatically. Ingenthron quotes journalist/historian Edward Pollard:

> The remote geography of the county, the rough character of the people, the intensity and ferocity of the passions excited, and the reduction of military operations to a warfare essentially partisan and frontier, gave to the progress of the war in this quarter a wild aspect, and illustrated it with rare and thrilling scenes . . . the order of the day was open robbery, downright murder, and freedom to all crimes.[11]

Particularly notorious was Alf Bolin, who "with a coterie of followers almost as diabolical as himself . . . robbed, raped and murdered persons from Union families over a wide area between Ozark, Mo., and Crooked Creek, Ark."[12]

William Gideon may have been among Bolin's victims, or perhaps he fell prey to another band. What *is* known is that in December of 1863, Gideon, described as "a man of quiet and peaceful disposition . . . honorable in character,"[13] left the relative safety of Springfield to visit his aged father in Christian County. As a Union recruiting officer, Gideon would have made a prime target for any bushwhacker—and he was indeed whacked, at his father's place, on December 16, 1863.[14]

In that same chaotic year— April 8, to be exact, just weeks before Gettysburg and the Confederate surrender at Vicksburg[15]—James David Young came into the world. His father, James Monroe, had married a preacher's girl, Mary Ellen McCrosky. Mary Ellen's family, like James Monroe's, had come to the Missouri Ozarks from Tennessee. Significantly, Mary Ellen was back in Tennessee when the child was born.[16]

A woman didn't want to be birthing in the Ozark hills of 1863 if she could help it. Ingenthron and others insist the war had practically depopulated the region. Families of Union sympathy had long since fled north and east. St. Louis was the closest safe haven for Union sympathizers. Little Rock served as émigré center for persons of southern sympathy.[17] James Monroe Young may or may not have served under the rebel flag,[18] but it seems clear that his family evacuated Christian County for the duration of the war.

The cessation of formal hostilities did not equate to peace in the Ozarks. Lincoln's "better angels" must have been busy elsewhere. Ingenthron states the problem succinctly: "Each survivor, each returning refugee, hated someone."[19]

It is perhaps appropriate then that, three months after Lee's surrender, the myth of the gunfighter was born on Springfield's Public

Square. Former Union spy James Butler "Wild Bill" Hickok and ex-Confederate Davis "Dave" Tutt had come to cross purposes over a poker game and a watch, with a woman thrown into the mix.

"The sun was bright," writes Hickok biographer Richard O'Conner, "and the heat of midmorning was already oppressive." The two men squared off at a distance of seventy-five yards. It was unlikely either could hit the other at this distance, but Tutt drew first. Hickok, shooting left-handed, drew last.[20] The Hickok-Tutt duel would become a myth-template—operative word, "myth." Wild's Bill's own demise, from a shot in the back while playing poker in the Dakota Territory town of Deadwood, was far more representative of frontier gun violence than what happened in Springfield, Missouri, on July 10, 1865.

Among the spectators that bright, sunshiny day was the Greene County Sheriff. Hickok was charged with murder. It took the jury all of ten minutes to come back with a verdict that drew this forlorn response from *The Missouri Weekly Patriot*:

> The citizens of this city were shocked and terrified at the idea that a man could arm himself and take a position at a corner of the public square, in the centre of the city, and await the approach of his victim for an hour or two, and then willingly engage in a conflict with him which resulted in his instant death; and this, too, with the knowledge of several persons who seem to have posted themselves in safe places where they could see the tragedy enacted. But they failed to express the horror and disgust they felt, not from indifference, but from fear and timidity.[21]

If the courts were indeed paralyzed by "fear and timidity," then "horror and disgust" would be expressed in the form of vigilantism. In his exhaustive 1883 *History of Greene County,* R. I. Holcombe endeavored to explain: "Robberies and horse stealings were so common as to be every day occurrences, and even murders were not rare." As the law seemed impotent to deal with the crisis, some of the "best citizens" of the county banded together to form what was called the "Regulators" or "Honest Men's League."

The Honest Men began regulating in earnest in May of 1865. Their first target was Capt. Green B. Philips, a Federal officer who had given "valiant and valuable service at the defense of Springfield," but "incurred the suspicion and fell under the ban of the 'Regulators,' as a sympathizer with and an aider and abettor of crime and criminals."

Aiding and abetting was broadly defined; the very act of bailing an accused person out of jail was enough to draw the righteous wrath of the Regulators. Philips was caught unaware in his barnyard; when he tried to flee, he fell over a hog, and was shot and killed trying to get back up.[22]

Holcombe, along with others, lay much of the post-war bitterness at the feet of Missouri's Drake Constitution. As the price of suffrage, Missourians were required to "solemnly swear" they had always been "truly and loyally on the side of the United States, against all enemies therefore, foreign and domestic." Twenty years after the war, Holcombe would comment, "No wonder the ex-confederates and those who sympathized with them hated intensely the Drake constitution, and still retain vivid and bitter memories of the days when it was in force."[23]

There is reason to believe the "vivid and bitter memories" were passed down through the Young family. J. R. Woodside reports that James Monroe Young "often regaled his family with stories of his discoveries of the iniquity of those in office and power," and voiced "unquenchable hatred for carpetbaggers in particular and all governmental agencies in general."[24] The lessons would be passed down to his grandsons.

As there is no record of James Monroe and Mary Ellen Young in the 1870 Census of Christian County, we can reasonably infer James was in no hurry to return from Tennessee and take the loyalty oath. Or maybe they were waiting for a suitable time between pregnancies.

Per scriptural mandate and regional imperative, "Be fruitful and multiply," James and Mary Ellen Young produced a new child every couple of years, until the total was up to eight: James David followed by Emily, Rachel, Lydia, Robert, another Archibald Alexander, John, and Franklin. By all accounts, the parents made every effort to raise their young in the path that leads to righteousness.

According to Woodside, firstborn James David "showed a consuming interest in the Bible. He grew into young manhood well fortified with a deep Christian faith and a smattering of much that was in history and geography books."[25]

On October 23, 1884, twenty-one-year-old James David Young wed Willie Florence Haguewood, with W. E. Vaughn presiding.[26] The Youngs and Haguewoods were obviously very close, as two of James David's siblings, Emily and Lydia, married into the same family.

The bride's father, James Madison Haguewood, was born in North Carolina. He and his wife Mary were living in north central Missouri when Willie Florence was born July 8, 1867. There were at least seven children: William Judson (who married Emily Young and figures into events of January 1932), Laura, Willie Florence, John Alonzo (future husband of Lydia Young), Luvena, Theodosia, and Major Clarence. The tribe was said to possess a strain of Native American blood, either the Narragansett or Pequot.[27]

Willie Florence would later remember her courtship:

> Almost from the first, I mean even when we was little shavers, we was pretty thick with each other. Whenever we could we would ride together over the hills and near the pretty creeks in Christian County. Them was happy days, and I was so proud to be with Jim, 'cause everybody else liked him too. He was a quiet sort, very quiet and always so respectful toward older folks. My parents never objected to having me go with him, and as we grew older and went higher up in school, we was free to do almost as we pleased. My folks knew Jim was a little gentleman, and his folks knew I was always a little lady, and they never cared how much we was together."[28]

The seventeen-year-old little lady exchanged nuptials with her little gentleman in a turbulent place and time. Just five days before their wedding, in the next county south, a Taney County jury declared Al Layton "not guilty" of murdering Jim Everett. There was no disputing Layton had fired the fatal shot, but the defendant claimed he was acting in self-defense. It was rumored the prosecutor had been bribed to go easy on Layton and that a Layton supporter greased the jury with a good supply of whiskey.

In disgust, Nathaniel Kinney—originally of Tennessee but more recently a saloonkeeper in Springfield, a farmer of 267 acres in Taney County, and a preacher on the side—called a select group of right-minded citizens to a meeting atop Snapp's Bald. Thus was the original Bald Knobbers organized. If the law could not protect Taney County from men such as Al Layton, then Nate Kinney and his ilk of neo-Regulators would take matters into their own hands.

The movement spread to adjoining counties. Perhaps most menacing of all was the Christian County chapter. Established less than a year after James David's marriage to Willie Florence, the Christian County Bald Knobbers wore custom-designed hoods that might have frightened Frankenstein's monster.

The stated purpose of law and order was quickly lost in a flood of personal vendettas. If a Bald Knobber coveted his neighbor's land, he could simply call his fellows together for a torch-lit night ride around the neighbor's front yard. A pile of sticks delivered the unambiguous message: leave the land—or else. The "or else" might mean a bullwhip or even a hangman's noose.

In Christian and Taney counties, insists Ingenthron, circumstances forced men to take sides: You were either with the Bald Knobbers or against them. It isn't known for sure where James David positioned himself. Perhaps he simply tried to mind his own business. But just as the first years of his parents' marriage had coincided with war and retribution, J.D.'s marriage to Willie Florence commenced in a climate of vigilante terror.

As it appears that most of Christian County was present for the hanging, we can speculate J.D. brought his wife and small children to the county seat town of Ozark May 10, 1889, to witness the end of Dave Walker, Dave's son Billy, and fellow-Knobber John A. Mathews. On March 11, 1887, Walker-led Bald Knobbers had made a night ride to the cabin of James Edens, intent on avenging a perceived insult. Three couples and two children were asleep inside. By the time the masked men left, Edens and Charles Green were dead.

Sixteen Knobbers were indicted, among them Pastor C. O. Simmons, arrested two days after officiating at the funerals of the slain. Simmons admitted riding with the others to the Edens' home, but insisted he tried to prevent the killings. Despite the pastor's protest that he was more innocent of this crime than was Pontius Pilate "of the blood of our Saver" (sic), Simmons was sentenced to twelve years in the penitentiary.[29]

Four men were sentenced to hang. One, Wiley Mathews, managed to escape, leaving three. The hanging itself went poorly. As Mary Hartman and Elmo Ingenthron tell it, the Christian County sheriff hadn't counted for stretch factor in the rope, so when the trap door was sprung, Dave Walker landed on his feet. A preacher who had come to administer final consolation hoisted Walker by the legs while the sheriff readjusted the rope.

It went even worse for teenaged Billy. The coil around his neck broke altogether and Billy hit the ground with a thud, very much alive—though not for long. To the consternation of the crowd, the sheriff took Billy back up the platform, and this time the rope held.

While what follows is pure speculation, we can imagine righteous J.D. telling his little boy Jarrett to behold the hanging men: *Son, it's like the Bible says: The wages of sin are death.* If so, perhaps it made an impression. Of the five sons of J.D. and Willie Florence, first-born Jarrett would be the only one never to run afoul of the law.

The first three issued from Willie Florence's womb—Loretta, Mary Ellen, and Jarrett—do not figure prominently in our story. Next came Oscar, then Paul, followed by Major Jennings. Exact birth dates are unknown, but as 1919 Missouri State Penitentiary records list Paul as age twenty-three and Jennings twenty-one, we will infer the latter came into the world circa 1898.

It may be instructive, in gauging the ideas of J.D. and Willie Florence, to consider the name given their sixth born child: Major Jennings. "Major" was from the Haguewood side of the family; of more interest is the middle name—the name by which the child would be known.

In the presidential campaign of 1896, a little known Nebraskan named William Jennings Bryan captured the Democratic nomination, largely on the strength of what is remembered as the "Cross Of Gold" speech. Two decades earlier, the United States had followed Europe's lead in adopting the "gold standard." In theory, the gold standard should have assured monetary stability. In practice, it was perceived as serving the interest of large financiers to the detriment of the "little guy."

Speaking to the Democratic Convention in Chicago, William Jennings Bryan electrified the delegates: "We have petitioned and our petitions have been scorned. We have entreated and our entreaties have been disregarded. We have begged and they have mocked us when our hour of calamity came." Then the big line: "You shall not press down upon the brow of labor the crown of thorns. You shall not crucify mankind upon a cross of gold."

Bryan was standing up for a constituency characterized by Charles Morrow Wilson: "the depression-tormented farmers, the unemployed laborers, the ill-paid teachers and preachers, and the independent shop-keepers"[30]—people like James David Young, who would have also been attracted by the candidate's overt Christian religiosity.

On Tuesday evening, November 3, 1896, the *Springfield Leader-Democrat* reported:

IT AMOUNTS TO A SILVER LANDSLIDE
The Wall Street Contingent Is Given A Black Eye By The Voters Of Springfield And Greene County.

Good order prevailed at all the booths and no disturbances or fighting occurred in the city.

Southwest Missouri was voting for William Jennings Bryan! Bryan would carry the state! But the Wall Street Contingent got the last laugh. The next president would be William McKinley. J.D. and Willie Florence named their next-born for the loser.

Times being what they were, men like him routinely crucified on a "cross of gold," J.D.'s prospects were limited. But he was, after all, grandson of the original Archibald Alexander, who had relocated to the Ozarks when the land was new (new to the Anglos, anyway) and built something for himself. What was to prevent James David from doing the same in a new country?

CHAPTER FOUR

Oklahoma

"It was in Oklahoma that the leaves were painted to tint the family tree."

—J.R. Woodside, *Young Brothers Massacre*

In 1901, James David Young ventured to Lawton, Oklahoma, to participate in a land lottery. The Federal government was offering 4,639 square miles of prairie, formerly the unbounded habitat of the Comanche, Kiowa, and Plains Apache, then, per the Medicine Lodge Treaty of 1867, a reservation the size of Connecticut. At the turn of J.D.'s century, the reservation had been canceled. Unlike the Osage in the Ozarks, these indigenous persons would not be driven off the land; they would even receive parcels to call their own. Tribal ties were to be marginalized, red Americans mixed with white Americans in a great grid of individual enterprise.[1]

J.D. was one of 200,000 entrants. Thirteen thousand would be awarded parcels of 160 acres each. First names out of the hat received first choice of location. The most attractive of the lottery parcels were in the vicinity of Lawton. James David came back to Missouri holding one of the *least* prized, a location in the extreme southwest corner of the state, what would be called Tillman County.

J.D.'s acreage was two miles east of the town site of Gosnell, soon to be renamed Frederick—as in Frederick VanBlarcom, scion of the Blackwell, Enid, and Southwestern Railroad VanBlarcoms. The Blackwell, Enid, and Southern was laying new track south and west. The route would go through either Gosnell (named for the founding Baptist pastor), or the neighboring community of Hazel. One community would be blessed, the other consigned to anonymity. Baptists would be with them always. This being their only opportunity to attract the railroad, the townsfolk of Gosnell voted to rename the village for a son of the VanBlarcoms and thereby sealed the deal.

In the spring of 1902, Willie Florence and the girls arrived in Lawton via passenger train. Daughter Holly Gladys remembered they got "the last room in an old wooden hotel where everyone else was quarantined with small pox." J.D. and the boys followed three days later in a chartered boxcar containing the family's worldly possessions. These were loaded onto a wagon, whereupon the reunited Youngs set out across the prairie.

Having reached their acreage, J.D. nailed together a two-room dwelling place. Rooms were added with the years and the property diligently improved. In the spring of 1904, Willie Florence went back to Missouri long enough to give birth to her ninth child, a son named Lyman Harry.[2] Much later, his mother would say of baby Harry, "He was a big, fat boy with blue-eyes—pretty and nice as any boy you ever saw."[3]

Following the birth of two more daughters—Lorena in 1906 and Vinita in 1909—J.D. and sons built a new five-bedroom house on the property, complete with dining room, kitchen, bathroom, and parlor. The parlor was graced by an upright piano that figures in the events of January 2, 1932. The family's first automobile was purchased in this period. Oklahoma had been good to J.D. Young—so far.

A family portrait: J.D. and Willie Florence are seated outdoors, in front of their new home, surrounded by all eleven children. The patriarch is attired in his best Sunday-go-to-meeting. The crown of his bullet-shaped head is bald, a shock of dark hair on either slope, gone gray at the ears; Zapata-ish moustache, eyebrows fixed in straight-line clanmarking, pronounced dimple at mid-chin, hands joined together in his lap. This is an altogether serious man.

After eleven children, Willie Florence brings to mind a Faulkner character, "The gray woman not plump and not thin, manhard, workhard . . . her face like those of generals who have been defeated in battle."[4] Particularly notable is the deep set of the eyes. She wears a dark, full-length dress, belted at the midsection. The only touch of color is a white bow at the neckline.

The baby of the family, Vinita, stands in front of her parents in a long white gown. Vinita is cute as a button. On the other side of mother's knee is Lorena, a head taller than her younger sister, hair cut in a boyish manner, offering scant hint of the beauty she will become.

Seated to J.D.'s immediate right is Loretta—"Rettie"—the first-born of the eleven. She has her father's eyes and facial construction; her dark hair is pulled back and parted in the middle. Rettie is garbed in matronly fashion almost identical to her mother's. Standing to Loretta's right is adolescent Holly Gladys, who will grow to be the family historian, a pretty girl in a light-colored, western-style dress.

Behind Gladys, the back row starts with Jennings, still identifiably a boy, but posing as a man, black hair severely parted to the right. The face is as serious as his father's; perhaps this is what J.D. looked like in his own youth.

To Jennings' left is Jarrett, the all-American young man, shoulders back, sporting a light jacket and bow tie.

Oscar has the raw-boned look one might associate with a ballplayer—or a machine gunner. He is the most conventionally handsome of the Young brothers, perhaps the genetic gift of the Haguewood side of the family.

Next is Paul. If Jarrett and Oscar have crossed over to manhood, Paul appears yet on the boyish side of the line, face much fuller than will be seen in mug shots ten years later. One might more expect this countenance to evolve into that of a rural parson than career criminal.

To Paul's left, a head shorter than her brother, is Mary Ellen, a younger, fresher version of her mother. Seated in front of Mary Ellen is Florence Willie, visage obscured by a flaw in the old photograph.

And, finally, at the fringe of the family portrait, is young Harry, seven or eight years old, already looking like trouble. This would appear to be a sullen little boy. There will later be suggestions Harry was "spoiled" by his older sisters—and this picture does nothing to discourage that notion. He has his mother's deep eye sockets, hair not quite combed, jaw set in defiance, mouth in a deep pout. Indeed, the pose is remarkably similar to what will be seen in his adult crime portfolio. This may, of course, be a trick of imagination, reading the future into the face of a child. Or maybe not.

Writing in 1915, Mrs. J.M. Smith Sr. marveled at her hometown of Frederick, Oklahoma. A hamlet born in 1901 with "about 40 people and 800 prairie dogs" had grown to a town of four thousand, boasting school houses "as fine as can be found in any city twice this size," an electric light plant with seven miles of line, a state-of-the art telephone exchange, fifteen miles of concrete sidewalk, seventy-five miles of "wide, graded, rolled streets," twice-a-day mail delivery, three banks, fourteen lawyers ("and any of them would be glad to look after your legal affairs"), nine doctors, four dentists, two newspapers, three hotels, ten grocery stores, a thirty-ton capacity ice cream factory, ten dry goods enterprises, four hardware stores, over a hundred brick business houses, and a variety of mills to serve the farmer.

A Carnegie library was under construction. You could get your car fixed at one of three garages, be entertained at the opera house or one of Frederick's three "picture shows," get your clothes cleaned in a laundry that "does such high class work that it is often necessary to look closely to detect the right from the wrong side of the fabric because of the laundry's fine finish," join the Protestant church of your choice, and/or hope to be chosen for one of the "secret orders": the Masons, Odd Fellows, Royal Neighbors, etc. One could *not* join the Merry Wives Club, for the MWC was restricted to "old settlers": "It was first organized with fifteen members. We do not fill vacancies but continue the club with what members remain."

Mrs. Smith reports: "Our police department is small in number, but large in size. Frederick is very peaceful; there is very little crime committed." Deterrence may have been a factor. Reading from the Works Project Administration's Depression-era guide to Oklahoma:

> It was from Frederick that President Theodore Roosevelt started on April 8, 1905, on a wolf hunt that became famous because Jack Abernathy, a young ranchman of the region, caught a coyote with his bare hands and Roosevelt wrote about the feat. Later, after leaving his job as United States marshal, Abernathy repeated his coyote-catching stunt for the movies.[5]

Surely, even the most hardened criminal would think twice before tangling with a barehanded coyote-catching marshal!

And there is this note from Mrs. Smith's account: "Frederick was the first city in the territory to vote out saloons and pool halls, and since statehood, it has been the leading prohibition town in the state."

When one considers that Oklahoma was the first state in the union to vote "bone dry," Frederick could well claim to be Prohibition's Ground Zero. If Willie Florence Young later comes across as obsessive to the point of comical on the issue—more concerned about allegations of her sons' drinking than accusations of murder—it must be remembered where she came from.

On the other side of personal and family devastation, Willie Florence would retain cherished memories of Oklahoma: "At nights, the boys would take a wagon sheet out in the yard and they'd all sit out there and talk with their daddy. Maybe they'd sing. People passin' would wish their sons would stay home like the Young boys."[6]

So what went wrong? Why did the Youngs pack up and move back to Missouri? Perhaps it had something to do with world war. The time-line invites such speculation.

The Youngs held a public sale on September 17, 1917. The first of the Frederick boys bid farewell for arms two days later, and the day after that, the 20th of September, J.D., Willie Florence, and family take their own leave, destination Christian County, Missouri.

The newspapers of the period brim with patriotic stories of men lining up to serve. In Greene County, Marcell Hendrix had registered on June 5.[7] Though not ultimately called to fight, the young farmer and father of two small sons had done his patriotic duty. In contrast, it is suspected that Paul Young shot three toes off his right foot in order to avoid the draft.[8] Did such issues enter into the family's decision to leave Tillman County?

Many years later, Vinita told Paul and Mary Barrett the issue was economics: "Daddy couldn't make it and we moved back to Missouri."[9] There are indeed signs of ongoing economic struggle.

In November of 1911, J.D. and Willie Florence transferred title of the farm to J.M. Young of Tillman County for $4,000. It would appear that J.D.'s daddy had come to live with his family and apparently drove a hard bargain. The property carried two mortgages totaling $1,300. As this coincides with the period when J.D. was building the new house, perhaps the transaction had something to do with financing the construction. Two years later, September 1913, J.D. and Willie Florence regained possession from J.M., in the identical amount of $4,000, still carrying the same two mortgages.[10] But times were undeniably hard.

J.D. supplemented his income working as a carpenter in town. The devout Baptist may have been particularly gratified by his participation in the construction of Frederick's handsome red brick Baptist church. A wonderful photo from the congregation's archives shows a mule at ground level, serving as a hoist for raising a cast iron bell up to an impressive tower. Perhaps J.D. is among the men in the photo, sitting atop the brick tower, waiting to receive the crown of their creation.[11]

In later remembrance, Willie Florence would deny that poverty was an issue. Yes, some times were better than others, "but always there was enough to eat."[12]

John R. Woodside offers a more colorful explanation for the return to Missouri:

The Youngs became proficient with guns of all kinds in early boyhood. Paul and Jennings used to boast of their ability and gloat over what would happen to anyone who gave them battle. This proficiency with firearms gave Harry also an unholy confidence in himself, and it wasn't long till he was toting a 'rod.' His father remonstrated mildly, but Mrs. Young upheld the boy on the pretext that Paul and Jennings and other boys did the same.

Always weary from toil on his acres, Father Young had little energy to cogitate upon the future of his sons, but any contemplation he did avail himself foretold a bad end for them unless somehow it would be possible to foster a different companionship for all. In the odd moments Senior Young snatched away from attention to corn and cotton farming, he thought of his old-time neighbors back in Missouri. For the sake of his family he wished to be back there again where their kin might have a wholesome influence on the children. This wish became an obsession with him and the family, excepting Paul, Jennings and Harry, agreed that they would gladly live again among early acquaintances.

When it was discovered that Paul and Jennings had come to know the taste of potent brew, the Young parents hastened to find a buyer for their Oklahoma property. At some sacrifice they sold and headed for the Ozarks. They cast about for awhile and then bought more than a hundred acres a few miles south and west of Springfield. Here they settled down with high hope in the heart of father Young, the Lord would intercede to lead his sons in the paths of righteousness.

J.D. and Willie Florence's "high hopes" would be short-lived. John Steinbeck wrote: "We'll start over. But you can't start. Only a baby can start. You and me—why we're all that's been."[13] The character of their sons fixed, there would be no starting over for James David and Willie Florence Young. Many years later, she would lament, "If we'd only stayed in Oklahoma, this never would have happened."[14]

CHAPTER FIVE

White Hats
Soaked in Blood

"It's almost more than I can stand hearing the women and children scream and cry as I drive past funeral parlors tonight."

—An unidentified taxi driver, quoted in the
Springfield Daily News, January 4, 1932

It's unclear exactly how news of the disaster first reached Springfield. In the account that has Virgil Johnson driving his car off the road, word is called into town from a rural telephone.[1] J.R. Woodside, on the other hand, reports Virgil arrived at headquarters, "like an arrow in its flight," having "zoomed his car over holes in the road, over cross-road humps and railroad tracks." Even as "he slid the wheels to stop" in front of the station, Johnson was barking, "We want more men and guns, they've killed the Sheriff and more at Young's."[2]

Frank Pike would remember the wounded Tony Oliver wondering what was taking so long, "They must have gone to Kansas City or they would have been back by now."[3] Of course, the minutes must have seemed like hours to men under fire.

We might wish Virgil had stopped at one of the apple mansions, just up the road from the Young farmhouse, and called from there. This surely would have expedited matters—though probably not enough to save any lives. What seems clear is that the crisis was first reported to City Police Headquarters at College and Market, then relayed to the Greene County Jail.

One of the "perks" of the sheriff's job was residence at the Greene County Jail. The jail itself was a vermin-ridden disgrace, with only a sliding wooden door separating the residence dining room from upwards of 150 prisoners in space intended for forty. That's where Maude Hendrix took the call that changed her life forever.

According to the caller, Maude's husband had been "seriously" wounded at the Young place, Wiley Mashburn with him. Thankfully, Marcell's sister, Orpha Bischoff, happened to be visiting, so Maude didn't have to face this alone. Orpha tried to lift flagging spirits with a happy memory from just the night before. Marcell had come home "holding his jaw as if he had a toothache." Asked what was wrong, the sheriff, "looked slyly over at Mrs. Hendrix and said, 'My tooth is just aching for one of those good apples upstairs.'"[4]

The Hendrix boys, twenty-year-old Glenn and eighteen-year-old Merl, came roaring in, grabbing jail-issue revolvers, insisting they were going to the Young farm to help their dad. Maude pleaded with them not to. Greene County Prosecutor Dan Nee, who had come to take charge of the jail, added his voice to their mother's: Glenn and Merl were needed here.[5]

There was a third child, nine-year-old Maxine. Maxine doesn't remember much of anything from that night; she speculates she took refuge in her room and just stayed there.[6] Something bad had happened to her daddy.

In a remembrance published January 3, 1960, a *Springfield News & Leader* reporter, Lucille Upton Morris, recalled she had been at the courthouse around 3 P.M., when Hendrix and Mashburn came tearing out of the prosecutor's office, saying, "We may have a story for you after a while."[7] Morris returned to the newspaper building, at the southeast corner of Jefferson and McDaniel, south of the public square. About 5 P.M., she was at her desk typing when an editor yelled, "Get over to the county jail as fast as you can—Marcell Hendrix may have been shot!"

From the newspaper office, Morris took a Boonville Avenue streetcar north to the jail, wanting to believe the report was false. "The minute I saw Jailer Frank Willey, however, I knew the news was true . . . though there was still hope the sheriff might be found alive." According to the reporter, the full extent of the tragedy was not known until around 8 P.M.

At police headquarters, where Wiley Mashburn's red Durant was still parked as he left it before the raid, Chief Ed Waddle was working the phones: coordinating with the governor in Jefferson City, requesting authority to use a machine gun, discussing the feasibility of an aerial bombing, scrounging for firearms, purchasing eight hundred rounds of ammunition—"bullets that would fit any type of high-powered rifle or revolver"[8]—alerting officers within a 225-mile radius to be on the lookout for the fugitives. Radio stations were contacted and thousands of cards prepared for mailing with detailed descriptions of the Young brothers.

While darkness seemed to preclude bombing the farmhouse, it was suggested a plane could first drop flares to illuminate the countryside, *then* release the bomb. A plane was readied at the municipal airport, east of town, waiting for a "go" from Waddle, who had been authorized by the governor to do whatever was deemed necessary. But there was the additional issue of what to use as a "bomb"—something not readily available in Springfield, Missouri. As it turned out, there would be no aerial bombardment on the night of January 2, 1932, which, given the tragic misadventures of earlier in the day, was probably just as well.[9]

Ed Waddle covered a lot of bases Saturday evening; the one thing he didn't think to do was order an immediate roadblock *into* Springfield. It would be said of Ed Waddle that "The most likeable trait about the Chief is the utter lack of ego, as he expressed it himself, 'I was one of the boys before I was made Chief, and I am still one of the boys, and my name is still Ed.'"[10]

In Ed Waddle's case, the "lack of ego" may have been warranted. The only reason "My Name Is Still Ed" was chief in the first place was because his predecessor, Frank Pike's father, had been sent to Leavenworth Federal Penitentiary for taking bribes from bootleggers. Springfield Mayor T. H. Gideon, also under Grand Jury indictment, hadn't promoted the former retail grocer for his fighting spirit (if the mayor had wanted a fighter, he would have advanced Tony Oliver). Gideon wanted someone who wasn't going to make waves—and in this regard, at least, Ed Waddle was imminently qualified.

Ed's dad was a cop, though perhaps not a very good one. Henry Waddle had been among those censured by a 1906 Grand Jury investigating the lynching of three black men taken by a mob from the Greene County Jail, subsequently "hanged and roasted" on the public square. Grand Jurors went on record that Fred Coker and Horace Duncan had certainly *not* assaulted the white woman, Mrs. Edwards, whose "reputation for virtue and chastity is not good." According to the Grand Jury, it was doubtful Mrs. Edwards had been assaulted at all—and certainly not by the hanged men.

Will Allen was the last of the three to die, almost as an afterthought, it seems (two "Negroes" apparently weren't enough to satisfy the bloodlust). By the time Allen met his end, Saturday night had turned to Easter Sunday morning.

The Grand Jury exonerated Sheriff Horner, who had seen trouble coming and sent in vain for reinforcements. In contrast, the city police force was severely criticized for standing by and doing nothing while the mob formed. Several officers were singled out for "laughing and talking while the mob were bringing Allen up to the square." Among them was Henry Waddle, Ed's dad.[11] In 1932, old Henry was still on the police payroll.

Ed Waddle sent young Rancy Burch over to North Sherman Avenue, residence of the Tony Oliver family. Tony's wife Maude answered the door. She'd heard about the shooting. Burch stammered. Maude Oliver didn't: "Tony's dead, isn't he?"[12]

Wiley and Maude Mashburn lived at 945 N. Robberson, very near the county jail. Their daughter Erma and her newlywed dairyman husband, Albert McClernon, had come by for a Saturday afternoon visit, perhaps intending to sit with Erma's anxious mother through this latest raid. They waited for Wiley to come home, and waited some more, and then it was time for the cows to be milked, so Albert went back to the farm. The phone was ringing when he got there, Erma saying, "They've got father."[13]

Then the ambulances started coming into town. Hendrix, Oliver, Meadows, and Houser were all in the back of the Floyd Fox hearse; W. L. Starne carried Ollie Crosswhite.[14] Coroner Murray Stone (himself a cadaverous looking fellow) ordered the bodies transported to the Herman Lohmeyer mortuary for collective examination. The convergence of ambulances at the stately two-story mortuary on Walnut Street, east of the square, was the magnet for an enormous crowd.

The five bodies were "laid in line on stretchers in a large parlor." Coroner Stone, who was still out at the farm, had given instructions that only the immediate families were to be allowed inside the mortuary for viewing. But there were so many people outside Lohmeyer's, the collective grief so enormous, that finally the mortuary doors were opened "to allow all who wished to file through the room where the shooting victims lay. The white shrouds were turned back, revealing to all who passed the blood smeared faces of the officers whose daring had cost them their lives." Hendrix was the only one not shot in the head.[15]

Mashburn alone was missing from the tableau. He had been rushed to Springfield's Baptist Hospital. While some reports have Mashburn talking incoherently to the ambulance driver, Woodside quotes him saying, "The boys got me. I guess we didn't do any good about there."[16]

Remarkably, having reached the hospital, Mashburn was actually able to stand as his bloody clothing was torn away.[17] Men didn't come any tougher than Wiley Mashburn. According to Woodside, the dying man asked for his wife, sobbing, "It's dark. I can't see." The *Press* reported: "As he lay in bed, blood staining the sheets, anxious relatives paced the corridor, peering cautiously at the door which shielded the fatally injured man from numerous curious bystanders." Death was pronounced at ten o'clock.[18]

A reporter was given access to the sisters. In these first, chaotic hours, "Vinita and Lorena lay on a cot in a police cell here, unconscious of the cause of the commotion in the police station." Lorena "wore a fitted brown dress and a becoming turban" and seemed primarily concerned about her daughter, little Natalie. Asked about the '31 Ford that led to her arrest, Lorena repeated what she'd told the officers: Her brother Paul had brought it up from Texas last Wednesday. She had no idea it was stolen. Other brothers? Well, there was Oscar, of course, who lived in the vicinity, but Lorena professed ignorance as to the whereabouts of Harry and Jennings.

Vinita, "plainer than her sister," but with "a direct way of talking and opening her eyes wide," said she and her mother never heard much from "the boys"—which was okay with Vinita. "The trouble they've been in before has been such a worry to mother," she said, adding, "This will just burn mother up."[19]

"Mother" was being questioned by Assistant County Prosecutor James Horn Bostel, but Willie Florence was "so wracked and exhausted from crying that she hardly could understand the prosecutor or answer his questions coherently."[20] This first round of questioning took place at the city police station, but it was then decided to move Willie Florence to the county jail, perhaps to put distance between mother and daughters. Though in county custody, Ma Young would be just a sliding door removed from Maude Hendrix.

Even as the bodies were being brought from the farm into Springfield, citizens of Ash Grove, Missouri, gathered at their Baptist church for collective mourning, the preacher challenging, "Let us engage in a prayer of personal dedication, dedicating ourselves to the strictest obedience of the law of the land, to the stamping out of all lawlessness in our town."[21]

It was entirely appropriate that the official mourning should begin in Ash Grove, a small town in the northwest corner of the county Marcell Hendrix had sworn to defend. The sheriff's last workday had started in Ash Grove with a raid on "rural racketeers" who had terrorized the local citizenry. The primary illicity was booze, the gang "making liquor on a wholesale scale and running it to important cities of three states."[22]

The bootleggers brooked no interference. Alleged outrages included the torching of two Frisco railroad bridges leading into town. Ash

Grove was afflicted by "wide open gambling," auto theft, large-scale chicken stealing, and "daring hold-ups." When the criminals needed extra capital, they made unauthorized withdrawals from local banks. The safe at Farmers' Bank was blown in January of '31, $1,600 removed. The Bank of Ash Grove had been taken for $3,750 over the summer.[23] Townsfolk appealed to the county for help, but the gangs warned law enforcement "had better lay off Ash Grove. We will put them away if they come up here."[24]

The Ash Grove raid was carefully orchestrated by Sheriff Hendrix and Greene County Prosecutor Dan Nee. Nee had come to office in the election of November 1930. He was a large fellow whose physicality might remind the modern-era reader of actor John Goodman, and was a thoroughly capable and experienced man.

On May 31, 1917, Dan Nee had been a twenty-nine-year-old assistant prosecutor whose boss was out of town, so when J. Holland Keet showed up first thing in the morning to report a missing child, Nee handled the report. Baby Lloyd Keet had been taken from his bed in one of Springfield's most exclusive neighborhoods. Ransom was demanded in the amount of six thousand dollars. The Keets were more than ready to pay, but the transfer went poorly. The child was found floating in a cistern on June 9.

The primary culprit was twenty-year-old Claud G. Piersol, whose father was a veterinary surgeon in Springfield. Four others were implicated; one of these was arrested in Kansas City by Detective Tony Oliver. Adding to the sensation, Piersol claimed he was in the employ of the German government and the ransom demand was part of an organized plan to raise money for the Reich.[25] Piersol got thirty-five years and Nee enlisted to fight the Hun.[26]

In the raid of Saturday morning, January 2, 1932, Hendrix was joined by Deputy Sheriffs R.E. Hodge and Wiley Mashburn from Springfield, John Bright from Bois D'Arc, and John Hilton of Ash Grove. Ash Grove Constable Joe Johnson and City Marshal John Daniels were also listed as part of the operation, though it may have been sprung on them as a surprise. According to the papers, local officers "had not been informed in advance of the impending raids."[27]

The action started at 4 A.M. First stop, the Gott brothers, Orville and Sutton.[28] By ten o'clock, nine men were in custody. Claud White, a "high-cheeked, large, powerful-looking man,"[29] was thought to be the ringleader. White's place was a mile west of town, near a lime quarry. When Mashburn and Hodge came to visit that morning, they saw liquor on a shelf. Mashburn seized the container. White knocked it from his hands and ran into the next room. Mashburn followed and beat the daylights out of White.[30]

In what would be remembered as "Mashburn's Last Photo," a glowering Wiley and R.E. Hodge are posed on either side of Claud White, both officers wearing white felt hats and black winter coats. Mashburn's coat is open, revealing a white shirt, dark tie, and overalls.[31]

Hendrix himself experienced what must have been a nervous moment. He found Lonnie Cowell chopping wood, ax in hand. Nevertheless, the sheriff walked right up with an arrest warrant. The *Press* reported, "Cowell dropped his ax in surprise. He scratched his head, looked carefully at the warrant. Without saying a word he slipped on his jacket and marched to the sheriff's waiting auto."

Prosecutor Nee announced, "I believe we have broken up one of the best organized bands in this section. There is no doubt but that much of the criminal activities occurring through this section could be laid at the doors of this gang."[32]

Per court order, "All of the confiscated liquor was poured out on the street. . . . A crowd gathered to watch Sheriff Hendrix empty a half-gallon jug found at [Danie] Dotson's home, and the liquor confiscated at the place of Zunnie McCall."[33]

The Sheriff stands in the middle of main street Ash Grove, Missouri—a small town taken over by bootleggers. The criminal element had warned the Sheriff not to interfere. Mind your own business. Stay in Springfield. Don't you dare come up here! Marcell Hendrix dared. In his hands, he holds the fruit of the pre-dawn raid: Home brew. Sin in a bottle. Crime in a container.

A tall man, the Sheriff is all the more imposing in his white Stetson hat and great coat, the ubiquitous chaw of tobacco between cheek and gum. An eagle graces his badge of office, a small diamond stud grasped in its talons. The Sheriff is armed with two pearl-handled Smith & Wesson revolvers: one, a nickel-plated .38; the other, a .44 hand-injector—big guns for a big man. These are carried in a suspender/holster rig beneath his coat.

With the wrongdoers in custody and the town watching, Hendrix turns the cursed jug on end. The prohibited beverage splatters on the street. The law WILL BE ENFORCED in Greene County, Missouri.

That was early Saturday. Very late the same day, as detritus from the killing yard floated into police headquarters in Springfield, someone brought in a white hat soaked in blood. Initialed on the brim: M.C.H. And it was remembered that a month or so ago, Hendrix had come into fifty dollars as a reward for bringing in an escaped federal prisoner. Christmas was fast approaching; Sheriff Hendrix used the money to buy new wide-brimmed, western-style felt hats for his deputies, and liked the look so much, he bought one for himself.[34]

The white hat was surely ruined now. Nevertheless, it was not immediately discarded, but sent on to the mortuary, reunited however briefly with the good guy who had worn it into battle.

CHAPTER SIX

The Queen City of the Ozarks

"SPRINGFIELD (1,345 alt., 61,238 pop.), Missouri's fourth largest city, is in the southwestern part of the State at the northern edge of the Ozark Highlands. The business district is concentrated around the Public Square, which lies near the center of the city. Within the square is the 'pie,' a slightly raised concrete safety zone approximately 75 feet in diameter, around which traffic moves to the right. . . . Around Commercial Street, the principal industrial and commercial district extends along a tier of railroad tracks. Here are creameries, furniture and garment factories, cooperages, chicken and egg establishments, and the railroad shops."

—Workers of the Writers' Program of the
Works Project Administration in the State of Missouri,
"Missouri: A Guide To The 'Show Me' State."[1]

Marcell Hendrix was elected Greene County Sheriff on the sixth day of November 1928—what had been a very turbulent year in Springfield, Missouri.

Seven months before the county election, city voters had gone to the polls, choosing Thomas H. Gideon as their new mayor. Gideon was no stranger to the local political scene. Having received a law degree from Washington University in St. Louis and served a short stint as a government attorney in the "Old Oklahoma Indian Territory,"[2] Gideon returned to Springfield, where he entered the family law firm. Further following the footsteps of father and uncle, he threw his hat into the political ring. Gideon was elected first to the City Council, then judge of the county probate court.[3] Gideon married Della Stowe on August 14, 1901. In 1915, it was reported that Thomas, Della, and their children were "members of the Christian church and its teachings are an influencing factor in their lives."[4]

Like the Youngs, the Gideon clan is an archetype of western expansion. The mayor's ancestors immigrated to America from Ireland in the era of the American Revolution, settling in New York State. One of the mayor's great-great uncles, Edward, was killed in the Revolutionary War. The Revolution complete, Edward's brother, James Gideon, moved his wife Nancy and his sons Edward, William, Isham, James, and John to North Carolina. Their son William Gideon was the mayor's great-grandfather.

After a tenure in Tennessee, William Gideon brought his family to Southwest Missouri in 1836, settling on two hundred acres of land north of the village of Ozark, where they would have been neighbors of Archibald Alexander Young. The second William Gideon, William C., was twelve at the time.

In addition to changing locations, the elder William changed his religion. After forty years as a Baptist, William Gideon converted to the tenets of Universalism, rejecting traditional Trinitarian formulas and embracing the utopian conviction that a loving God would not forever damn a soul for eternity, therefore all will be saved. The idea did not take firm root in the region. In 2004, the Springfield/Branson Yellow Pages carried over fifty listings for Assemblies of God, a like number of Southern Baptist fellowships, thirty-some Methodists congregations—these being only the largest of a multitude of Trinity-based denominations and non-denominations. The Unitarian Universalistists, on the other hand, listed but one small membership church.

We have chronicled William C.'s death, bushwacked while visiting his father in 1863. (C. died in a state of Methodist grace.) His marriage to Melinda Bird produced eight children, including two sons who would make names for themselves in the practice of law: Thomas J. and James J. Gideon. In their generation, the family morphs into the archetype of another kind of American mobility, moving "upward" into the professional class.

James was himself a Civil War veteran, having run away from home at age sixteen to enlist in the United States Cavalry, eventually rising to the rank of corporal. After the war, he went back to Christian County, farming, and reading law books as he could.

James Gideon was admitted to the bar in 1872. Politics beckoned. He was elected Christian County prosecuting attorney and represented his county in the state legislature. This Gideon relocated to Springfield in 1886—perhaps not coincidentally, the height of Bald Knobber violence in Christian County. In Greene County, J.J. reprised his role as prosecuting attorney, before being elected judge of the criminal court.

In light of the circumstances of his father's violent death, it is somewhat startling to read that James J. Gideon provided legal counsel for some of the most notorious of the Bald Knobbers—including those hanged on the Ozark town square in 1889. Perhaps he admired their attempt, however misguided, to bring order to his old home county.

James' older brother, Thomas, was also a veteran of the Civil War. Thomas had served alongside his father in Company F of the Fourteenth Regiment of the Missouri State Militia. Thomas was severely wounded in the battle of Springfield, January 8, 1863, but continued to serve in a recruiting capacity. He was elected to his first public office in 1866, married to Letitia F. Williams in 1868, and admitted to the Missouri bar in 1877, five years after his younger brother.

It would be said of Thomas J. Gideon, "As both a lawyer and a citizen he was widely known in this section of the state and his integrity was unimpeached, and when he was summoned to his ultimate reward, on November 7, 1913, there were many to express a regret at his loss to the city and county."[5]

The word "integrity" would not be widely attached to the third born of Thomas' five children, Thomas Harry Gideon[6]—at least not in the years 1928-1932.

Springfield Daily News, April 17, 1928
MAYOR GETS OATH AND REPEATS VOW OF 'ENFORCEMENT'
Installed As Chief Executive, Gideon Reiterates That Springfield Must Have A Moral Cleanup

Law enforcement or lack thereof had been a major theme of Thomas Gideon's mayoral campaign. As reported in the *Leader,* "He assailed the laxity of the police force as a whole, and the ability of individuals."[7] Thomas Gideon promised change: "Police will be more than car markers when I get into office."[8] The majority of the force had been appointed by two-term incumbent W.E. Freeman; when Freeman finished third in the 1928 primary, the department pinned its hopes on retired newspaperman E.E.E. McJimsey. When Gideon prevailed by a count of 6,915 to McJimsey's 5,892, the reckoning was immediate.

On his first day at work, the bespectacled, balding Gideon fired nineteen officers—almost half the force.[9] These were replaced by men who had supported Gideon's election. The new hires included Sid

Meadows, Charlie Houser, and Francis DeArmond. Tony Oliver and Wiley Mashburn were rewarded with promotions to the Detective Bureau.[10] As if in grim foreboding, the *Daily News* characterized the terminations "The Police Massacre":

> The mayor belongs to that ancient school founded upon the 'golden rule': that to the victor belongs the spoils. He is building a political organization, a machine, just as thousands of other office holders have built one. When he becomes a candidate for reelection there shall be no hesitancy or doubt upon the part of those under his domination. He has told them as bluntly and as clearly as a man can that his favors shall go to those who favor him.[11]

The paper's use of the term "machine" is significant. This was an era of machine politics; perhaps the most efficient of all was running full-speed just two hundred miles to the north, in Tom Pendergast's Kansas City, Missouri.

In the foreword to his 1942 study, *Tom's Town,* William M. Redding offers the "full-blown stereotype" of a machine "boss." Let's see how Springfield's new mayor measured up: "A man of Irish features [if not stereotypically Irish in features, Gideon certainly qualified in ancestry], self-made in life [the description would have better fit his father and uncle, though the stint in "Indian Territory" does stand out], genial [by all accounts], hard-drinking [alleged], cigar-smoking [and proud of it, though he would famously claim to get sick on a bad one], corpulent [no] and customarily wearing a derby hat [not in any of the pictures this author has seen]."[12]

Gideon took exception to the charge of politics as usual. "Springfield must be 'cleaned up' morally as well as physically," insisted the new mayor. "I have said before and I say now that I am in favor of law enforcement. By this I mean the enforcement of all laws, which includes the eighteenth amendment to the constitution."[13]

As this story gets soaked in illicit liquor, it is important to note that, according to Fairbanks and Tuck, "whiskey was in almost universal use," during Springfield's early years, but "the temperance people never ceased in their opposition":

> In 1849 there was a genuine temperance revival. A division of the Sons of Temperance was organized and soon numbered seventy-five members. In April there was a grand all-day celebration, with marchings,

sermons and general demonstrations against the liquor foe. Later on the temperance people were strong enough to erect a two-story brick building, on the northeast corner of the public square and St. Louis street. This was quite an addition to the town. It stood through all the days of war, and was finally destroyed by fire in 1875.[14]

There had been major (albeit unsuccessful) temperance campaigns in 1873 and 1887, aimed at running "the liquor foe" out of Springfield. In 1910, Missouri held a statewide referendum on the issue. "Wets" carried Springfield proper, while the rural/county vote went "dry" by a large margin. Going to press in 1915, Fairbanks and Tuck could state with confidence that "The days of the saloon in Springfield are certainly numbered."[15] Numbered everywhere, as it turned out.

National prohibition was first instituted as a wartime measure to ensure that America's grain harvest went into food rather than spirits. Then, in a wave of post-war patriotic virtue, giving thanks to God (presumably "dry") for victory over the Hun, prohibition was codified into the Constitution of the United States of America.

William Jennings Bryan celebrated the moment: "When you remember that King Alcohol has slain a million more children than Herod ever did, what language can more appropriately express the joy in the hearts of parents today than those words, 'They are dead that sought the young child's life.'"[16]

In an admittedly highly partisan 1943 volume titled, *The Wrecking of the Eighteenth Amendment,* published by the Alcohol Information Press, Ernest Gordon makes a strong argument that national prohibition started well. For instance, in 1917, pre-prohibition Connecticut imprisoned no less than 7,314 persons on charges of drunkenness. That's a lot of drunks. In 1920, the number dropped to 943. In a three-year period following the passage of the Eighteenth Amendment, automobile death rates fell by 40 percent. The Massachusetts Society for the Prevention of Cruelty to Children reported a huge drop-off in caseload.

Gordon is not alone in asserting that where the law was enforced, people seem to have largely obeyed. Real wages increased, poverty decreased. Men brought their paychecks home, rather than squandering them at the saloon, with obvious benefit for wives and children. The increase in living conditions for women translated into a marked decrease in prostitution. Jane Addams, of Hull House fame, is quoted as saying, "During those first two years, beginning with 1919, we were all elated by the marked decrease in disorderly conduct." Testifying at national hearings on repeal in 1930, Thomas Edison said, "I feel that Prohibition is the greatest experiment yet made to benefit man."

Author Gordon attributed the "wrecking" of the amendment to poor enforcement, starting at the top. President Harding, characterized as a man "without sharply defined principles," was sworn to uphold the law, yet was guilty of personally "cocktailing" in the White House. Harding's successor, Calvin Coolige, was vilified for appointing the hated Andrew Mellon to the office of Secretary of the Treasury—an act compared to putting a fox in charge of the hen house. Even Herbert Hoover, whose victory in 1928 seemed the ultimate affirmation of the Eighteenth Amendment, abandoned the sacred cause in 1932. William Randolph Hearst and other "presstitutes," John D. Rockerfeller, even General Pershing, Jews, Roman Catholics, politicians bought off by the liquor lobby, Wall Street financiers—each of these and many others are counted by Gordon as part of a vast "wet" conspiracy to undermine the way of righteousness. (What was Wall Street's interest? Liquor had been a prime means of tax revenue. If the "little guy" wasn't buying rum, the tax shortfall would weigh on the wealthy.)[17]

In a less hysterical study of the effects of prohibition in Washington State, Norman Clark wrote, "It seemed clear that the fatal erosion of the prohibitionist's faith occurred at the level of municipal enforcement. . . . Early in the decade, the chief of police in Seattle, William B. Severyns, observed that 'the dry law has created an opportunity for graft in law enforcement such as never before existed, and it is surprising that no more policemen go wrong than they do."[18]

Bringing us to mayor-elect Gideon's choice to head the Springfield Police Department: G. Claude Pike. Claude Pike was fifty years old when he ascended to the highest office in Springfield law enforcement. He had previously served eight years as chief of police in Eureka Springs, Arkansas. The *Leader* reported that Springfield's new top lawman, "bears the reputation of having arrested more bank robbers, outlaws and other criminals than any other man in the Ozark section and he often has been called back to Arkansas to aid in detective work there."

Immediately prior to his appointment by Gideon, Pike had been a deputy game warden in the district serving Missouri's Greene and Webster Counties. How a stalker of bad men wound up as a warden of game is not explained, though politics likely had something to do with it. The *Leader* noted Springfield's new chief "always has been prominently identified with the Republican Party."[19]

As Pike's second-in-command, Gideon tabbed Spanish-American War veteran H. L. "Hank" Teaff, a practicing attorney whose resume included eight years on the Springfield police force, law enforcement experience in Tulsa, and a stint with the Frisco Railroad detectives.[20]

In a May 13 *Leader* article, Mayor Gideon was said to be "elated" with Pike and his team. They certainly seemed off to a strong start: "174 Arrests Made and $1,073 Collected in Fines During 26 Days Under Chief Pike, Who is Gaining Confidence of People Rapidly." Municipal Judge C.A. Hubbard said of Pike, "he is a real chief of police."

But then, on the 18th of June, Newell "Dobb" Adams[21] went looking for his estranged bride, Meada. The inebriated wife-beater took a taxi to the home of Zella St. Clair on West Division Street. Driver Roy Wells honked his horn. Ms. St. Clair emerged from the house. Dobb told Zella that a mutual friend was in town and wanted to see her. St. Clair made the mistake of getting into the back seat.

According to the cabby, Dobb initially seemed in good humor—but the mood quickly changed. Cab in motion, Dobb accused Zella of causing trouble between him and his wife, demanding to know where Meada was hiding. Seven miles north of Springfield, Dobb told the driver to pull over and get out of the car. Dobb dragged Miss St. Clair from the auto, cursed her, and shot her in the stomach.[22]

The cab driver having fled on foot, Dobb hitched a ride back into town, to his mother in-law's place at 1701 W. Webster. Dobb's exertions had made him thirsty; the mother-in-law, Sarah Whalin, drew him a drink of water from the well. Dobb played a jazz record on the phonograph in the company of his sister-in-law, sixteen-year-old Mrs. Edith McCrary. As Mrs. McCrary later testified, Dobb suddenly turned nasty, and said "I am going to shoot the hell out of both of you and kill myself if you don't tell me where Meada is."[23] As good as his word (the first part, anyway), Dobb pinned Mrs. Whalin against a wall, put three bullets into her abdomen, then clubbed her with the gun.

Edith McCrary tried hiding in a closet. Dobb pried the door open with a knife, stabbed Edith in the back and left side, then forced her to go to the phone and call a taxi. Desperately trying to save her own life, the pregnant Edith suggested Zella St. Clair might know of Meada's whereabouts. Dobb's response: "Hell, I've already seen her."[24] Dobb rode away in the taxi, the cops were called, and the game was afoot.

Around seven that evening, police were tipped off that Dobb Adams was inside a house on College Street. Fourteen city officers approached the dwelling, among them Tony Oliver, Francis "Ted"

DeArmond, and W. K. Webb, who entered the house together. DeArmond reached for a light switch, shots erupted, DeArmond was hit.[25] Oliver called for assistance that was not forthcoming.

Tony Oliver would be described as "big and handsome, one of the city's most popular officers." In a file photo, Detective Oliver's fedora is cocked down to his left eyebrow, a jaunty expression of "Bandits Beware."[26] Dobb, who was under no illusion he could best Tony Oliver, offered to surrender. When Dobb came out with his hands up, Oliver hit him over the head with his gun.

Oliver's heroics notwithstanding, June 18, 1928, had been a black day for the Springfield Police Department. Ted DeArmond was dead. Of the fourteen men who made the raid, eleven had run away, including Chief Pike's boy, Frank. But at least Frank made an appearance. As Tony Oliver was stalking a crazed killer, Chief Pike had been home eating dinner.

The *Leader* headline of June 19: "Policemen 'Yellow?' Mayor Orders Probe." The next morning's *Daily News* screamed, "Pike Defends Cops on Cowardice Charge." None of the officers would be suspended or otherwise disciplined.

It was an age of speedy trials. Dobb Adams' case was heard in July at the Polk County Courthouse in Bolivar, thirty miles north of Springfield. The *Daily News* of July 18 reported:

> Amazing stories of cowardice and unbelievable cruelty were woven together yesterday in sensational testimony. . . . How Adams tortured his sisterinlaw, Mrs. Edith McCrary, and how Tony Oliver, police detective here, vainly called for help to fellow officers during the gun battle in which DeArmond was slain.

Called to the stand, Officer Frank Pike testified he entered the house with Oliver, DeArmond, and Webb, but "when the shots were fired at DeArmond, I stepped back three steps onto the back porch."[27]

Newell "Dobb" Adams was sentenced to hang. Escorted from the courtroom by Deputy Sheriff Ollie Crosswhite, the condemned was heard to say: "Well, boys, they sort of poured it on me."[28] In a post-verdict interview that must have gratified prohibitionists, Adams traced his ruin to his first taste of rum.[29]

Now the gloves came off. On July 30, the *Leader* published an anonymous letter suggesting a mayoral recall election might be in order. Gideon smelled conspiracy, surely orchestrated by newspaperman Edson K. Bixby.

"Bix," the product of an Oklahoma newspaper family, had purchased the old *Springfield Republican* from E.E.E. McJimsey, remaking it into the *Daily News*. The first edition rolled off the press New Year's Day 1927, setting off heated competition with the established *Leader*. Then, in May of 1928, Bixby purchased the majority of *Leader* shares, giving him a practical monopoly on advertising and opinion in Springfield and vicinity. The *Daily News* was published in the morning, the *Leader* in the evening, and combined on the Christian Sabbath as the *Sunday News & Leader*.[30]

It's hard to tell who hated the arrangement more: local advertisers or the new mayor. No longer could department stores and other retailers profit from the competition of a two-paper town; they paid Bixby's rates or were shut out. Long-standing "gentlemen's agreements" between the press and city hall were as defunct as the *Republican*. Bixby wrote of his editorial policy:

> The News (and now the Leader too) shall be just what its name implies, preeminently a NEWSpaper. It shall be drastically independent but never neutral when wrong seeks to usurp the seats of authority. It shall ever stand for right causes, right principles and right men under whatever banner they appear, for civic righteousness in city, state and nation. It shall acknowledge but one master, the people of the great empire which it serves and of which Springfield is the undisputed capital.[31]

The righteous (sometimes *self*-righteous) impulse of Edson K. Bixby would collide head on with the power politics of Thomas H. Gideon, the latter lumping his critics together as "the Bixby crowd."

Regarding the anonymous letter published in the July 30 *Leader*, Gideon fired back that very evening, reminding hearers at a Methodist church that "Rome wasn't built in a day and even the Lord took time to fulfill his work."[32] The mayor would welcome a recall contest "like flowers in May." That's what he said. But then the Feds showed up.

The *Springfield Sunday News & Leader,* November 4, 1928, reported:

RAID RUM DEN NEAR POLICE STATION!
U.S. Sleuths Seize Liquor Cops Missed
  Springfield's most brazen and notorious speakeasy, operating within 100 feet of the Central police station, fell Saturday before a federal raiding squad.

It was the Keystone bar, 422 College street, operated by pictur-
esque old Tom Fuzzell, a popular bartender in the days when bar-
keeping was a legitimate calling. To the well informed it was simply
'Tom's place'—where those whom Tom knows get hard liquors or
soft served freely across the fine old bar, where many city policemen
loaf and where wholesale shipments of liquor are delivered within 75
feet of the police station.

Bixby and staff had been engaged in some serious investigative journalism, reporting the ease with which liquor might be obtained in
Springfield at pool halls, rooming houses, and from rum runners who
would bring the brew directly to a thirsty man's automobile at a price
of fifty cents a quart. Some of the best-known drug stores in the city
were selling liquor without prescription. Most notorious were
Springfield's speakeasies, "scattered among the residence districts,
both south and north sides," some catering "to the younger generation
and college students."

The paper took its readers inside a place on Cleveland Street, operated by J. E. Smith Jr., where sixty-eight gallons of homebrew and
forty-eight gallons of "on the way beer" were confiscated. Implicated
with Smith were Clara Wilburn and Lenora Shoflar:

> Entrance usually was gained through the rear door. Sometimes a
> 10 or 12-year-old boy, a relative of one of the women, would answer
> the door. Admittance rarely was refused.
>
> Once inside the customer had little to do but lounge in any of the
> four small rooms and quaff the beer.
>
> Describing an atmosphere "hazy with smoke of innumerable ciga-
> rettes," reeking "with the odor of stale beer and fresh beer just foam-
> ing over," the report continued: "An expensive phonograph played
> cheap records. . . . The women never seemed to sleep. They would
> smoke cigarets and drink a friendly bottle of beer with a customer
> anytime, day or night. T hey always urged that 'you take one more.'"[33]

On the editorial page, Edson K. Bixby noted that, just days earlier,
Chief Pike had issued a report to the mayor and City Council extolling
his team's record in cracking down on liquor violators.[34] The editor's
tongue-in-cheek essay was titled, "Springfield Wasn't Dry After All."

Amidst all the sordidness, in this very same edition of the *Sunday
News & Leader*, November 4, 1928, readers could hardly miss the
large boxed political advertisement:

Vote For Marcell Hendrix For Sheriff

What His Neighbors Say:

We, the undersigned friends and neighbors of Marcell Hendrix, nominee for Sheriff on the Republican Ticket, irrespective of party, state that he has resided in this neighborhood all his life.

And we commend him to the voters of the county as a man of sterling character, unswerving honesty and integrity, rugged manliness and fine neighborly qualities.

Mr. Hendrix's neighbors evidenced their esteem and confidence in him by giving him 140 votes out of the 145 Republican votes cast in his township at the primary election.

In our judgement no worthier or better qualified man ever asked for the office of Sheriff of Greene County, and should there be any rumors started against him the last days of the campaign his life of industry, honesty, and integrity is a complete answer.

Sterling character. Unswerving honesty and integrity. Rugged manliness *(He won't run away when the shooting starts)*. These qualities must have sounded attractive indeed to voters disgusted by what they were reading elsewhere in the Sunday paper. And the election was only two days away.[35]

Marcell Hendrix was born April 26, 1887, to Daniel and Rosella West Hendrix. Marcell was a true son of western expansion, born in Missouri to a father born in Tennessee, whose own father was born in North Carolina. Rosella West Hendrix died when Marcell was very young. Daniel Hendrix remarried, pledging his troth to Effie Trogden of Greene County. One gets a sense of the propriety of the courtship, as well as the man, from a letter written to Effie, February 6, 1890: "Friend I would like the Privilage of having a conversation with you If agreeable with you on keeping company with you. Please answer soon whether accepted or not. Daniel E. Hendrix." [36]

The conversation must have gone well, as Daniel and Effie were married less than two months later. To Daniel's children by the first marriage, Orpha and Marcell, five were added in this second union: Lillard, Dae, Thelmah, Wanda, and Thomas.

Daniel's marriage to Effie also brought her brother into the family, John Parker Trogden, characterized in Fairbanks and Tuck as "a type of our better class of farmers, a man who uses more brains than brawn in operating his place. He has been successful both as a farmer and a merchant and also as a dealer in live stock."[37]

John Parker Trogden had connections. He was a member of Masonic Lodge #328, the Odd Fellows, Modern Woodmen of America, and the Nichols Anti-Horse Thief Association. He was also active in Greene County Republican politics, serving as Brookline Township Committeeman. Perhaps Uncle John was the conduit for his nephew's own participation in many of these same organizations, including the Republican Party.

Daniel Hendrix died on February 3, 1917, in Phoenix, Arizona, where he'd been living since the previous September in hopes that a change in climate would improve his health. According to his obituary, Daniel was "one of the most widely known citizens of Greene County."[38] Brought back to Brookline for burial, an estimated seven hundred persons gathered at his gravesite.[39]

As Lillard Hendrix plays a prominent role in this narrative, it may be useful to compare the brothers in a family portrait, circa 1915. Marcell, father of two little boys, is already losing his hair, while Lillard sports a thick rug parted down the middle, curled inward at the sides. Though the two men's eyes are not dissimilar, Lillard's heavy jaw gives his face a much rougher cast than his elder half-brother's.

Marcell photographs every bit the church-going, Baptist farmer he in fact was. Prior to assuming office as sheriff of Greene County, Hendrix had exactly zero law enforcement experience—in fact, he would be quoted as saying he had never so much as read a detective novel.

Marcell had married Maude Brown on December 8, 1909. Maude was the second born of Sam and Ida Brown's eight children. She was a comely young woman with a full round face that the years would turn lean. Photos indicate she was not averse to experimenting with hairstyle. As a new bride, Maude's dark hair is carefully sculpted in the shape of a Siberian hat. In young motherhood, a much shorter cut is swept to the side in a manner that would not be out of place eighty years later. In the early 1930s, she was wearing the exaggerated perm popularized by movie stars of the flapper era—a "marcel wave," the style was called.

On January 26, 1925, Marcell and Maude Hendrix were baptized into membership at the Brookline Baptist Church. It isn't known if Willie Florence Young was present. She had joined the congregation by transfer of membership January 16, 1921.[40]

It would be said that Marcell Hendrix had long aspired to the job of sheriff.[41] He launched his campaign on March 31, 1928, putting down five dollars to register as an official candidate. Hendrix wouldn't have to face incumbent Albert Owen. Missouri state statute imposed strict term limits on sheriffs: one four-year-term and out.[42]

Hendrix narrowly secured the Republican nomination in a crowded August primary. In contrast, November's general election was no contest. Democrat Ward Mackey was gracious in defeat, saying of Hendrix, "The citizens of the county have elected a good clean man."[43]

The sheriff-elect certainly hadn't been hurt by the national Republican landslide, paced by Herbert Hoover (dry) over Al Smith (wet) at the top of the ticket. Greene County Democrats took such a thumping, they held a mock parade, some leaning on crutches, others marching with their heads bandaged. A sign on a calliope read, "Scott Curtis For President," in reference to the lone Democrat to have been elected—and that to the relatively minor position of constable of Campbell Township.[44] We will hear more of Scott Curtis.

Having paid a $25,000 bond as guarantee that he would "at all times during his term of office . . . faithfully and punctually discharge all his duties,"[45] the new sheriff took office without ceremony at the stroke of midnight, the first day of 1929. To the surprise of many and delight of some, Federal prohibition agents had been abruptly removed from Springfield, so the *Leader* could forecast a festive night: "Spies To Be Away As City Toasts 1929!"[46] As a Republican replacing a Democrat, per tribal custom, Hendrix brought in a new team of deputies. Among the casualties was Deputy Sheriff Ollie Crosswhite. The few holdovers included veteran jailer Frank Willey—surely a wise call.

Willey (pronounced "Willie") had been "keeping evildoers in their place" since 1909. "The aged brick bastile back of the courthouse" had been his responsibility the past seven years, and it was a matter of personal pride that no prisoner had ever escaped his custody.[47] Frank Willey was well-acquainted with the Young brothers. In the previous administration, Willey and Sheriff Albert Owen were bringing Jennings in for stealing clover seed, when Jennings jumped out of the car—only to be quickly recaptured.[48]

Little Maxine Hendrix was age six at the time of her daddy's election.

Trying to adjust to very new surroundings, the child found a friend in Frank Willey. Seventy years later, she remembers she loved the old man: Maxine sitting in his lap, surely making a nuisance of herself, Willey not minding. [49]

Changes were also underway at City Police Headquarters, including a promotion for Frank Pike. Claude Pike's boy was moving up from the motorcycle squad to the newly created position of Day Patrol, where he would be partnered with Wiley Mashburn. The Day Patrol was to "tour the residential district of the city at regular intervals" and "bend special efforts to locating stolen motor cars."[50]

Also notable were alterations in the journalism landscape. On March 4, 1929, the day of Herbert Hoover's inauguration, the *Springfield Press* came on line, declaring itself "Drafted For Service": "A vast number of citizens petitioned for the launching of *The Press*—otherwise the project never would have been undertaken."[51]

The publisher was veteran Springfield newspaperman, H. S. Jewell. Petitioning citizens included merchants eager to break up the Bixby advertising monopoly. Mayor Gideon surely lent his own encouragement, as he was thoroughly sick of Edson K. Bixby and the *Daily News* and *Leader*.

For anyone trying to piece together the astonishing events of the next several years, the timing could not be more propitious. From 1929 through 1932, Springfield was blessed with lively journalistic debate, including intense competition in covering a series of local stories that would rock the region, then the nation—beginning and ending with the Young Brothers.

CHAPTER SEVEN

Brothers in Crime

"Devotees of the art of criminology will be interested in noticing the photographs and descriptions of the Young brothers in one detail.

"All their eyebrows meet. Penitentiary descriptions note that fact, and examination of the pictures reveals that the line of the brows is unbroken across the center.

"Pictures of Paul and Jennings Young, the two nearest in age, were so much alike that officers observing them last night said they looked like twins in both the front and side views."

—*The Springfield Leader,* January 4, 1932

Upon returning to Christian County in 1917, James David Young first rented, then purchased, 128 acres along the Finley River. The seller was L.P. Gipson; the price, $13,000.[1] Just ten weeks later, J.D. turned around and sold this same property at a five hundred dollar profit, relocating his family to the west edge of Greene County on land purchased from Ed R. and Maude Jackson. The new home was situated on 98⁴⁹⁄₅₀ acres north and east of Brookline, and was sometimes referred to as the "Judge Perkins farm."[2] Again, the purchase price was $13,000. Granted, this was 29²⁹⁄₁₀₀ fewer acres than the Finley River property, but the new acreage was flatter and presumably more tillable. Perhaps the romance had quickly gone out of the hills once J.D. tried to farm them.

The neighborhood was certainly first rate, the farmstead located immediately south of the vast Haseltine Orchards and the stone mansions of the apple-barons. The greatest of these was Hazelcrest, built at the turn of the century to rival anything in Kansas City. Hazelcrest boasted five thousand square feet of living space, twenty-two rooms, and "an elegant roofed porte-cochure" to welcome "carriage-borne guests in style."

The apple mansions featured pressurized water systems—indoor running water!—practically unheard of in the rural areas. Each of the baronial estates had its own water tower, though one put a large tank in the attic and this doubled as a swimming pool for the children.[3]

No one was going to confuse the Young's new spread with Hazelcrest; still, compared to the plain cube dwelling in Tillman County, the house may have appeared genuinely upscale. Features included twin gables and a handsomely fenestrated porch. It wasn't a large house, but the family was getting smaller all the time.

Jarrett had married a lawyer and was living in Arkansas. Oscar was in France, serving as a machine gunner with General Pershing.[4] Mary Ellen had wed a Frederick boy in 1906 and was settled in Oklahoma. Gladys would be going back to Frederick, too, as soon as her beau came home from the war.

That said, J.D. and Willie Florence's move may have been motivated less by property values than their sons' behaviors. Paul and Jennings made an immediate impression on the town of Ozark, sporting flashy clothes and their very own automobile. Paul was remembered as a good conversationalist, and townsfolk remarked on the brothers' "polished manners."[5] But the young men didn't seem to have any jobs. How could Paul afford fourteen or fifteen suits and his own car, with no visible means of employment?[6]

Paul H. Barrett and his wife Mary wrote a book on the massacre, published in 1988. Mr. Barrett, whose distinguished legal career would be crowned as a justice on the Missouri Supreme Court, grew up in Christian County. According to his narrative, young Barrett and his fellow adolescents were in awe of the "only fellows in Ozark with access to an automobile":

> The "punks" were duly impressed by the Youngs' opulence and sophistication and by the car. They noticed that there was a new battery-operated spotlight attached to the left side of the Ford and, in the back seat, some small tools and automobile accessories.
>
> Gathered around the Ford, the cowboys and Indians were all silently but excitedly aware that some of the articles, particularly the spotlight, could not have come into the possession of the Youngs by purchase. Even the "punks" knew that Paul and Jennings could not have paid for these luxuries.[7]

Steinbeck wrote of two punishments among the migrant peoples: "a quick and murderous fight or ostracism; and ostracism was the worst.

For if one broke the laws his name and face went with him, and he had no place in any world, no matter where created."[8]

While life was certainly more settled in Christian County than in the migrant camps of California, the region was, after all, only a couple of generations removed from the Bald Knobbers. "Murderous fights" were largely a thing of the past, but perhaps not ostracism. Hence the supposition: J.D. and Willie Florence couldn't bear the reproach of their neighbors, resulting in the quick move out of the county.

The Youngs had been in their new Brookline area home only a matter of months when the law showed up, searching the barn. There was more than a needle in these haystacks; stolen merchandise from six Christian County business establishments was recovered.

Paul and Jennings were taken into custody. According to the *Christian County Republican* (subscription price: $1a year in advance), the boys had planned to fence the goods in Oklahoma, via an accomplice in Frederick: "The property found consisted of jewelry, automobile accessories and an assortment of dry goods. In all, the property taken is valued at between six and seven hundred dollars."

Paul confessed, implicating not only himself and Jennings, but "another well known boy of the community . . . of which under the circumstances no further mention will be made." The paper concluded that, "This is a lamentable case, of two young men, who had previously borne the best of reputations, sons of parents who have always been highly respectable people in the communities in which they have lived, the whole affair being a shock to the friends and acquaintances of the family."[9]

In May of 1919, Paul and Jennings were sentenced to ten years each in the Missouri State Penitentiary. Their mug shots are indeed startling in similarity. In addition to sharing uni-brows, the brothers' hair is cut and combed in identical fashion, with a touch of curl and parted toward the right side; Jennings' color is listed as medium chestnut brown, Paul's medium *light* chestnut brown—though it's hard to tell any difference in the photographs.

The profiles of Numbers 21852 and 21853 are interchangeable, frontal expressions chiseled from the same mold, the visage of raw, lean men. Both have blue eyes. Jennings is slightly heavier, weighing in at 133 pounds, while Paul tipped the scales at 125. Paul's height is measured at five foot eight-and-a-quarter inches, Jennings at five foot eight without the quarter.

Upon closer inspection, however, one does perceive the age difference. Paul looks not three years older, perhaps—more like three years *harder.* That said, neither Paul nor Jennings has the almost simian look of baby brother in mug shots yet to be taken. [10]

It would have been in one of these first winters back in Missouri that Harry took a hard fall on the ice. He was fourteen at the time, so his mother remembered. After the fall, Harry was prone to fits of violence, "beating door panels with his fists and even breaking out windows." One doctor diagnosed him as insane. The disorder gradually seemed to pass, "although he retained a certain nervousness."[11]

In another version, the fits were brought on by an attack of the German Measles.[12] Or maybe he was just spoiled rotten—"the meanest kid who ever lived"—and the claim of mental affliction was merely an excuse.[13] Who knows? There was clearly a problem with this child.

It would be said that the shock of his sons' criminality killed James David Young.[14] Death came at a sanitarium on Jefferson Avenue in Springfield, November 4, 1921[15]. This would have been the Ozark Sanitarium, formerly known as the Johnson Sanitarium—a story in its own right.

Dr. Samuel A. Johnson had practiced at the Missouri asylum in Nevada, north of Joplin. In 1911, he moved to Springfield, setting up his own private facility for the treatment of mental and nervous disorders in what had formerly been a Catholic church and school.[16] On November 26, 1917, the physician was ax-murdered by an elderly patient, who explained he just wanted to go home.[17]

The extent of James Davids Young's mental and/or nervous disorder is not known. Friends reported, "There was nothing wrong with him except that his mind and body had been sickened by grief and worry over his boys"[18]—but that was apparently enough. This much is certain: the last years of J.D.'s life were not happy ones.

The patriarch was buried in McCauley Cemetery, a small private ground west of Ozark in Christian County.[19] The State of Missouri escorted Paul and Jennings from Jefferson City, but arrived late, so the boys missed the service—one final disappointment for a man who had died of disappointment.[20] Ten years and two months later, McCauley Cemetery would be the scene of great excitement: A fresh-dug grave for two, roads clogged with spectators and reporters waiting arrival of the would-be occupants. These too would be disappointed.

In family crisis, wrote Steinbeck:

> Men stood by their fences and looked at the ruined corn, drying fast now, only a little green showing through the film of dust. The men

were silent and they did not move often. And the women came out of the houses to stand beside their men—to feel whether this time their men would break. . . . Women and children knew deep in themselves that no misfortune was too great to bear if their men were whole.[21]

Now that Willie Florence's man had suffered the ultimate break, what was to become of her? J.D. had left the land and buildings free and clear, with some insurance money, but how was she supposed to keep a farm going? By 1921, the rural economy, which had boomed during the war years, was bust again. The twenties might have been roaring elsewhere, but not in rural America, where depression set in long before Wall Street crashed. Telling statistics from the Jonathan Daniels' study, *The Time Between The Wars:* "Net total farm income dropped from $10,061,000,000 in 1919 to $9,009,000,000 in 1920 and to $4,138,000,000 in 1921"[22]—the year J.D. left Willie Florence to fend for herself.

Her husband was dead. Two of her sons were in prison. Harry was, well . . . undependable, perhaps even insane—and given what had become of J.D., the fear of herditary insanity had to wear on Willie Florence. That left Oscar, back from the war, but Oscar would soon be starting a family of his own and didn't have any more operating capital than she did. It might have made sense for Willie Florence to sell, but with farm values in post-war decline, it is easy to understand her wanting to hold on and hope . . .

Sentenced to ten years each, Paul and Jennings served just over three. The brothers were released on the 29th of April 1922.[23] Paul wasn't out long. He ran afoul of the law in Texas and was sentenced in January of 1924 to ten years in the state correctional facility.[24]

While Paul was doing time in Texas, in April of 1924, Frisco railroad detectives again raided the Young farmstead, this time in search of goods taken from a boxcar parked at nearby Nichols Junction. According to the *Leader,* "The officers found nine tires and tubes, three large rugs and 200 pounds of copper wire. . . . A large quantity of other goods, supposed to have been stolen in this vicinity, was also discovered but was not confiscated."[25] As Scott Curtis later remembered it, the house was covered with rugs, as many as six piled on top of each other.[26] Willie Florence admitted she had "noticed the articles around the house, but did not know her sons stole it."[27]

Jennings, twenty-five now, was the primary suspect, but brothers Oscar and Harry were also charged. This was Harry's first arrest. The newspaper reported him as age seventeen, but he must have been fudging a couple of years, hoping for leniency on account of misrepresented youth. Willie Florence was charged with receiving stolen goods.

Oscar had lived thirty-two years without being convicted of anything—though by now it was routine for him to get picked up along with his brothers. At the time of the Nichols Junction arrest, he and Jennings were awaiting trial on a charge of stealing guns from a hardware store in the Christian County town of Billings.

That case was heard in May of 1924, in Mount Vernon, on a change of venue from Ozark, the brothers claiming they couldn't get a fair trial in their old home county. Jennings and Oscar were represented by future Senator Roscoe Patterson. The Lawrence County jury judged Oscar "not guilty" but hung on Jennings. The prosecutor vowed to try again, but it became a moot point when Jennings confessed to Nichols Junction, taking a three-year term in Leavenworth in exchange for the dropping of all charges against his mother and brothers.[28]

Harry himself broke into the conviction column in November of 1925, accused of defacing the registration number on a motor vehicle. He got off with a $100 fine and court costs, but it was a harbinger of things to come.[29]

The Springfield Leader, February 7, 1927
TWO ARRESTED FOR ROBBING OIL STATION
Harry Young and Roscoe Tuter Held—Latter Said To Have Confessed

It didn't take police long to crack this one. Harry's accomplice, Roscoe Tuter, was behind on his rent at the Baltimore Hotel. With six dollars and forty-one stolen cents in his pocket, Tuter went straight to the Baltimore to pay up. Police arrived shortly thereafter. Roscoe confessed:

> I was staying with Young and for several days he had been trying to get me to help him rob a filling station at Jefferson Avenue and Grand Street. Yesterday Young and I visited the station two or three times. Last night about 10 o'clock, we went to the station but returned to Young's home.
> We returned around 12:30. Young knocked the glass out of the front door and entered. While he was doing that I called a taxi. Before the taxi arrived, we decided to run down an alley.[30]

Roscoe called a taxi? Some folks just aren't cut out for a life of crime. Tuter was perhaps fortunate that Harry didn't take to homicide right then and there.

Butch and Sundance hid the checks under a culvert. Harry told Roscoe they'd taken $12.83 in cash and gave Roscoe half, keeping the extra penny for himself. Harry may have been less than entirely forthright with his fellow thief; according to Chief of Detectives Al Sampey, the cash take was closer to $75.

Officers Scott Curtis and Jesse Teaff found Harry in his room at a boarding house on Mt. Vernon Street, two revolvers beneath his pillow, sleeping alone, apparently[31]—a significant detail in its own right.

The year before, March 9, 1926, Harry had wed Frances Lee O'Dell, who assured the justice of the peace she was over twenty-one, though census records indicate she could have been no older than seventeen.[32] Frances Lee was a farm girl. Like Harry, she had attended the Brick School, due west of the Young place. The union was ill-fated and short-lived—and coincided with Harry's emergence as a genuine criminal in his own right.

August 15, 1926. The crime: buying and receiving stolen goods, specifically, "one household rug, one kitchen linoleum, four dining room chairs, and one mattress all of the aggregate value of $75.00."[33]

September 19, 1926. Harry did "wilfully, unlawfully and feloniously take, steal and carry away one Ford Roadster automobile of the value of $400.00, the personal property of Joe Cromer."[34]

September 27, 1927. Harry did "break into and enter the store of the L.C. Shackelford Café . . . to steal, take and carry away: one small safe of the value of $25.00, good and lawful money of the United States of the value of $325.25, 2 pocket knives of the value of 50 c each, one Elgin Watch of the value of $15.00, 2 fountain pens of the value of $4.00 each, and one wrist watch bracelet of the value of $6.50, all of the aggregate value of $380.75."[35]

In spite of the mounting charges, Harry kept getting released on bail, the money posted by a combination of Willie Florence and his in-laws. Through thick and thin, Willie Florence held to a consistent explanation for the criminal behaviors of her sons: They were influenced by bad company, and Harry was the most vulnerable of the bunch.

In early 1927, Harry was spending a lot of time with the aforementioned Roscoe Tuter—and Willie Florence didn't like it one bit. The concerned mother called Deputy Sheriff Ollie Crosswhite, imploring him to intervene and make Tuter leave her impressionable son alone. Speaking to reporters in June of 1929, Ma Young remembered:

Harry was living with me on South Avenue then. Francis was married but he left his wife and came and roomed next door to us for three or four days. I was afraid he would get Harry into trouble and called Mr. Crosswhite to come and tell Francis to go away.

Harry came running in and said, 'Mamma, what did you call the sheriff for?' I told him that I felt Francis was going to get him into trouble. That night they robbed that filling station. That Francis was always a mean boy.[36]

Wait. *Francis* was a mean *boy?* We're confused. Was Francis perhaps Roscoe's middle name? No, his tombstone at Brookline Cemetery reads W. Roscoe. The only Francis/Frances in Harry's life seems to have been his wife. Either the reporter bollixed the story, or Willie Florence's synapses were not firing at full capacity.

At the time of the 1929 interview, her Harry had just been accused of murdering a law officer. Perhaps Roscoe Tuter and Frances Lee O'Dell Young had somehow been conjoined in a distressed mother's memory—the real problem *not* the ne'er-do-well accomplice in petty crime, but the temptress who had enchanted her youngest son, leading him along evil paths.

On March 28, 1927, in the court of Judge C. A. Hubbard, Lyman Harry Young confessed to the crime of larceny regarding the City Services Oil Company filling station. All other charges were dropped. Harry's sentence: Three years in the Missouri State Penitentiary at Jefferson City.[37]

Much would later be made of Harry's resolve that he was never going back to prison. The implication: Harry was so traumitized by his experience in Jefferson City that he would rather die than return. By all accounts, the Missouri State Penitentiary of this era was itself cruel and unusual punishment. Nevertheless, by the standards of the day, Harry's first and only prison stint seems to have been relatively cushy.

In January of 1932, Frank Jones, a member of the prison board, told the Springfield papers that most of Harry's eighteen months were served at the penitentiary dairy farm. "I recall him as a very energetic and efficient young man," said Jones. "He had charge of sanitary conditions and weighing of milk, and was always very accomodating."

There was one severe bump along the road to the straight and narrow: Frances Lee was threatening divorce. Concerned that Harry might run away, prison officials returned him to the Big House—but that was only temporary and Harry was soon back among the cows.

Frank Jones said that Harry "was such a fine young man I never expected to hear of him being in trouble again."[38]

Bill Padgett, who had been a guard at Prison Farm No. 3, and in 1932 was operating a lunch counter in Springfield, agreed that Harry was a model prisoner. According to the *Leader,* "The former guard also said Young frequently tipped the guards as to the attitudes of the inmates."[39] This did not endear Harry to other inmates.

A fellow ex-con said that Harry Young "was a regular rat. He snitched his way into a trusty's job and spent most of his time ratting on his fellow inmates. It was the height of his joy for him to find some of the boys in possession of a little change or something which they were not supposed to have, then run and blab to the guards."[40]

The *Leader* report noted that "Young's former fellow prisoners said it was known in the penitentiary that Young was placed on the prison farm away from the 'tough muggs' who had planned to do him harm because of his tattle-tale disposition."[41] From which we may infer that Harry's aversion to prison life perhaps had less to do with "hard time," than a snitch's fear of his fellow inmates.

According to Missouri Penitentiary records, Prisoner #31358 was five foot, six-and-five-eighth inches tall, possessed of medium light chestnut hair, blue eyes, with medium fair complexion. His formal education had terminated after the ninth grade. He is listed as a Protestant farmer. The three-year penal clock started March 28, 1927. Meritorious service would have put Harry out on December 27, 1928, but Harry did even better than that. He was granted ninety-two additional merit days and released on September 26, 1928.[42]

Steinbeck's Tom Joad: "But when a bunch of men take an' lock you up four years, it ought to have some meaning. Men is supposed to think things out. Here they put me in, an' keep me an' feed me four years. That ought to either make me so I won't do her again or else punish me so I'll be afraid to do again."[43]

Meritorious service notwithstanding, Harry Young's experience at the Missouri State Penitentiary served neither purpose.

These were hard times for Willie Florence. There are references to a nervous breakdown.[44] She may have supplemented her income as a seamstress.[45] Vinita was enrolled at the high school in Springfield, and mother and daughter lived in a succession of downtown boarding houses.

Oscar and his wife Mabel seem to have taken up residence at the farm. The machine gunner had come back from the war to dim prospects. With the rural economy in shambles, Oscar could not hope to buy land of his own. What bank was going to lend him any money?

He certainly couldn't count on inheriting the farm on Haseltine

Road. Eighteen acres had already been sold off, and the remaining eighty were heavily mortgaged. Lawyers like Roscoe Patterson didn't come cheap and the revolving door of bail money for Harry only added to the family misfortune. Is anyone surprised at suggestions of tension between Oscar's wife, the former Mabel Conn, and her in-laws?

The house appears not to have been big enough for all of them. When Willie Florence moved back to the farm after Vinita's graduation, Oscar and Mabel moved out, living as farm renters on land near the old Wilson's Creek Battlefield.

After the combat of August 10, 1861, the Confederates held the field along Wilson's Creek. Union dead were disposed of without ceremony, dumped into natural sinkholes. For years and even decades to follow, corpses would occasionally bubble up to the surface. Did the lingering putrefaction somehow infect the vicinity with violence? Men like Oscar might be immune, but perhaps the ghosts could work with a Harry Young.

CHAPTER EIGHT

The Republic Scuffle

From the pages of *Startling Detective Adventures Magazine*
"I Survived Missouri's Posse Massacre"
By Frank Pike

"Do you know Harry Young?" the sheriff asked those gathered around the body after it was found by Lillard Hendrix.

"Sure," almost everyone said.

"But that young fellow didn't do this," one man asserted. "He's as mild looking as they make them."

The sheriff stooped over the body.

"Between that shot," he said pointing to the wound in Noe's chest, and then pointing to the one in his head, "and that one, Harry Young wasn't mild looking. Mark Noe looked into the eyes of a killer before that last shot. Young didn't have to kill Noe to get away after he wounded him. He shot that last bullet deliberately, like a damned fiend."

The narrative follows the Frisco track. At the beginning of the Civil War, the rails from St. Louis terminated at Rolla, a hundred miles east and north of Greene County. The railroad reached Springfield in 1870, going through north of town.

Wherever the tracks stopped for a time, another settlement sprang up. First stop west of Springfield: Nichols Junction, a.k.a. Junction City, where the main line intersected with rails leading to Kansas City. Haseltine, serving the apple barons, was the next station.[1] From Haseltine Station, Haseltine Road went due south, past what would be the Young farm, while the railroad continued building at an angle of south and west.

In the fall of 1871, at another stop in the tracks, Brookline was born. The town's nucleus was business and residents transplanted from Little

York, which, having been bypassed by the railroad, was doomed to extinction. Brookline was never much of a town, though, and it was soon eclipsed by the next stop on the line: Republic.[2]

In 1929, Republic, Missouri, had a heck of a baseball team. On the evening of June 2, many Republicans had gone to Billings, seven miles further down the tracks, for what would be remembered as the best game of the season. The rival town teams were tied at the end of nine innings, the contest not decided until the fourteenth, when the visitors scored three times to post a 5-2 victory. Townsfolk returned to Republic in a state of elation.[3]

We don't know if Harry Young actually attended the ball game. Oval LaFollette would tell Marcell Hendrix that he and Harry had just been driving around—down to Billings, over to Clever, and back to Republic.

If there was joy in Republic that Sunday evening, perhaps Harry's life felt more like Muddville. Earlier in the day, Harry had accompanied other family members in a visit to his father's gravesite at McCauley Cemetery. Did his mother ruminate about James David's righteousness and good standing in the community, how it broke his heart when his sons ran afoul of the law, her humiliation when Paul and Jennings were late for the funeral, and all the tragedy that had befallen her since?

If so, perhaps that wasn't the worst of it.

Harry's marriage had very recently ended. After his release from the penitentiary, he and Frances Lee tried making a go of it, living with her folks, south and east Republic, but Frances Lee finally gave up. Harry moved out, taking a room in Springfield. On June 2, 1929, his address was listed as 602 West Harrison.[4]

According to Frances Lee's divorce pleading, she had "faithfully demeaned herself and discharged all her duties as the wife of the defendant and at all times treated him with kindness and affection." But Harry, "wholly disregarding his duties as the husband of plaintiff had offered such indignities as to render her condition intolerable." Furthermore, the defendant was said to be "quarrelsome and abusive" and "often threatened" Frances Lee. His criminal record didn't help matters, of course.

Harry didn't bother to appear at the proceeding. On May 16, 1929, a jury found that Frances Lee was the "innocent and injured party." The divorce was granted and her maiden name restored, so that she was once again Frances Lee O'Dell.[5]

On the night of June 2, 1929, Harry was driving a gray Ford coupe. With him was a "farm boy" named Oval LaFollette. Oval was only twenty years old, but one of those had been served in the Missouri State Penitentiary on conviction for what the newspapers termed criminal assault,[6] but was recorded by the Missouri State Penitentiary as "rape."[7] After making the circuit—Republic to Billings to Clever, and back to Republic—the coupe cruised up and down Main Street, while Mark Noe watched from inside Owen & Short Hardware.

Mark Noe (pronounced No'-ee) was forty years old and married to Bernice. He was from one of Republic's founding families. Noe was an affable looking fellow in his first year of law enforcement, having received all the customary training—which is to say none at all. Prior to his election as constable, Noe worked in the hardware store. He would be characterized as "popular in business and well-liked among the business men." His obituary would make note of the constable's sense of "duty."

When the gray coupe stopped in the middle of Main Street, and Oval LaFollette climbed out from the passenger side, Mark Noe left his perch at Owen & Short and went out to do his job.

The inquest was held the next evening, June 3, 1929, in the Boy Scout Room on the second floor of the hardware building. Greene County Coroner Murray C. Stone called D.E. McNabb to testify regarding events of the previous night:

> McNabb: "There isn't much to tell. I was walking up the street, Mark was in Owen and Short's hardware store. He asked me to come in and have a friendly chat with him."
>
> Stone: "What time was that?"
>
> McNabb: "Somewhere around ten o'clock. We saw a car parked in front of Ryan's café and Mark said he believed it was a stolen car."
>
> Stone: "Did you see who got out of the car?"
>
> McNabb: "Yes."
>
> Stone: "Did you know who they were?"
>
> McNabb: "I wasn't quite sure."
>
> Stone: "What did Mark do?"
>
> McNabb: "We went in the back room of the hardware store and Mark checked the license number of the car. When we came back from the room, the car was gone. They drove up and down the street six or eight times. They first stopped at the café on the east side of the street, then they drove north, came back and stopped in the center of the street. One of the two got out of the car, spoke to some boys

who were standing there, and went inside the restaurant. As he got out of the car, Mark said, 'I believe that he has a bottle of whiskey in his shirt. I believe I'll go out and get that gentleman.'"

Oval LaFollette, a scary looking young fellow in his own right, possessed of black hair, deep slate eyes, and ruddy complexion,[8] gave this testimony:

> Coroner Stone: "Where do you live?"
> LaFollette: "About five miles northwest from here. We were driving down the street a time or two."
> Stone: "Who was with you?"
> LaFollette: "Harry Young."
> Stone: "About what time?"
> LaFollette: "About eleven o'clock."
> Stone: "Whose car?"
> LaFollette: "Young's car."
> Stone: "Did you ride around a while?"
> LaFollette: "Yes. We saw some boys go into the cafe. We stopped the car in the middle of the street."
> Stone: "Which café?"
> LaFollette: "Ryan's café. I went in the cafe, came out and started to get in the car when Mark Noe said to me, 'Get in.' I did."

Noe seems to have intended that Harry would steer the coupe to the home of Republic's justice of the peace, where Harry would be charged with disorderly conduct.[9] According to Oval, he himself was in the coupe's middle front seat, sandwiched between Harry and Noe. Harry had a pistol. Noe reached across to take it. Harry was not inclined to give it up. Noe had a gun of his own and may or may not have used it to hit Harry on the head. Harry's firearm went off. LaFollette slid out from underneath Noe and ran away, leaving the constable and Harry still in the car.

Bernice Adams, being duly sworn, testified as follows:

> Adams: "About eleven o'clock last night I was out in front at the gas tank and I heard what sounded like a pistol shot up the street. I looked up and I saw a Gray Ford Coupe coming down the street in low and passed by. I could see someone fighting in the car. They drove down by Fikes' and stopped and as soon as the car stopped one fellow jumped out and ran, came back up the street and turned the corner at the Baptist Church and went down the alley. About the time he got to the corner, another shot was fired in the car."

Stone: "Was the car standing still?"

Adams: "Yes, and I heard someone call for help and then the car started again. The car was on the left hand side of the road, then crossed to the right hand and when they got over there they shot again. They then went right out of town."

Stone: "How many shots did you hear?"

Adams: "Three."

Stone: "One while the car was moving?"

Adams: "Yes."

Stone: "One while the car was standing?"

Adams: "Yes."

Stone: "Another one after it started up?"

Adams: "Yes."

Stone: "All sounded like the same gun?"

Adams: "Same gun."

The killing weapon was a 32-20 caliber revolver, a heavy weapon discharging a steel-nose bullet.[10] The coroner would determine that Noe had been shot in the right arm, the chest, and the back of his head—quite probably in that order.

Startling Detective Frank Pike told readers Harry acted of out premeditation. Some months earlier, Mark Noe had taken a gun away from Harry. Harry became abusive. Noe slapped him. Harry hissed, "You have arrested me for the last time, Noe."[11]

In Pike's telling, on the night of June 2, 1929, Harry Young was deliberately provoking Republic's constable, knowing his "reckless driving on the main street of Republic" was a challenge the "courageous and well-loved" marshal could not ignore. While Frank Pike is not always the most reliable of sources, a pre-existing hatred does make sense, given what turned into—by the third bullet, at least—an execution.

That's the *Startling Detective* version. We will return to the presumably firmer ground of sworn inquest testimony, with Detective H. G. Snyder on the stand:

Stone: "You arrested LaFollette about what time?"

Snyder: "About four or four-thirty."

Stone: "Where was he?"

Snyder: "At his brother-in-law's, six or seven miles from here. Brother-in-law's name is Kates."

Stone: "Was LaFollette in bed asleep?"

Snyder: "Yes."

Stone: "What did Lafollette do?"

Snyder: "The first thing I did when I went in and awoke him, I asked him what he did. He said nothing. I told him that we had been sent after him and asked him if he didn't run off from the marshal last night. He said, 'Yes.' We told him that he would have to go with us and that we would have to take him to town, as we figured Young had bumped Mark off."

Lillard Hendrix was called.

This morning about six or fifteen after six, I was standing outside and two men came up the road going north and stopped and hollered to come there right quick. They said a man was lying dead at the corner. . . . As quick as I looked at the man, I knew it was Mark Noe.

Lillard and Marcell Hendrix farmed neighboring acreage in Brookline Township. Marcell's farmhouse was just yards off the Frisco tracks, south and west of Brookline on the way to Republic; Lillard's place was on the county road due north of Republic. In dumping Mark Noe's body on Hendrix home turf, was Harry sending a not-so-subtle message? *You Hendrixes think you're so high and mighty. Come and get me, Marcell—if you can.*

As an exclamation point to his disdain, Harry seems to have taken his own sweet time about getting away. He went back into Springfield to his room on West Harrison and packed a grip before hitting the road—not exactly the behavior of a desperate man. Even then, he made no attempt at stealth. Instead of entering by the "separate outside door" to his room, Harry woke up the whole house, banging on the front door. There are suggestions of "the odor of liquor."[12]

Harry was positively identified around 12:30 A.M. Monday, servicing his car in Halltown, west of Springfield on Route 66. Another clue pointing in the same direction: The clothes he'd been wearing Sunday night—black trousers, overalls, a faded shirt (all bloodied now)—were found on the side of the highway west of town. Harry had apparently tried to burn the clothes, but soaked them in kerosene, which lacks the burn factor of gasoline.

Hendrix, Mashburn, and Oliver took up the scent south and west: Joplin; Picher, Oklahoma; Wichita (where it was said Harry could be found hiding at sister Rettie's); Tulsa; Cherryville, Kansas; Independence, Missouri.[13] No Harry. Of course, a close watch was kept in the Young's old stomping ground of Frederick, Oklahoma.

The Missouri Penitentiary supplied photos of the suspect, and these received wide distribution. As described in the *Springfield Leader*:

> They pictured the alleged killer as a short, stocky man, light complexioned, with weak slate blue eyes and light chestnut hair. He is not quite five feet, six inches tall. One of the man's distinguishing marks is a small scar three inches below the left ear lobe near the chin, and there is another scar on the back of his head.

The *Press* added, "He is slightly bald."[14]

There was a flurry of excitement from central Missouri. Harry had reportedly been seen in Sedalia and his mother was rumored to be headed that way. But Ma Young was quickly located, still in Springfield, and the Sedalia tip was dismissed as a hoax.

The first Willie Florence heard of Harry's predicament was from a *Leader* reporter who showed up at 211½ W. Walnut, asking for her reaction. Her response: "I can't believe it. It all seems like a dream to me."[15]

The widow's rented room was described as "dark, dingy and poorly furnished." Mention was made of a recent nervous breakdown and continued poor health.[16] But Willie Florence wasn't going to hang her head for anybody. "I've tried to live right," she said later in the week, "My mother and father had a Christian home and taught me to do right. I had 11 children, all living, if Harry is alive, and I tried to teach them to be good. Whenever they got into trouble it was because they got into bad company."[17]

Per macabre journalistic custom of the gangster era, Mother Young was asked if it wouldn't be a comfort to learn her son was dead—as opposed to him living in constant fear of arrest and trial. "'No, I wouldn't want him dead,' she sighed. 'No mother wants her boy to die. But I do wish he could get away somewhere where they could never find him. Of course, I could never know where he was, or ever see him again.'" And be sure of this, said the fugitive's mother: "If Harry did do it, I know he shot in self-defense."[18]

As for Harry's "companion in the carousel which led to murder,"[19] Oval was held in the county jail on charges of carrying a concealed weapon. Turns out he was related to William Jennings Bryan's pal, the late Wisconsin senator Robert M. LaFollette. That nugget was gleaned from Oval's dad, who said of his boy, "Oval isn't bad, he's just fallen in with bad company."[20]

The *Republic Monitor* mourned the passing of a friend, writing of Mark Noe:

> He gave his life in an effort to keep Republic, our home and our town, a clean little city, gave his life to make this a better place to live, a safer place for the people, Republic's visitors and its boys and girls. He was a straight-forward clean thinking gentleman with high ideals. Every citizen keenly sympathizes his tragic end, and sincerely hopes the cruel lawless fiend shall quickly receive justice according to law and order.[21]

There would be nothing "quick" about justice and Harry Young— not this time. Hendrix, Mashburn, and Oliver returned from the chase empty-handed. Willie Florence's concern that she "could never know where he was, or ever see him again" proved overly pessimistic; over the next thirty-one months, the fugitive would occasionally show up at the family farm for a short, nervous visit. In contrast, Marcell Hendrix would not again set eyes on Harry until January 2, 1932—and then only for a moment.

Strong Cigars

"The report by a 'citizen's committee,' composed of Preachers Hale and C.B. Jeans, Mrs. J.C. Dubuque and Albert Hayward deserves some attention. This report was published in yesterday's newspaper. I happen to know that as usual, Edson K. Bixby is at the bottom of it. At a meeting behind closed doors night before last Edson K. Bixby, C.B. Jeans and Albert Hayward were in consultation together with Preacher Hale. I defy them to deny it."

—Mayor Thomas H. Gideon,
The Springfield Press, October 17, 1929

Harry Young had disappeared into the vast expanse of the American southwest, but Springfield would not lack for excitement in his absence. Dobb Adams' date with the hangman was set for September 27, 1929, in Bolivar. On the morning of September 9, still housed at the Greene County jail, Adams asked to see Sheriff Hendrix. Hendrix arrived shortly after noon, asking what Dobb wanted. As reported in the *Daily News*:

> "Mr. Hendrix," he started slowly. "I just want to tell you how much I appreciate what you have done for me. You've treated me like a man and I want to thank you."
> The sheriff explained that it was his intention to treat all prisoners alike, regardless of what they had done.
> "Well," Dobb continued, "I couldn't have expected better treatment."

Hendrix went to take a phone call. While the sheriff was away, Adams collapsed. Hurrying back to the cell, Hendrix asked, "Did you take something?" Yes, Dobb had: A dozen blue-green poison pills—bichloride of mercury.

Dobb's wife, Meada, was called. She had tried to poison herself the previous year, when the guilty verdict was first announced. It was speculated Dobb was in possession of the pills even then; that he and Meada had made a suicide pact, but Dobb hadn't been able to swallow his end. In death throes now, he wanted Hendrix to know, "I wasn't myself when I killed the women." (Mrs. Whalin and Miss St. Clair.) "I was just crazy about my wife. I wanted to know where she was. They wouldn't tell me."

To those disappointed that Dobb had cheated the hangman, the *Daily News* reported this consolation: "By the time the jailer and the Sheriff got him out of the cell and placed him on a small cot in the outer office of the jail, he was in an agony of pain. From that time til the end, he suffered a thousand deaths."[1]

Then, on Friday, October 11, 1929, a Federal grand jury in Kansas City indicted Springfield Police Chief G. Claude Pike on the charge of violating the national prohibition law. Specifically, Pike was said to have taken ten gallons of confiscated whiskey from the police station for the purpose of his own consumption. The grand jury heard testimony from several Springfield police officers, including Wiley Mashburn.

Pike was arrested, bond posted at $2,500. The chief termed the charges "absolutely malicious and false"—a conspiracy hatched by the Bixby crowd "to win the recall election against Mayor Gideon."[2] The timing *was* interesting. The much-anticipated mayoral recall vote was scheduled for October 18, just a week away.

On the intervening Sunday, prince of the First Baptist pulpit Lewis M. Hale left no doubt where he stood. "Take for instance the prohibition law," he told his congregation. "Every public official is sworn to do his duty in enforcing the laws of the land. It is manifestly plain that no public official, then, has a right to himself violate these laws."[3]

Lewis Milton Hale, who photographed as a pensive fellow, with light wavy hair and a dimple in the middle of his chin, was never one to duck the hard issues. It would be remembered that "Dr. Hale viewed very seriously the problems of the 1930s: depression, rising threats of war in Europe, Asia and Africa, repeal of prohibition and changes in moral values and practices which he described as people 'playing the devil in general.'"[4]

Born in 1882, the son of a small town preacher, Hale graduated from Southern Seminary in 1913 and was married to Harriett Babb the same year. Harriett was herself a soldier of the cross. First Baptist celebrated its Diamond Jubilee in 1927, with what Wayne Bartee described as "a week of special services climaxed by an elaborate pageant in the Shrine Mosque. . . . The Spirit of War, portrayed by C. F. Baggett and looking much like the defeated Kaiser stalked through parts of the pageant, but was overcome by the Spirit of Christianity in a white robe, portrayed by Mrs. Hale."[5]

In his controversial sermon of October 13, 1929—the Sunday before the mayoral recall election—The Reverend Mr. Hale insisted he wasn't telling anyone how to vote, and he certainly wasn't "saying it because I think it is popular to say it, for I don't think it is"; rather, he was motivated out of "profound Christian duty." Hale's hearers owed it to themselves, their community, and their God to go to the polls on Friday and "vote intelligently."[6]

As if the Federal position needed further illustration, prohibition agents swooped back into Springfield on Wednesday, October 16, with a series of high profile liquor raids lasting into Thursday morning.[7]

For the coup de gras, a "Citizen's Committee," headed by none other than Reverend Hale, issued a statement declaring Mayor Gideon unfit for office. Their report, printed in Thursday's *Daily News,* included the accusation that on a recent trip to Jefferson City, Gideon and Pike had packed "an abundance of liquor." Mayor and chief imbibed freely on the way, and Gideon arrived in the state capitol "in a sickly, drunken condition." This had been witnessed by Mose Kelton, former head of the County Children's home.

The "citizens" incorporated a complaint from Ollie Crosswhite regarding the police department's cozy relationship with "known bootlegger" Sam Goldstein. But the most damning charge came from within Pike's own ranks. The October 17, 1929, *Springfield Daily News* headline read "Nine Policemen Say Mayor, Chief linked to Crime." Beneath it ran the subtitle "Statement Declares 'It Appears Chief of Police and the Mayor Are in Accord with Underworld.'"

An excerpt:

> We know that conditions are bad. We have not done many things which we should have done if unhampered in our official duties. We have protested frequently against the keep-still requirements of Chief Pike, but it appears that the chief and the mayor are in accord with the underworld and do not want gamblers, bawdy houses and bootleggers molested. Anyway, they have frowned upon efforts on our part to clean up the joints and without cooperation of our superiors in office we can do but little.

The nine signing officers included W. K. Webb, who had done himself credit in the Dobb Adams shootout, and Wiley H. Mashburn. Mashburn, a six-year veteran of the force, had been born and raised on a local farm. Moving into Springfield, Mashburn first worked for an ice company, then as a streetcar motorman, before joining the police department. In signing the declaration, Mashburn was putting his job on the line, but it may have seemed the smart bet. Those who sided with Gideon would surely be ousted if, as seemed likely, the mayor was recalled.

The report of the Citizen's Committee and dissident officers appeared on Thursday morning—the day before the election. That evening, Gideon struck back via the *Press*, castigating his opponents for this "eleventh hour" attack:

> To resort to this cheap and vicious trick is to admit the charges could not have been made at an earlier hour when the facts could be developed and the real truth shown. The winding up of this campaign in the very despicable and damnable fashion by Bixby and his crowd should and will meet with the rebuke it merits on the part of the people.

The mayor specifically denounced Ollie Crosswhite as "a bitter partisan against me from the start."

Even before this last-minute flurry, Edson K. Bixby was sufficiently confident that he wrote of the outcome as forgone conclusion:

> The News & Leader have no candidate for mayor. They shall have none after Mayor Gideon has been recalled. Their interest in the election of Mayor Gideon's successor shall be only that of every good citizen, that the mayor, whoever he may be, be a man of honesty and sincerity and of such a type and character that Springfield need no longer blush at the mention his name.[8]

Voters went to the polls the next morning, Friday, October 18, 1929. The results were ruefully reported in Saturday's *Daily News*: *Final Count Shows 6224 for Removal of Mayor to 7511 Against; Riotous Demonstration Staged by Gideon's Friends and Members of Police Force.*

Sirens screamed in celebration as cops raced motorcycles around the public square. "Guns roared in the main business district"; an effigy of Edson K. Bixby was toted through town in a W. L. Starne (remember that name) ambulance. Someone threw a stink bomb into the office of the *Daily News* and *Leader,* which offered this comment: "The victors were speaking in the language they knew best."[9]

Not all Springfield officers joined the celebration, of course. Wiley Mashburn and his fellow signatories were summarily fired.

The *Press,* on the other hand, reported the results as vindication of G. C. Pike, "victor in a just cause." Supporters "swept him onto their shoulders, cheered him like a football captain, and followed him through the city, shouting confidence in him."[10]

That confidence was not shared by the Federal grand jury, which, on November 6, added a charge of bribery to existing indictments against the chief. Pike had asked for a "speedy trial." He got it.

The proceedings began Monday, November 19, 1929, given extensive coverage by the Bixby papers. Among the first witnesses called by the prosecution was Greene County Sheriff Marcell Hendrix. District Attorney W. E. Vandeventer "asked Hendrix how long he had known Chief Pike. The sheriff said about 15 months."

> Vandeventer: "Did you talk with him at the police station about the law violations?"
>
> Hendrix: "He called me to his office one day last spring when I was at the police station."
>
> Vandeventer: "Did you discuss liquor violations?"
>
> Hendrix: "To an extent, yes."
>
> Vandeventer: "What did Chief Pike say?"
>
> Hendrix: "He said, 'You have been elected sheriff and you have juristiction over the city and the county. I have jurdisdiction over the city only. I wonder,' the chief said, 'If we couldn't arrange so that you would keep you hands off the city and let me take care of it while you watch the county.'"
>
> Vandeventer: "What did you say?"
>
> Hendrix: "I told him no. I explained it was my duty to look for law violations in both the city and the county."

The implication seemed clear enough: Pike wanted Hendrix to stay out of city business—particularly liquor enforcement, or lack thereof. Pike later testified he was only trying to help the sheriff.

Pike had a lot of explaining to do—for instance, those ten gallons of whiskey transported from the police station to his home. Pike cited a recent veterans reunion in Cape Giradeau. Old soldiers had raided the local police station in quest of confiscated whiskey to lubricate their party. A similar gathering was scheduled for Springfield. At the advice of Mayor Gideon, Pike removed the whiskey for the good of the veterans, so they might avoid temptation. The prosecution suggested Pike was slandering veterans. Prosecution: *Why wasn't the liquor just destroyed?* Pike: *It was evidence.*

Damaging testimony was given by Pike's former second-in-command,

Hank Teaff, who admitted he'd served as Pike's "bagman" in receiving payoffs from illicit establishments such as Tom Fuzzell's Keystone Bar. The defense countered it was Teaff, not Pike, who was the scuzzball.

The defense called Thomas Gideon to the stand. The mayor confirmed Pike's testimony concerning the soldier's reunion. The prosecution wanted to know more about this trip to Jefferson City.

> District Attorney Vandeventer: "Isn't it a fact that when you got into the restaurant you were so drunk that you laid your head down on the table, and that you vomited right there on the floor?"
> Mayor Gideon: "I got sick on a cigar."
> Vandeventer: "Don't you smoke all the time?"
> Gideon: "I got a hold of one that was too strong for me."
> Vandeventer: "Did the cigar make you unconsious?"[11]

To which, reported the *Leader,* "There was no intelligable answer, but the mayor was evidently confused and indignant at this part of the proceedings."

Vandeventer returned to the liquor taken from police headquarters. The soldiers' reunion had come and gone without incident, had it not? "Gideon admitted this, but repeated that he had wished to take no chances," reported the *Leader.*

Vandeventer: "You mean that there was no use taking chances that the veterans of the World war were burglars and robbers?" This prompted an objection from defense counsel.

Charles Newman addressed the jury on behalf of Pike:

> Gentlemen, seldom has it fallen to the lot of twelve men to decide a case more important than this one. Here stands a man who has spent his life in useful production, until his hair is streaked with gray, who lives here in Springfield with his family, serving as chief of police, which office you know would not have been given to him if he had not had an honorable and good name.

Chet Keyes spoke for the prosecution:

> The whole thing is a mess—just a dirty rotten mess—that's what it is. If you men were walking through a woods and you came upon a rattlesnake, you would kill that snake without hesitation, so that its venom and its sting might not reach your homes and your families. It is your duty to go to the jury-room, to carefully consider the evidence, and if you find that a verdict of 'guilty' is justified, to be fearless and true to your oaths, and to return that verdict.

While unable to reach unanimity on the charge of bribery, the twelve jurors were agreed re the count of transporting confisacted liquor: Guilty. Pike was fined $500, but, to the considerable consternation of the Bixby papers, remained in control of the police department—albeit temporarily.

Amidst a subsequent firestorm of criticism, Pike announced he would resign on January 1, vowing to return upon his vindication by the courts. Gideon appointed Sergeant Ed Waddle to fill the vacancy. To say the *Leader* was not impressed would be an understatement; the paper characterized Ed Waddle as one of Gideon's political cronies and called his appointment, "Just another strong cigar."[12]

The Feds were not done with Pike. The first jury had hung on the bribery charge. In April, the prosecution tried again. Far from being vindicated, on April 11, 1930, Pike was found guilty of accepting pay-offs from bootleggers and sentenced to a year and a day of Federal time in Leavenworth. The *Leader* described his adieu in maudlin terms that sounded almost conciliatory:

> This afternoon he was on his way to prison to begin the serving of his sentence. He and 22 others—bootleggers, gamblers, white slavers—were herded into a special car attached to the 3:15 Sunnyland.[13]
>
> It was a tragic and somewhat pitiful farewell. Gone was the proud arrogance that had marked his police regime and as a man. Deep in humility and with a newfound friendliness in his misfortune, he clasped the hands of those who had called him "chief" and said, simply, "I'm sorry."
>
> Wearing a blue serge suit and white sombrero, Pike was dressed exactly as the men had seen him day after day for two years. However, the clothes were not as neat appearing as they had been in the past. The trousers bagged at the knees, long streaks of shine on the back of the coat and around the elbows told of its age, and he made no effort to brush aside the ashes that had fallen on his vest from the end of a huge cigar.[14]

Less than a week later, G. C. Pike was joined in Leavenworth by Jennings Young. Jennings had graduated from box cars and hardware stores into big time car thievery. He was arrested in Texas and tried on three counts of violating the Dyer Act—transporting stolen cars across state lines. The axis seems to have been Frederick to Fort Worth; autos from as far away as San Diego were smuggled across the Oklahoma line into Texas, then sold in Tarrant County.

Jennings arrived in Leavenworth on April 17, 1930—six days after

Pike.[15] Did Jennnings and Pike strike up a relationship in this period? Surely Pike had known *of* Jennings and vice versa. Did one seek the other out in the time they shared at Leavenworth? As will be demonstrated, this is not an idle query.

Having first bagged Deputy Chief Hank Teaff, then used Teaff to get to Pike, the Feds now went for the top of the food chain: Mayor Gideon himself. Unlike Teaff, however, Pike showed no sign of rolling over on his boss. The trial was scheduled for October. In September, Gideon went on what was described as a "good will" tour of the Ozarks. The Bixby papers suggested he was trying to influence potential jurors.[16]

Federal Judge Albert L. Reeves came down from Kansas City to officiate. Reeves, whose visage was right out of *American Gothic,* would preside over some of the most sensational trials of the era, including the 1936 Pendergast voting-fraud scandal, where he earned this review from Senator Harry Truman: "A Jackson County Democrat has as much a chance of a fair trial in the Federal District Court as a Jew would have in a Hitler court or a Trotsky follower before Stalin."[17]

In the Gideon trial of 1930, prosecutors reprised evidence from the Pike proceedings. The mayor was called to answer for some of his appointments to the police force. Fred Walker, for instance. Was it not true that Walker had pled guilty to indecent exposure in Marshfield, yet remained on the force? And how about Ben Bilyeu?

> Vandeventer: "Didn't you appoint a man to the police force by the name of Ben Bilyeu who was charged with murder in Christian county, who has been convicted of felonious assault?"
>
> Gideon: "He is not on the police force. I only gave him a commission without pay to do special work."
>
> Vandeventer: "Well when you gave him that commission didn't you know he had been convicted?" [18]
>
> Gideon allowed he had read something like that in the newspaper, but in any event, Bilyeu was no longer on the police force.
>
> Vandeventer: "He's still got his badge and commission doesn't he?"
>
> Gideon: "I don't know whether he's got a badge or not. If he's got one he bought it."
>
> Vandeventer: "He's carrying a gun like a regular officer, isn't he?"

Gideon said he didn't know about that, either, whereupon the prosecution moved on to more questions about Fred Walker, the indecent exposer.

The *Leader* was poised to report the verdict, having situated correspondent Beth Campbell "directly across the hall from the courtroom." A "special telephone wire" had been "stretched, without switchboard connections" from Campbell's courthouse perch, north of downtown, to the *News & Leader* editorial office south of the town square. In the Bixby building, a reporter "sitting with the headphone to her ears called the report from the court room, word by word, to a staff that grouped, with feverish pulse, around her."

> "All right," she cried, repeating the sound of the voice at the other end of the wire. "The jury has knocked upon the door . . . now they're coming in . . . they look solemn . . . must have reached a verdict . . . the foreman hands it to the judge . . . some of the defendants and attorneys aren't there . . . the judge is sitting there toying with the verdict...turns it over in his hands . . . ALL SET . . . "
> "Stand by," the managing editor cried.
> Then: "Gideon guilty!" shouted the reporter at the telephone.
> "Gideon guilty!" went the cry of the pressroom below, where the big presses were waiting.[19]

The joy in Leaderville was tempered when Gideon declared he would remain in office while the verdict was appealed. The *Daily News* reported: "Springfield yesterday began a year or more under the rule of a man under sentence for two years to the federal penitentiary and a $10,000 fine for conspiracy to violate the prohibition laws."[20]

If this wasn't enough excitement, even as the Gideon trial was underway in Springfield came the sensational news that Jake Fleagle had been shot in Branson. Fleagle was the kingpin in one of the most high-profile crimes of the era. In May of 1928, he and three others had taken $219,000 from the First National Bank of Lamar, Colorado, killing the bank president, his son, a teller, and a Kansas physician— the latter after being kidnapped and forced to treat one of the wounded bandits. Jake Fleagle had consequently been the subject of an intense national manhunt, but "the earth seemed to have swallowed him."[21]

As it turned out, the "Wolf of the West" had been hiding for over a year in the Branson area, under the alias "Walter Cook." Jake and his brother Lee leased a farm south of Branson near Hollister, where they socialized freely with their neighbors, even hosting a square-dance. Alas, another brother, Ralph, had been arrested re the Lamar bank job and was sentenced to hang. Jake wrote to the governor of Colorado asking "clemency" for Ralph, and the letter was traced back to the the Ozarks.

On October 14, Fleagle walked into a trap set by government agents at the Branson train station. He was mortally wounded, expiring at Baptist Hospital in Springfield.

The *Leader* hoped gangsters had been taught a lesson:

> The Ozarks section of Missouri is not a good hiding place for hard-boiled criminals, although they seem to have conceived the idea that it is. We are not so remote. There is no wilderness here and not much 'fastness.' Ribald and spectacular writers in a search for atmosphere have pictured the Ozarks region as the end of the world and a place where one may disappear and be lost from the world. Mr. Fleagle fell for that bunc. . . .
>
> The Ozarks have railroads, fine highways, some rather large towns and many progressive small ones. It is not a good place for the criminal to hide out, and if there are any more lurking about they would be wise if they moved on. Otherwise they may be shipped back home in a pine box.[22]

Harry Young must have missed that edition.

CHAPTER TEN

Jailbreak

"There shall be kept and maintained, in good and sufficient condition and repair, a common jail in each county within this state, to be located at the permanent seat of justice for such county. 'Good and sufficient' as used in this section, means good and sufficient in a modern sanitary sense, and connections with water mains and city gas should be maintained to protect the health and safe-keeping of inmates of jail."

—Article 9, Section 8524,
Revised Statutes of Missouri, Volume 2, 1929

Photograph, circa 1910: It's a bright, sunshiny day. A little girl stands on a wide lawn, parasol in her right hand, the left on the backrest of a child-size rocking chair. Behind her looms a massive, two-story brick building.

Cut the picture in half, viewing only the portion to the child's left: what remains is a large Victorian/Gothic dwelling. Features include a multi-peaked roof and pleasant white frame porch (it's the porch that puts the "Victorian" into what would otherwise just be "Gothic"). This is the residence of the Greene County sheriff.[1]

Now, the other half of the photograph, directly behind the little girl: Large smokestacks rise from a flat roof; the windows at ground level resemble cannon openings at Fort Sumter; the second story casements are large rectangles, ceiling-to-floor length we presume, but there is no danger of anyone falling out, as these are heavily barred. This is the Greene County Jail.

Put the photo back together and fast forward two decades: Sheriff Marcell Hendrix, his family, and upwards of 150 inmates are housed here—and everyone agrees the place is a blight on the county.

Built in 1886, the jail suffers from overcrowding and is entirely insufficient "in a modern sanitary sense." Persons arrested for minor offenses are thrown in with genuinely dangerous characters. Marcell Hendrix has been particularly vocal on the need for a separate holding facility to isolate the "violently insane."[2]

The report of a 1931 grand jury does not make for pleasant reading. Highlighting some of the more descriptive phrases:

- "obsolete and badly deteriorated in every way."
- "constructed in the beginning to house approximately forty people, and now has approximately one hundred and thirty."
- "absolutely unsanitary in every particular."
- "only two bath tubs and three toilets to accommodate the entire jail."
- "necessary to scrub the floors of the cells and bull pen three or four times daily, the water therefrom seeping down through the steel floor into the concrete below which remains there and becomes sour and stagnate."
- "necessary for the prisoners to sleep doubled up in cells, on top of the cell block, and on the floor."
- "a breeding place for vermin of all kinds and the spreading of disease."[3]

The grand jury wasn't blaming Hendrix; in fact, jurors heartily commended his "splendid effort" in making the best of a hopeless situation. But times were hard. Where was money for improvements going to come from? The county couldn't even pay salaries on a regular basis, and the road and bridge fund was already heavily overdrawn.

There had been talk of converting the third floor of the County Courthouse into jail space, but that had drawbacks, too—including concern that odors would waft down into the courtroom.[4] So, for the time being, things would remain as they were, with Maude and the Hendrix children separated from the prisoners by the width of a sliding door that hopefully kept most of the smell out.

Newspaper coverage of the January 27, 1931, jailbreak is noteworthy in and of itself. The *Press* could offer a first-hand account, as one of its reporters was on the scene as events unfolded. On the other hand, the Bixby papers let readers know the prisoners wouldn't have escaped in the first place were it not for the *Press* reporter's ill-advised request for a photograph of Tommie Vaughn.

At age twenty-three, James T. "Tommie" Vaughn already possessed a crime sheet from Detroit when he, Sam Bass, and get-away driver

Clifford Hawley were arrested for holding up the Half-a-Hill T-House, a popular Springfield restaurant southeast of town. Bass pleaded guilty and was sentenced to twenty-five years. With Vaughn and Hawley waiting their turn, the *Press* persuaded jailer Frank Willey to have the duo pose for pictures.

The actual photo shoot seems to have gone well enough.[5] Standing beside the much taller Hawley, Vaughn has the appearance of a runt shopkeeper, but he was in fact a thoroughly dangerous fellow, who now saw opportunity and seized it. As Willey was returning Vaughn and Hawley to the "lower bullpen" (one of the jail's two large holding rooms), Vaughn managed to overpower the much-older jailer, beating Willey over the head with a heavy lock from the cell door.

The bullpen door now partially open, fifty men had a choice to make. Among them was Bert Oglesby, a doe-eyed fellow whose hairstyle resembled Shemp of Ted Healy's Stooges. Oglesby had been incarcerated following a botched holdup attempt at Springfield's Princess Theatre, compounding his offense by shooting City Patrolman Otis Larson in the hand. Bert Oglesby also stood accused of stealing $1,750 in Tulsa, and "looting a cockfight at John McCoy's farm near Springfield."[6] The latter was no chicken-feed operation, yielding a take of $8,000.

Oglesby seized Frank Willey's gun. An alert "trusty" managed to close a steel outer door, cutting off the escape route, but Vaughn and Oglesby threatened to shoot Willey, with the desired effect. Six men eloped: Vaughn and Half-A-Hill partner Sam Bass, the crime team of Oglesby and Leonard "Tex" Hayes (a.k.a. "The Jackson Jellies"; "jelly" translating to good-time guy),[7] "confessed street car bandit" Howard Walker, and William Michaels, charged with the November kidnapping of a fourteen-year-old newspaper boy.

These were (with the exception of Michaels) genuine gangsters, now availed of weaponry procured from the jail arsenal. Frank Willey grabbed a rifle, gave chase, and started shooting. Citizens were grateful school wasn't in session. The senior high was located just east of the jail, and one of Willey's bullets went through a window into a classroom.

Bass and Michaels disappeared down an alley. The quartet of Oglesby, Vaughn, Walker, and Hayes drew most of the attention. Warren Hedges, who lived in the 900 block of North Jefferson, was putting his shiny new Marmon sedan into the garage when the four men hijacked him, ordering Hedges to drive them out of town. An alert construction worker blocked their path with his own vehicle; the Marmon was stuck in the driveway. By this time Willey was approaching on foot, rifle blazing.[8] The fugitives returned volley and fled on foot. Hayes and Vaughn were apparently wounded, though not badly enough to prevent escape.

Fight and flight flowed east. After another abortive attempt at hijack, the escapees' luck turned on the campus of Drury College, where basketball coach Albert L. Weiser had parked his 1929 Essex—perfect for a fast break. Vaughn, Oglesby, and friends were not the only ones desperate for transportation. Sheriff Hendrix "commandeered" an auto belonging to Willard Huckins—but too late. The fugitive sextet had made the proverbial clean getaway.

First apprehended was William Michaels, last seen running down an alley with Sid Bass. Perhaps the thief, Bass, didn't want anything to do with the alleged child molester. Some hours later, Michaels was reported wandering haplessly around Brookline, where he surrendered without further incident to Deputy Sheriff R. E. Hodge.[9]

Hendrix was on the hunt north of Springfield. Ollie Crosswhite, hurriedly deputized for the occasion, tracked Coach Weiser's car to the hills around Pleasant Hope. A farmer reported coming across the Essex and its four occupants hopelessly stuck in the mud. After extracting the auto with his mule team, the good Samaritan saw the quartet drive away in the direction of Bolivar. From Bolivar, the desperados could have headed in any of multiple directions—most likely either north to Kansas City or west toward Tulsa, home turf of Hayes and Oglesby.[10]

When the Essex was in fact found abandoned in the Tulsa area, attention focused there, with Crosswhite dispatched to work the case on site. On February 9, Bass and Vaughn were apprehended in Guthrie, Oklahoma. They were well dressed for the occasion, having robbed a Tulsa "cleaning establishment" and absconded with several suits.[11]

Hendrix and Crosswhite escorted the prisoners back to Springfield. Bass, a swarthy-looking fellow, whose wise-guy pose belied his tender age of sixteen, was immediately sent to Jefferson City to begin serving the previously decreed twenty-five-year sentence. Greene County Prosecutor Dan Nee announced he was seeking the death penalty for Vaughn,[12] but eventually settled for forty years.[13]

The capture of Bass and Vaughn also served to flush Bert Oglesby and Tex Hayes from their Tulsa hiding place, finally resulting in this headline in the *Springfield Press* on March 7, 1931:

WOMAN'S LOVE OF OGLESBY LED TO BANDITS CAPTURE
Florida Officers Hold Hayes and Oglesby for Serious Charges There

The woman was Mabel Dameron, alias Mabel Wertz. According to the *Press,* "The sheriff figured that Oglesby would not be far from his sweetheart and that Hayes would not be far from Oglesby and events proved that the sheriff was correct."

Hendrix and Crosswhite located Mabel's place in Tulsa, but she and the Jackson Jellies had already fled south and east. After a wild chase, in the course of which Oglesby and Hayes committed acts of robbery, kidnapping, and murder, the Jellies were trapped by a posse of two hundred Floridians in a swamp near the panhandle town of Milton.

Hendrix telegraphed Florida authorities, asking that Oglesby and Hayes be returned to Greene County for prosecution; but given the scope of their crimes committed in the Sunshine State, Florida was determined to bring the Jellies to justice there. Prosecutor Nee reluctantly ceded Bert and Tex to Florida, where they were sentenced to long prison terms.[14]

The sixth and final escapee was recaptured on the second day of April. Hendrix didn't have to go out of state, or even the county, this time, as Howard Walker was found in the Frisco rail yards, holed up in a passenger coach.[15] What had started with a bang on January 27 ended with a whimper—and a ten-year sentence for Walker in the Missouri State Penitentiary.[16]

Given the debacle of January 2, 1932, some have dismissed Marcell Hendrix and his ad hoc team as Keystone Kops. They most assuredly were not. Oliver and Crosswhite, in particular, were very capable men, tested by fire. What Hendrix himself lacked in training and experience, he made up for in character and determination. Through no fault of his own, six men had escaped the sheriff's charge in January of 1931, among them several hardened criminals; by April, all six were back behind bars.

Do not underestimate the capabilities of Marcell Hendrix. During his three years in office, Hendrix successfully hunted down every culprit he was looking for—with the one exception: Mark Noe's killer. And that one exception really stuck in his craw.

Constable Scott Curtis remembered accompanying the sheriff to St. Louis after receiving a tip that Harry was hiding there. St. Louis officers offered to help in the capture; Hendrix said that wouldn't be necessary. He had known Harry since Harry was a kid and Harry wasn't going to give him any trouble.[17]

If Marcell Hendrix can be said to have had a fatal flaw, it was not lack of courage or capability, but rather what seems to have been a cognitive disconnect. He was unable or unwilling to identify the little boy who attended Brick School and Brookline Baptist with the monster who fired that third bullet into Mark Noe "like a damned fiend" and dumped the body in front of Lillard Hendrix's house.

Then, at an unspecified date in 1931, a lawyer from Tulsa showed up in Springfield. This lawyer had a client who was accused of car theft, and the client was swearing he had purchased the auto in good faith from one "High" Young, believed to be Harry. This much was certain: the car in question had been stolen from Springfield. Marcell Hendrix's antenna went way up.[18]

Apparently trying to dupe Harry, Hendrix spread word around Brookline that the heat was off; the sheriff thought Harry was probably in Mexico—at any rate, Hendrix wasn't looking for him anymore. Frank Pike may have been prone to exaggeration and even invention, but this line in *Startling Detective* is surely on the mark: "Harry Young would come back. Old haunts would draw. We waited and watched"— no one more keenly than Marcell Hendrix.

CHAPTER ELEVEN

The Dying Year

"The typical policeman is never yellow. He is a HE man. He may be rough spoken. His fist may carry a terrific wallop, but he has charity in his heart and respect for the rights of others. We may not know it and he may not claim it, but in many of the essentials he has Christian characteristics that make him an all round good citizen."
—*The Springfield Press,* January 5, 1932

Sometime in 1931 (Maxine Hendrix McIntyre speculates it was part of their Christmas), the Marcell Hendrix family sat for a photograph. Father is dressed in a suit and tie. His hair has thinned to non-existent. There is a kindliness about his countenance one might more readily associate with the Christian farmer he had been than the county sheriff he was. If chasing the likes of Harry Young and the Jackson Jellies had hardened Marcell Hendrix, you'd never know it from this picture. He is a man of straight posture, head held high. Casting an actor to play the sheriff's life on film, the first thought might be Gary Cooper in his *High Noon* years.

Maude's face is not nearly so round as in earlier photographs. Perhaps the severe hairstyle, in permanent wave swept to one side, contributes to the perception; or perhaps time and the times had made her lean.

The Hendrix boys stand behind Marcell and Maude. Though younger than his brother, Merle is the taller of the two, more closely resembling the physicality of their father, including prominent ears. Merle faces the camera head on, eyes wide open, mouth and brow solemnly set. Merle would serve in the Navy during World War II, then move his family to California following the war, fashioning a thoroughly successful life.

Glenn more closely resembles his mother, a notable brashness to his countenance. In 1948, Glenn Hendrix would be elected sheriff of Greene County. Term limits no longer applying, Glenn served sixteen years before losing unexpectedly in 1964, then died before he had a chance to run again.

In the center of the portrait is nine-year-old Maxine. More than seventy years later, still living in Springfield, Maxine doesn't remember much from that period. Things were different then, she reminds us. In the early years of a new millenium, a child who lost her father under such violent, traumatic circumstance would surely receive grief counseling and every encouragement to talk about it. Not so in 1932. The grief was to be buried with the dead. And she wonders, now, about the long-term emotional toll. But that's just the way it was.

Maxine has kept a yellowed newspaper clipping from her father's abbreviated term as sheriff, part of a *Press* series in which community leaders addressed the question:

IF I WERE 21
Marcell Hendrix

I really do not know what business I would go into. That's a problem. Another thing, it depends on how a man is fixed. If he has no backing he has to start in where he can build up. I like farming extra well. Under ordinary conditions a farmer can be independent. Farming is a great trade if you can make money at it.

I never worked as an officer a day in my life until I got into this office but I always had a wish to be a law enforcement officer.

Crime is getting to be about the biggest business. In practically all the cases we make, we have to pick up our information from the public. The public should get behind the officers and the prosecuting attorney closer.

When I first came in office it was a big proposition. The work was new to me. After I worked at it a few days it never bothered me a particle. I like this work. There is something new in it every day. It's hard work. A man has a heavy load on his shoulders all the time. In any case this work should be handled on a secret basis. A fellow working in this line has very nearly got to handle it that way to insure success. A fellow has to do a lot of thinking. Officers get very little help from the public as a rule. It's a little surprising that the majority of the public will back down when it comes to standing pat and doing their part in helping the officers and coming out in the open when it becomes necessary.

A fellow likes to do things for the public. It's got to be done by somebody. An officer gets to the place where he thinks very little about the danger. I have my mind set to get the suspects. I never read a detective story in my life. They are bosh to a certain extent. Criminals will do anything to help each other.[1]

At age forty-four, Marcell Hendrix was a "man in full," well-respected in his community, a beacon of honor in a sewer of civic corruption, blessed with a strong family life. The holiday season had been a time of reunion. As reported in the mournful January 3, 1932, edition of the *Sunday News & Leader,* "Only a few weeks ago Mr. Hendrix appeared at his office in the court house one afternoon beaming happily. 'I bet I did something today no other man in Springfield did,' he said. 'I took five women out to lunch.' The women were his wife and four sisters."

Though this was bizarre: In the last days of 1931, the Associated Press Wire Service was said to have queried Springfield regarding a report that the Greene County sheriff and several of his deputies had been killed. Asked for reaction, "Mr. Hendrix laughed and replied, 'Well, I'm still here. They may get me of course, but I'm sure here now.'"[2]

Perhaps the incident contributed to what was reported as a premonition. On the fateful day of January 2, Hendrix is alleged to have said: "I feel that something awful is going to happen to me. I've tried to shake it off, but I can't get away from it." Jailer Frank Willey would himself say he had "felt all day like something terrible was going to happen. It's just seemed like something awful was wrong."[3]

This must be balanced, however, by reports that Hendrix was in a jovial mood that afternoon. Perhaps, having survived the morning raid in Ash Grove, he assumed the "something awful" was now behind him.[4]

Christmas 1931 was likely a quiet occasion for Willie Florence Young. In former holidays, she had cooked for large gatherings, but her family was long since dispersed by geography, death, and crime. Vinita was still at home, and Oscar and his family were in the vicinity, so she wasn't totally alone. But it must have been quite a contrast to Christmases in Oklahoma, when James David sat at the head of the table amidst a rowdy din of growing children.

Down in Houston, Claude Walker was spending Christmas with his new bride, to whom he'd been married only a few weeks. At least, she *thought* his name was Claude Walker.[5]

If Tony Oliver's political plans came to pass, next Christmas he and his large family would be packing to move into the sheriff's residence at the jail.[6] The prospect may have made Maude Oliver shudder. At least two other candidates had their hats in the ring: Ollie Crosswhite and Wiley Mashburn.[7]

It is highly unlikely the job was discussed over the Oliver's Christmas dinner. Particularly after the Dob Adams business, neither Tony nor Maude could have any illusions about the danger.[8] "He didn't talk about it, much," she told the papers later, "hardly every mentioned it." In fact, he "never tells me when he is going out now." Though perhaps the Harry sighting had given even the fifty-year-old veteran detective pause. "He mentioned to me just a few days ago," said Tony's Maude, "that he was running a great risk of being shot."[9]

There would be no large family Christmas for twenty-eight-year-old Charles Houser. Charlie's parents, a grandmother, and a brother had all perished in the influenza epidemic that raged through the Ozarks in the war years. Another brother died in a motorcycle accident. Perhaps the quotient of loss made Charlie all the more appreciative of his young bride, Augusta, age twenty-four, who he at various times called "Dinky," "Mutt," and "Dynamite."[10]

Houser, a "hail fellow well met," had been with the Springfield police force three years, starting as a motorcycle cop, moving up to desk sergeant. Currently, Charlie was driving the paddy wagon, a position for which he was well qualified, given his eight years of experience with the Albatross bus line. Houser had very recently moved to the day shift. Charlie actually preferred working nights, but Augusta wanted him home after dark and "his first thought always was for her."[11]

According to Augusta, the devotion was entirely mutual:

> I guess there never was a sweeter love affair than ours. He was a big, jolly fellow, you know, but about the most bashful you ever saw. It was killing the way he proposed to me—if you could call it proposing.
>
> We'd been going together about two years, since 1926, and one night we were with some other kids and somebody said something about getting married. 'I wouldn't get married,' I bragged. Charlie came up to me and tipped my chin and said, 'Wouldn't you.'
>
> Well, it wasn't but a few days after that, I guess, till he came over one day with the license, and showed it to me. I was willing so we didn't fuss about that. We went to Joplin on the motorcycle, but we left it there and went on to Vinita, Oklah., in a car with Lester or

maybe it was Leslie Albright and Virginia Albright. They were friends of Charlie's and I haven't seen them since.[12]

I can't remember much about the wedding except that I was awfully thrilled and excited and happy, and Charlie looked awfully handsome.

Charlie was always so good to me. He bought me a Studebaker Dictator sedan, a beautiful car, and he loved to have me drive it for miles and miles. He wanted to trade it in on a new one this fall, but I wouldn't let him, because it wasn't entirely paid for.[13]

In a photograph that would appear in the January 22, 1932, edition of Springfield's *Leader,* the couple stands together on what looks to be a front lawn. Charles, dressed in his police uniform, appears older than might be expected from other photos: a thin, gaunt man, a head taller than Augusta. She is pert and pretty, wearing an understated yet no doubt fashionable dress to a length just below the knees, where white stockings take over. Augusta is a woman of broad features. Her dark hair is parted just left of center, with what appears to be a bit of a wave, the coiffure following the contours of her face down to the neckline.

Perhaps Charles and Augusta spent some of that holiday season with his younger brother Fred—the only remaining member of Charlie's family of origin. Fred, himself a driver with the 209 Taxi Company, would say of Charlie, "He was always laughin' and he did love excitement. I've never seen him mad in my whole life."[14]

Though even Charlie surely would have been furious if he'd been around to see what Fred was going to do to Dinky.

At year's end, a booklet was being prepared—a piece of Gideon campaign literature thinly disguised as a "Souvenir Review" of the Springfield Police Department.[15] Positioning Mayor Gideon as a reformer, the pamphlet advised:

> There was a time when about all the qualifications a man need possess to be appointed to the position of a police officer was to be six foot in height, weigh two hundred or more pounds, be able to walk a "beat" and swing a club, look wise and vote right. Let us be thankful that time is past so far as Springfield is concerned.

But perhaps no so *far* past.

Big Sid Meadows, a Gideon appointee in 1928, fit the "qualifications" to a T. Now forty-four years old, the former Frisco employee had been married to Lilly Wilhite five years. Lilly brought three children into the marriage: Hazel, Elvie, and Homer. Hazel would describe her stepfather as "one of the best men there ever was."[16]

It would be said that a sixteen-year-old niece had dreamed of Uncle Sid getting shot through the middle of his forehead. Told about it, Sid Meadows "had grinned and said, 'I don't believe in dreams.'"[17] The niece to whom the dream was attributed denied such a thing ever happened.[18]

If it's omens we are looking for, consider the officer's full name: Albert Sidney Meadows. We can only speculate that someone in the family was an admirer of Albert Sidney Johnston, Jefferson Davis' favorite general, who caught Ulysses S. Grant unaware at Shiloh, only to get shot out of the saddle and bleed to death as the Confederates snatched defeat from the jaws of victory. Sid Meadows might have lived longer voting for E. E. E. McJimsey.

Things were not merry and bright at the Crosswhite home, 1154 Mount Vernon Street. Ollie was out of work—again. He'd been on the city payroll in December, one of the extra men hired to patrol downtown during the holiday shopping season. But the holiday shopping season was over and with it Ollie's employment.[19]

Crosswhite hadn't held a steady job since the county election of 1928. This was certainly no reflection on his skills. When a big case broke—such as the 1931 jailbreak—Marcell Hendrix was quick to call on Crosswhite as a "special deputy." Missouri statutes permitted such hires "in case of emergency," for a period of not longer than thirty days, at a wage of two dollars per day to be paid from the county funds.[20] But that was no substitute for regular income. The recently completed six-week holiday gig netted Ollie Crosswhite a paycheck of $86.[21]

But that wasn't the worst of it. Ollie's son, Keith, was in an Oregon jail, charged with shooting a cop.

Having ripped off a wiener roast on the second night of October, Keith Crosswhite and Springfield preacher's kid Johnnie Owen fled the Ozarks in a stolen Chrysler. On October 18, Oregon Officer Amos Helm questioned them about a robbery in Idaho Falls. The interview ended badly, with shots fired, Helm falling. Keith and Johnnie Owen escaped, but were captured by a posse two days later. Ollie went out to Oregon to visit Keith in jail and was quoted as saying, "My son and I always were pals. My son was always a good boy until he came under bad influence."[22]

While that sounds a lot like Willie Florence Young talking about Harry, Crosswhite's son had indeed fallen in with rough company. John

Owen was almost ten years older than Keith. As reported in the October 21, 1932, *Leader* and *Press,* the son of a preacher had actually served a brief stint in the position of deputy constable, only to be fired for brutality against bootleggers. Accused of a "crime against nature" (sodomy) in March of 1930, John Owen plea-bargained to a charge of "common assault" and was sentenced to ninety days in jail. Other charges on his resume included petty larceny, disturbing the peace, and drunk driving.

Not that Keith Crosswhite was an innocent. On July 23, 1931, he was charged with the attempted rape of "a young Springfield girl." Young Crosswhite was out on $2,000 bond when he and Owen held up the wiener roast. When the two ran into Amos Helm on October 18, they were in the company of a sixteen-year-old girl. One wonders if her parents told police, *Our daughter isn't bad, she just came under bad influence.*

With the exception of a scar on his hip from what had been a life-threatening bullet wound, Ollie Crosswhite had little to show for fifteen years in law enforcement. He owned neither home nor property. His life insurance had lapsed; money that might have paid the premium was spent on the sad trip to Oregon. His wife, Ethel, was in poor health, having collapsed upon receiving news of Keith's arrest—and there were still five children at home to feed and care for: Lee, age fifteen; Carl, age twelve; Ethel Mae, age nine; Nellie Frances, age five; and Freddie Joe, age two.

Bad news piled on bad news. On the Wednesday between Christmas and New Year, it fell on Ollie to tell Ethel that Amos Helm was dead and Keith was now looking at a murder charge.[23] One can imagine Ollie's lanky 6'4" frame stooping under the load.

Ollie's old buddy, forty-eight-year-old Wiley Mashburn, had fared better. After his dismissal from the police department following the mayoral recall debacle, Wiley found succor from grateful Republicans, landing on the county payroll in the role of deputy sheriff. Hendrix was clearly glad to have him.[24]

Mashburn's wife, yet another Maude, had become accustomed to living with the danger incumbent to Wiley's work—that's what a friend told the papers, anyway.[25] After all, her husband had never been so much as wounded; though a bullet did come close enough once to put a "hole through the top of his high boots."[26] If anyone had cause for concern, it was the criminals. The fisticuffs at Ash Grove on the morning of January 2, 1932, were not atypical of the Mashburn's brand of law enforcement. Wiley Mashburn, characterized as "over-fond of rough physical contact to the extent of downright peculiarity,"[27] could more than take care of himself.

With the exception of Tony Oliver, these were men born and raised on farms, migrated to town. They had little in the way of accumulated wealth. Crosswhite, Houser, Mashburn, Meadows: none owned any property to speak of, each living in rented homes.

The *Leader* was not overstating matters in this editorial comment, two days after the tragedy at the Young farm: "In life we gave these men little, so pitiful is our appreciation of these brave men who defend us that they have left behind sorrowing widows and little children, scarcely able to comprehend the great tragedy that has befallen them, almost destitute."

One more stop with the ghost of Christmas past, this at the rented farm home of Oscar and Mabel Young near the old Wilson's Creek Battlefield.[28] If times were hard in town, they were certainly no less difficult for rural folks like Oscar and Mabel. The same *Sunday News & Leader* that would become a collector's item for its coverage of the massacre also contained an economic essay by correspondent Mark Sullivan:

> Here is how the price of wheat works: A farmer two or three or four years ago borrowed $5000 on mortgage. That is, he borrowed, as of that time, 5000 bushels of wheat. But today at present prices he owes 10,000 bushels of wheat. He can't pay it. It can't be done. The cutting in two of the price of wheat has doubled the burden of all debts.[29]

"It can't be done." What a brooding prospect going into a new year. Oscar may have been supplementing his income by working as a printer in town[30]; it's even possible, by this point, that printing had become his primary means of support, supplemented by whatever he could make off the farm.

We would imagine he spent some of the holiday season in the woods, tracking game with his dogs. Oscar and his brothers were crack hunters, partial to working with greyhounds and foxhounds.[31] The region's abundance of wildlife would have provided Oscar with sport, shared experience with his sons, and meat for the table. Among the weapons in Oscar's stock: a 25-20 rifle and a 12 gauge shot gun.

1931 and 1932 would be remembered as the very darkest of the Depression years. Nevertheless, the *Press* rang out 1931 with hopeful thoughts from staffer J. O. Waddell:

THE DYING YEAR

The close of the annual cycle is to many like the passing of a friend. Even Tennyson, who usually thought with wondrous clarity, once allowed himself to say, 'I've half a mind to die with you, old year, if you must die.'

The past might well be entirely forgotten but for the lessons it teaches. Its greatest lessons, for men and nations, have been surely learned and generally point to things to be avoided in the future. Man learns slowly—but he learns. And he steadily advances.

Human affairs sometimes find themselves in the 'trough of a wave,' as during economic and spiritual depression, but the crest of the succeeding wave shall always be the highest point yet achieved by mankind.

Standing here upon the threshold of 1932, our reasoned attitude must be optimistic, confident, based upon the certain knowledge that destiny forever drives the race to higher ground.

As these printed words were rolling off the *Press,* Lorena Young Conley was making her first pass at selling Clyde Medley a stolen car.

Part II

> *Gentlemen of the Clergy, Parents*
> *Of Growing Children, Philosophers,*
> *Insurance Men and Doctors*
> *as well as Law Enforcement Officers,*
> *Criminologists and Others*
> *Will Find Much of Interest in this*
> *True Account of America's*
> *Worst Peace Officer Massacre*

Inscription to *The Young Brothers Massacre,* John R.
Woodside, 1932

CHAPTER TWELVE

Manhunt

"Scott Curtis' voice boomed: 'I'm a constable. I'm Constable Scott Curtis. I'm a little out of my township but I guess you won't mind. I'm deputizin' every one of you men with rifles or shotguns or any other guns. We've got to spread out through these corn fields and find these killers. We'll find them if I have to track them the rest of my life.'"

—Edward Eddy, *Springfield Sunday News & Leader,*
January 3, 1932

Scott Curtis' mass "deputizin'" and subsequent dispersal of the mob into the fields likely saved the house from destruction. The constable later shared his story with the coroner's jury: "I think it was a little bit after five that I got the call from Sargent Crane at the Police Station, he notified me of the fact that they had killed the Sheriff and a number of officers, he said maybe five or six, I don't know; he said what they needed out there is some high powered riles, and if you can get some get out there as quick as you can."[1]

Curtis left his office in the company of four other men, including his son, Howard. "We got in the car immediately and went up on South Street to Rogers & Baldwin's,[2] and stopped there and told them what had happened, and asked them if they could let us have some guns, and they said they didn't have any"—whereupon Curtis and crew continued on to the farm.

By the time Curtis arrived, Virgil Johnson had already returned to the scene of the crime and was standing with Brown and others at the mouth of the farm lane, not at all sure what to do next. Curtis testified:

> They told me about what had happened and that there were five or six men up there dead, and that Ben Van Hook and some other boys had gone back to town to get a machine gun, and that they would be

there right away; the crowd kept increasing, excitement running high, and finally someone of the crowd suggested that they needed a leader, and asked me if I would accept it, and I told them I would do anything to help.

According to Curtis, it was deemed prudent to wait for the machine gun before moving on the house—but he was only going to wait so long. The hollering from Lon Scott and Lee Jones, having stumbled across Mashburn, seems to have been the signal for movement. Curtis and others climbed aboard the Floyd Fox ambulance, some on the front of the vehicle, others on the running boards. Curtis testified:

> It was well loaded. In fact, he could hardly pull it through there. And there was some other car, I don't know who was in it passed us; we all drove on up there as quick as we could, up in I guess twenty or thirty feet of the barn and cut off the lights of the car and all jumped off, unloaded out of the cars, all excited and didn't know what was going to be done; and first one and another kept saying, 'here is one man, and here is another one, and here is another one.'

At some point, the house was going to have to be entered—with no guarantee the killers weren't still inside. Curtis continued:

> Someone by me had a shotgun, I had a revolver, I didn't have any other gun; I told him to pour it on that door and I would go in; when he shot the door with that shot gun I went towards the door shooting as I went at the windows and the door, I figured if they was in there they wouldn't shoot while we was shooting in the windows, and the other boys was shooting likewise; we all run to the door, and when we got to the door we went against it, and it was locked, and I kicked it several times; Warren Hayes was there and helped me, and I don't know how many more, we kicked it open; Lee Jones came about that time with that gas gun and shot a couple of shots in the house at the window, I believe one on the north and one on the south; we went in there and (the gas) was so strong we had to run out; I think we made two or three different trips in the house, in and out; finally we got in the back room; I didn't ever find anyone until I got in the south-west room, in the kitchen, I found Mr. Hendrix, on the south side of the room, his face was facing north with his legs crossed, there was a little stack of wood there, his head was lying across this wood; I felt of him and seen that he was dead; there was very few lights there, I don't suppose there was over a half dozen flash-lights in the crowd;

when we lifted Mr. Hendrix up someone had a light, my boy was with me; we got hold of him and got him out the door.

In Springfield, the first of the *Leader* "extras" hit the street:

Desperado Escaped; Five Officers Killed
Mashburn Dying, Face Shot Away, Organize Posse

Eleven thousand copies went fast, and it was said many of the readers immediately made their way to hardware stores, looking for weapons.[3] There would be no shortage of guns out in Greene County this night. According to the *Press,* "Some had saw-off shotguns, some rifles, and some with firearms which wouldn't have been as effective as a pea-shooter had it been necessary for them to shoot at the bandits."[4]

In an extensive fortieth anniversary article for the *Springfield News & Leader,* reporter Frank Farmer remembered, "I was eight years old when my father walked into the house and announced in an anguished voice: 'Marcell Hendrix has been killed by the Young boys.' He was never one with much affection for fire arms, but my father dug out an old shotgun and loaded it."[5]

With townsfolk cheering them on, two truckloads of troops from National Guard Battery F, 203rd Coast Artillery, rolled out of Springfield in the direction of the battle zone.[6] The *Press* reported: "Among the volunteer guards was represented every cross section of southwest Missouri society. Men and boys, black and white, doctors, lawyers, preachers, laborers; white-collared men joined with all in a vigil that it was hoped would keep the bandits confined to the Young farm."[7]

The landscape was lit with bonfires and torches. Milk trucks making their morning run were stopped and searched; the headlights of these and other autos were turned into the fields.[8] Shots rang out intermittently. Men shouted. Dogs howled. "Tensity prevailed."[9] A young member of the National Guard fired at what turned out to be a small animal in the cornhusks.[10] One volunteer would later be quoted, "I was more afraid of getting shot by the angry mob than I was of the Young brothers."[11]

A "Dutch woman" called the police station confirming what was already rumored: The Young farm was riddled with a network of tunnels connecting house, barn and orchard. The Dutch woman had once lived on the property, so she ought to know.[12] In fact, however, no such "subterranean channels of escape" would ever be found.

Others tore up the countryside looking for caves—always a favored Ozarks hiding place. O. S. Traylor and a group of Legionnaires could report only frustration: "There ain't a cave in them hills. We'd hear there was one over the next hill and tear up the brush for acres, and not a cave. The neighbors didn't seem to know definitely where any were."[13]

It was Springfield's longest night. "A sad tempestuous confusion rumbled through the crowded rooms" of the police station.[14] According to the *Daily News,* "At 3 o'clock Sunday morning numerous automobiles still were being driven around the streets. Homes were lighted, revealing the sleeplessness within."

Around four in the morning, Frank Willey took a phone call at the jail. "How many was killed in the shooting out at the Youngs'?" Jailer Willey thought he recognized the voice of Harry Young.[15] The call originated in Kansas City, the most credible evidence yet that the fugitives were already out of the area and the direction they might be headed.

Willey had been off duty at the time of the raid. Described as "half-mad with grief," he was telling any and all who would listen that he had warned Hendrix and warned him again: "I told him that Harry Young would shoot him if he could. I told him not to go after him unless he was sure he could take him out of there."[16]

No doubt mindful of the 1931 jailbreak, Willey appreciated the good behavior of the 125 inmates this night. At one point, with the jailer and what remained of the sheriff's department otherwise occupied at the farm,[17] the prisoners were guarded only by Hendrix's brother-in-law, Al Bishoff, County Collector Jesse E. Smith, and a few other civilians who had come by to check on Maude. But there was no rioting, "not a single disorderly move on the part of any prisoner." Keeping to routine, the jail "trustees" prepared the evening meal, even serving coffee to Maude and those waiting with her on the residence side. "I'm proud of them," said Willey, the *Daily News* adding, "And coming from the jailer, the stern man that he is, those words meant what they said."[18]

At Herman Lohmeyer's funeral establishment, Coroner Stone closed the doors to the public and performed a preliminary examination of the bodies. His initial finding: three guns had done the killing—two rifles and a shotgun. One of the rifles was of a larger caliber than the other.

In these early hours of Sunday morning, it was assumed there were at least three killers, perhaps four. The likely suspects were, of course, the Young brothers: experienced murderer, Harry; mastermind older brother, Paul; and Jennings makes three.

And maybe Oscar? He and Mabel were taken into custody around 8:30 Sunday morning at their rented place near the old battlefield. The farmstead was described as "situated in a clump of trees much as the death house." This dictated great caution among the arresting officers, led by Greene County Deputy Sheriff Ernest Hodge.[19]

R. E. Hodge was Hendrix's senior deputy. He'd been serving papers in another part of the county Saturday afternoon, causing him to miss the raid and subsequent battle. Having deposited Oscar and Mabel at the county jail, Hodge told reporters he doubted they were involved, but this wasn't the time to be taking chances.[20]

Held on a technical charge of "investigation," Mabel admitted she and Oscar had been at his mother's place Saturday afternoon, but insisted they'd just come by to pick up a couple of mares, and were gone by 3:30 without seeing any of Oscar's brothers.[21] If Harry was in the area, it was news to her. She needed to go home now and see about her children. Mabel's guardians were unmoved by her plight.

At least one member of the family was having "a good time." When officers came to Etta Smith's home Saturday evening, looking for Willie Florence, police matron Margarite Hull had Lorena's daughter Natalie in tow.[22] The child was left with Mrs. Smith, who wanted to be clear on this: "She's no relative of mine."

Natalie had been with her mother and Aunt Vinita when they were picked up at Clyde Medley's. The child was fed a sandwich with a soda at the police station,[23] but headquarters was fast turning into a zoo, hardly a place for a little girl—particularly an offspring of the notorious Youngs. Not that Etta seemed any too happy to host little Natalie, telling reporters, "I didn't even know who she was when the police matron brought her out last night." Considering that Natalie had spent the morning and lunch hour in Mrs. Smith's home, the latter's statement seems disingenuous at best.

Natalie herself, however, seemed to enjoy the attention. "The child shook thick blonde locks back from peppy black eyes," while she told the *Press* that Santa had come to Houston and brought her a doll. "What does my father do? He doesn't do anything. He doesn't work and that's why we came up to the farm." She wanted reporters to see her new toy. "Here comes the bride," she chanted. "I'm four years old. I've got this doll and another bigger one and I'm having a good time."[24]

With the rising of the sun, the manhunt shifted into more purposeful gear, augmented by the arrival of American Legionnaires—"in blue overseas caps and a few in bright chromiumplated helmets"[25]—to help with much needed crowd control. All roads leading to the farm were jammed with the curious and mournful. Officers and Legionnaires were positioned approximately two hundred yards apart on Route 66 "and at closer intervals nearer the house."[26] The Legion was prepared for any eventuality, guns loaded with ammunition dispensed from the local armory.[27]

"No one was allowed to drive into the yard," reported the *Press,* "but thousands of persons parked a mile away from the buildings and walked through the field to stand around the fence and peer silently at the big white house." While denied entrance to the citadel itself, visitors could wander the killing yard and thrust "inquisitive fingers into bullet holes" in the soft maple trees.[28]

A wonderful photograph from Sunday morning would be published in the *St. Louis Post Dispatch*[29]: Sightseers in their church-going clothes are lined orderly along the wire fence immediately south of the farmhouse, "gazing about them as if unable to comprehend the terrible tragedy which had taken place yesterday afternoon at the very place where they were standing."[30] The men are hatted in straw boaters, but a little boy looks back at the camera out of a Knute Rockne-style football helmet. Perhaps the child simply liked the headgear. Or. Perhaps, his parents *insisted* he wear it, on the chance the Young brothers were nearby and bullets started flying.

Overhead, two airplanes flew "in constant circles above the vicinity."[31] If they couldn't bomb anything, at least the pilots could provide aerial surveillance.

Back at ground level, Coroner Stone added to the visual excitement, re-enacting the tragedy "with the aid of reporters and deputies."[32] A "small child" was reported missing. Officers conducted a hasty search and found the kid had slipped through the police cordon and gone inside the house.[33] Still wanting to burn something, "several more excited members of the crowd" tried to torch the barn, using kerosene to start a fire that was quickly discovered and stamped out.[34]

Also drawing a crowd were the respective mortuaries, the *Daily News* reporting: "Literally thousands upon thousands streamed in and out of the undertaking parlors where the slain officers lay. A morbid curiosity brought men and women seldom attracted by such an urge. Many mothers came with babies in their arms. None were denied entrance."[35]

There was a promising lead around nine o'clock. Two suspicious characters were spotted lurking around a house where the pavement ended on West Sunshine, near Brookline. This merited investigation.

A posse was dispatched, the house surrounded. Mindful of Hendrix's experience, the deputized approached very cautiously at first, then not at all, afraid to get any closer. Finally, a man named Ginsberg crawled on his hands and knees toward the silent house, shouting for whoever was inside to come out.

A hysterical lady emerged saying two men in leather jackets had come to her door, asking that she give them breakfast, including take-out for a friend. Told she had no food to give, the pair didn't press the point, wanting her to know: "We're not the fellows they're looking for." One was limping and probably carried a pistol in his hip pocket. That's what the lady, Mrs. E. T. Page, said.[36] Bloodhounds were brought to the scene, but lost the scent.

It had been a bad night for bloodhounds all around. Too many people at the crime scene, too many feet tramping all over the place, too many smells for the dogs to pick up a trail.[37]

From the Page home, team Ginsberg trudged on to a nearby farmhouse where, according to the *Daily News,* "The possemen riddled a chicken coop with shots and creeping up found only a few dead hens to reward their pains."[38]

The Christian Sabbath presented a dilemma for pastors such as R. W. Hoffman, shepherd of the flock at Springfield's Central Christian Church. Hoffman had planned a sermon titled, "Matching the Hour"— but this hour was unlike any other in his experience. When Hoffman got up to preach, "he felt the intense excitement of the people who were sorrowful and agitated at the murder of the officers." Therefore, the pastor matched his words to the hour and spoke of the need for calm. "Let us not be overcome by anger and hatred. A manhunt, when every person feels he must go armed, is a terrible thing for a community."[39]

On what was a communion Sunday in his congregation, Reverend T. Crowell of Woodland Heights Presbyterian likened the officers' sacrifice to the doctrine of substitutionary atonement: "They substituted for us in the enforcement of law even as Christ showed a willingness to be substituted for our sins."

At Grace Methodist, Dr. A. J. Croft told his Sunday School class, "If more persons were living Christ-like lives, there would not be such butchery." To which his hearers surely said, *Amen.*

And, of course, everyone would want know what Dr. Lewis M. Hale of First Baptist had to say. Marcell Hendrix's name was on the membership rolls at Brookline Baptist, but since his election to office and subsequent move to town, when the sheriff attended church, it was usually First Baptist in Springfield. At recent revival services, Hendrix, Mashburn, and others of the sheriff's department had attended First Baptist as a group and were given special recognition.[40] We would imagine, on that occasion, Dr. Hale made particular mention of his guests' heroic defense of the Eighteenth Amendment.

On Sunday morning, January 3, 1932, Lewis Milton Hale, no doubt attired in the formal coat and striped pants that were his custom to wear in the pulpit,[41] read from the gospel of St. Luke, "And it came to pass, when the time was come that he should be received up, he steadfastly set his face to go up to Jerusalem." Commented the vigorous man of God, "The six courageous officers went out to face danger because they thought it was their duty, even as Jesus set his face steadfastly toward Jerusalem because he believed it was his responsibility to do so."

The talkative Frank Pike was holding his first round of press interviews, offering no end of colorful detail:

> I heard Marcell say, "They got me."[42] The rest of us kept shooting, trying to stay behind shrubbery. Tony was crying "Kill 'em, kill 'em," and then he fell. After he was shot, he yelled, "They got me. Take out. You ain't got a fightin' man's chance." He's got guts. He died like a man.[43]

Frank Pike wanted to be clear on this: He ran away only *after* the dying Oliver had urged, "Run, Frank, they'll kill us every one."[44]

The Associated Press gave the younger Pike his own byline. On Monday, the nation thrilled to his exploits:

> Me and Wiley Mashburn and the sheriff all ran against the door and burst it open. Two shotgun charges were fired from the kitchen. Down came the sheriff, dead, and they hit me in the arm. Mashburn dropped down dead on the other side of me. Their blood spattered on my hat and clothes. The doctor later took a handful of shot out of my left arm and I picked out two or three more. The arm of my overcoat here is all cut up with buckshot.[45]

In reconstructing the scene, J. R. Woodside would suggest Frank Pike was in fact *not* at the back door with Hendrix and Mashburn; the "Startling Detective" was in the front yard when the shooting started, eventually wounded in the course of running away.[46]

At the Bixby newspaper office, phones were ringing off the hook, journalists calling from across America, "demanding details of the story":

> Additional telephone operators were summoned, messengers posted and other precautions taken well before the first calls came from outlying points. Soon the telephones began their mad cry. From Chicago, from New York,[47] from Detroit, from many cities came breathless demands for information. There was nothing to do but tell the complete, the bitter truth—so incredible that even hardened reporters in far-away cities gasped in unbelieving horror.[48]

The already fevered pitch was taken up a notch when a phone call came into police headquarters from Ohio. Bowling Green Chief of Police Carl Galliher was saying Floyd Mitchell, alias Charles Floyd, alias "Pretty Boy"—wanted for the April 16, 1931 murder of a Bowling Green patrolman—might well be among the Springfield killers.

A crime spree through Kentucky and Ohio had taken the "Phantom of the Ozarks" and accomplice Billy "The Killer" Miller to Galliher's town. Along for the ride were Rose and Juanita Ash, nee Baird—sisters who had married the Ash brothers, William and Wallace, themselves minor Kansas City mobsters. When Rose and Juanita took up with Floyd and Miller, the jilted husbands collaborated with Kansas City police to set a trap for their rivals. Pretty Boy shot his way out of the police trap, then went gunning for the Ash brothers. When they crossed paths with Carl Galliher in Ohio, Rose and Juanita were widows.

The foursome of Floyd, Miller, and the Baird/Ash sisters was coming out of Uhlman's Clothing Store when Galliher got the drop on them, ordering the quartet to put up their hands—which, of course, Floyd and Miller did not. By the time the firing stopped, "Killer" Miller and Officer Ralph Castner were dead on the street.[49]

Pretty Boy had escaped, but Galliher remained very much on the trail, having reliable information that Floyd was very recently in the Queen City of the Ozarks.[50] His connection to the massacre at the Young farm made sense. As the *Daily News* commented, Floyd was "one of the few men in the nation capable of such wanton butchery."[51]

The Young brothers might be unknown to most of America, but Pretty Boy Floyd was a criminal celebrity. The "baby face killer," whose "daring is matched only by the dexterity with which he drives an auto,"[52] had been implicated in "a score of Oklahoma bank robberies committed within the past 18 months" and "at least four slayings."

Adding to the intrigue, Floyd had served a sentence in the Missouri State Penitentiary concurrent with Harry's residency.[53]

The connection was reinforced when a Kansas City area tire salesman called Sunday afternoon to say three men had been at his place around two o'clock, looking to store "a dark blue Buick coupe" until nightfall. The Buick was "coated with yellow clay mud." Salesman R. S. Champ identified one of the men as Harry Young and another as Charles Floyd. Champ told the trio he didn't have a garage—just tires—and they drove away without incident. According to Champ, Harry "wore a bloody sheet around his right arm."[54]

Yet another lead came from Kansas City. Three men in a "Ford car which bristled with rifles" had stopped at an area filling station asking directions to the highway.[55] Adding to the suspicion, the license numbers were "covered with rags."[56]

The Kansas City sightings were followed by a call from Mount Ayre, Iowa, just north of the Missouri border, where a posse had three suspicious characters surrounded. Additional "vigilantes" were rushing to lend support.[57] Mount Ayre was a straight line from Kansas City.

But there were also reports of the fugitives in Oklahoma, including a promising lead from a druggist in Quapaw.[58] Had the killers split up, one group headed north, the other south and west?

By now, all sorts of stories were in circulation.

It was said Harry was so good with a gun that he could hit a half-dollar piece at fifty yards, thirty-nine out of forty tries. He could shoot fifty walnuts off a tree without changing stance. His rapid-fire pistol action could keep a spool spinning upright. He could throw marbles into the air and shoot them to bits. He'd been barred from competing in turkey shoots, so others would stand a chance.[59] Then Prosecutor Nee announced it was Jennings, not Harry, who was the crack shot.[60]

A barber on St. Louis Street was saying he'd cut Harry's hair on Friday—though he didn't know it was Harry at the time, of course. If he had . . . "With this razor in my hand, he wouldn't have dared to resist."[61]

It was said that five tubes of narcotics and an abundance of liquor bottles had been found at the crime scene.

It was said Willie Florence was prone to answer the door with a shotgun in hand.[62]

It was said the Youngs were at the center at a vast criminal enterprise, including, but not limited to, stolen cars.

It was said the brothers had partnered with Bert Oglesby and Tex

Hayes in ripping off the cockfight at John McCoy's farm in December.[63]

It was said a note had been found at Oscar's place, left by Jennings some six hours after the killings, next to a bunch of keys: "Give these keys to Lorena," read the note, "and tell her to move the cars at once."[64]

A farmer reported coming to the Young place on Friday, where he saw a stranger—definitely not one of the Youngs—on the front porch, "cleaning a peculiar looking gun," with "something on it that looked like a tomato can."[65]

Several sticks of dynamite were found in the barn—though the *Leader* was prompt to note the explosive "might have been used for a good number of legitimate purposes around the farm."[66]

It was said the fugitives escaped in a submarine, though no one seemed to take this very seriously.[67]

If the killers were in Kansas City, Iowa, Oklahoma, or on a submarine to Timbuktu, they must have had help getting away. Attention quickly focused on Jesse Moore, known to run with the Youngs, himself possessed of a petty criminal record. Scott Curtis had a witness who insisted that two of the Youngs were in Moore's car, out on Highway 66, between 8:30 and 9:00 Saturday evening.[68]

Jesse Moore lived on a farm approximately midway between the murder scene and Springfield. Constable Curtis raided the place about two o'clock Sunday afternoon. Jesse wasn't home, but his wife was—though she had little to offer in the way of information.

Curtis returned to the Moore farm at six o'clock that evening; again, no Jesse—though two men were seen running from the rear of the house into a field. Officers heard a motor engine start up, then a car roared past with darkened lamps. A little further down the road, the auto stopped and sounded its horn, leading to speculation the men on foot climbed into the car, which then sped off in the direction of Ash Grove and "vanished like mist in the night."[69]

Could there be a connection between Saturday morning's Ash Grove liquor raid and the massacre that evening? According to the *Press,* "Scores of possemen, armed with rifles and shotguns, beat the woods and fields near Ash Grove, leaving no barn unsearched, no hay stack unturned."[70]

At midnight, officers made a third raid on the Moore place. Jesse was still unaccounted for, but this time the law did not leave empty handed, taking the twenty-five-year-old Mrs. Moore and three farm hands into custody.[71] Jesse himself would resurface around noon on Monday, immediately taken in for questioning. Where had he been all this time? "Been down in the country." The answer did not satisfy, earning Jesse Moore a place behind bars.[72]

Oscar's brother-in-law, Hubert Conn, ran a grocery store and filling station on Route 66, north of the killing field. Mabel Conn Young may not have had the best of relationships with her in-laws, but the Conns and Youngs were family, as well as neighbors, so it made sense to take a look at Hubert.[73] That said, there is no evidence the Conns had anything to do with facilitating the get-away.

Not everyone was buying the theory the killers had left the area. Sunday afternoon, a posse led by none other than G. C. Pike converged on the very rural village of Bird Eye, fifteen miles northwest of Springfield. The disgraced former chief of police had been released from his imprisonment in Leavenworth, Kansas, December 20, 1930, having served eight months and ten days.[74] If Pike Sr. was operating under any particular legal authority this Sunday afternoon, there is no mention of it in reports of the raid.

Bird Eye was a remote hill hamlet, with something of a fractious history. In the wake of some long-forgotten civic strife, the town had once-upon-a-time moved "lock, stock and barrel," east to Frog Pond, but later returned to the original location.[75] In 1932, seventy-year-old William Judson "Judd" Haguewood—Willie Florence's brother— made his home in the vicinity.[76] Bird Eye had been mentioned by Lorena, as police tried to trace her brothers' movements since their Wednesday night arrival in Greene County. According to Lorena, Harry and Jennings had spent some of that time up at Judd's place.

G. C. Pike may have had many faults, but he seems to have been a natural leader of men. His eight-man pack included his son Frank, Ben Bilyeu, Officer Cecil McBride, and a reporter from the *St. Louis Post-Dispatch*.[77] According to the *Press*, "The posse in three automobiles left Springfield shortly after 3 o'clock. Led by Pike, who is familiar with that rugged section, the posse advanced in their cars, lights of only one burning."[78]

It was snowing when they reached the Haguewood farm. "As the cars passed the house, two or three men were seen. . . . "[79] Pike ordered the place surrounded, saying he would take the front door. Frank told him that was "the way the Sheriff and Ollie got killed." Pike settled for crawling toward the house, shouting for Judd and/or whoever was inside to show themselves. The only sign of life was "two dogs barking viciously and without hesitation."[80]

Finally, the former chief enlisted a neighboring farmer to give Judd a hail. Haguewood opened the door. Judd allowed that his nephews had been up here in recent days,[81] but the answers did not satisfy Pike. Judd Haguewood found himself employed as a human shield in his own home, Pike behind him, in the course of a room-by-room search.

Reported the approving *Press*, "The raid was typically 'Pike.'"[82]

Which brings us to an intriguing set of possibilities. A set of drawings had been discovered at the Young farmhouse—plans for a criminal hideout complete with trap doors, a secret chute, and tunnels to facilitate quick getaway. On the back of the page was "the printed notation: 'Bird Eye.'" Pike said he knew all about it; the design was for a house he himself had owned.[83]

Huh?

Pike was no longer in actual possession of the Bird Eye property, having sold it to a party presently living in Arkansas, but he had recently been actively negotiating a deal between the Youngs and the Arkansan. According to the *Press*, "Pike played a game of 'chess' with the would be purchaser of 'Bird Eye' farm. He made a trip to the place with the Young brother,[84] talked price and terms and even went so far as to make the brother believe he was about to buy the farm."

According to Pike, Bird Eye had been Harry's hiding place in the days immediately following the murder of Mark Noe in Republic. Harry had been in and out of the region many times since and had made arrangements with a used car dealer in Springfield to fence cars stolen in other places.

Pike insisted he was setting a trap for the Youngs, but given Pike's track record of consorting with bootleggers, one can only speculate as to the real story and what he and Jennings may have discussed during their shared time in Leavenworth.

Did Pike have personal reasons for wanting Jennings dead before he could talk? Or had Pike, in fact, been setting a trap, figuring to use Harry as his redemption and ticket back into law enforcement?

This much seemed clear to the *Press:* the Bird Eye affair proved "Killer Young had made extensive plans to branch out into what undoubtedly would have been the most powerful criminal organization operating between here and the Texas border."

In Washington, D.C., Missouri Senator Roscoe C. Patterson positioned himself in the story, revealing he had known "every person involved in the tragedy." He once represented Jennings and his older brother (Oscar, though Patterson called him Charles) in a court case that ended in "Charles'" acquittal (the stolen gun charge heard in Mount Vernon).

And just this past November, while visiting constituents in Missouri, Patterson received a phone call from a man identifying himself as Harry Young, asking for an appointment with the senator. Patterson gave directions to his office at the Federal Reserve Bank Building in St. Louis, but Harry never showed. Senator Patterson speculated that Harry "wanted to give himself up," but was scared off by "all those uniformed officers and guards stationed in and patrolling the corridors"—standard procedure for a Federal Reserve Bank Building.[85]

On the west side of the continent, tough-guy Keith Crosswhite finally broke down. Five days earlier, when informed that Patrolman Amos Helm had expired, Crosswhite was reported to have merely "whistled." Told he was facing a murder charge, Crosswhite "sang" in apparent contempt. But upon learning of his father's fate, the nineteen-year-old was so distraught that a physician had to be brought in to treat him.[86]

Back in the Ozarks, over in Thayer, recently the lair of the Barker gang, the massacre was the last straw for citizens concerned about mounting violence in the region. Shades of the Bald Knobbers! One hundred sixty Thayerites gathered at the Young Men's Christian Association to form a "vigilants committee," including "a subcommittee of five to investigate all strangers in the community whose actions arouse suspicion."[87]

After about forty hours at his desk, the office still swarming with folk, Ed Waddle "finally reached for his cap. 'I wouldn't go so far as to hint that you had all better go home,' he said, taking his revolver from his desk and slipping it into his holster, 'But that's where I'm going and I'd like to leave this office empty.'"[88]

If Waddle is to be criticized as a desk-jockey, it must be admitted that he rode with endurance.

And in Streetman, Texas, many miles from the Ozarks and Springfield, Missouri, Mrs. A. E. Gaddy, a telephone operator, went home after what had been an unusually interesting shift at the switchboard.

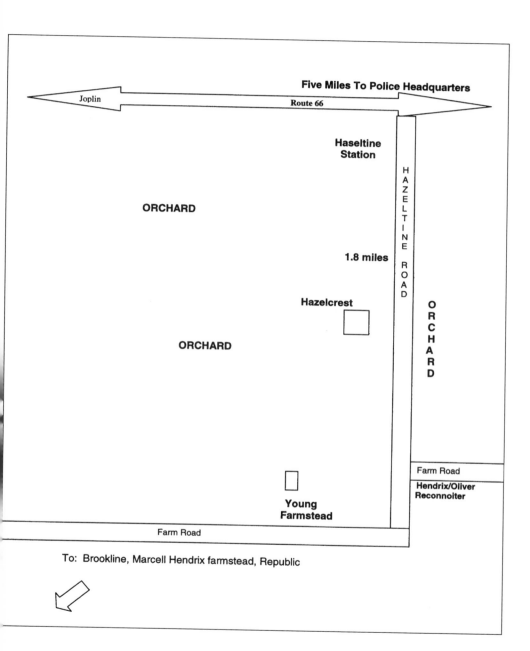

Five Miles To Police Headquarters

Joplin

Route 66

Haseltine
Station

H
A
Z
E
L
T
I
N
E

R
O
A
D

O
R
C
H
A
R
D

ORCHARD

1.8 miles

Hazelcrest

ORCHARD

Farm Road

**Hendrix/Oliver
Reconnoiter**

Young
Farmstead

Farm Road

To: Brookline, Marcell Hendrix farmstead, Republic

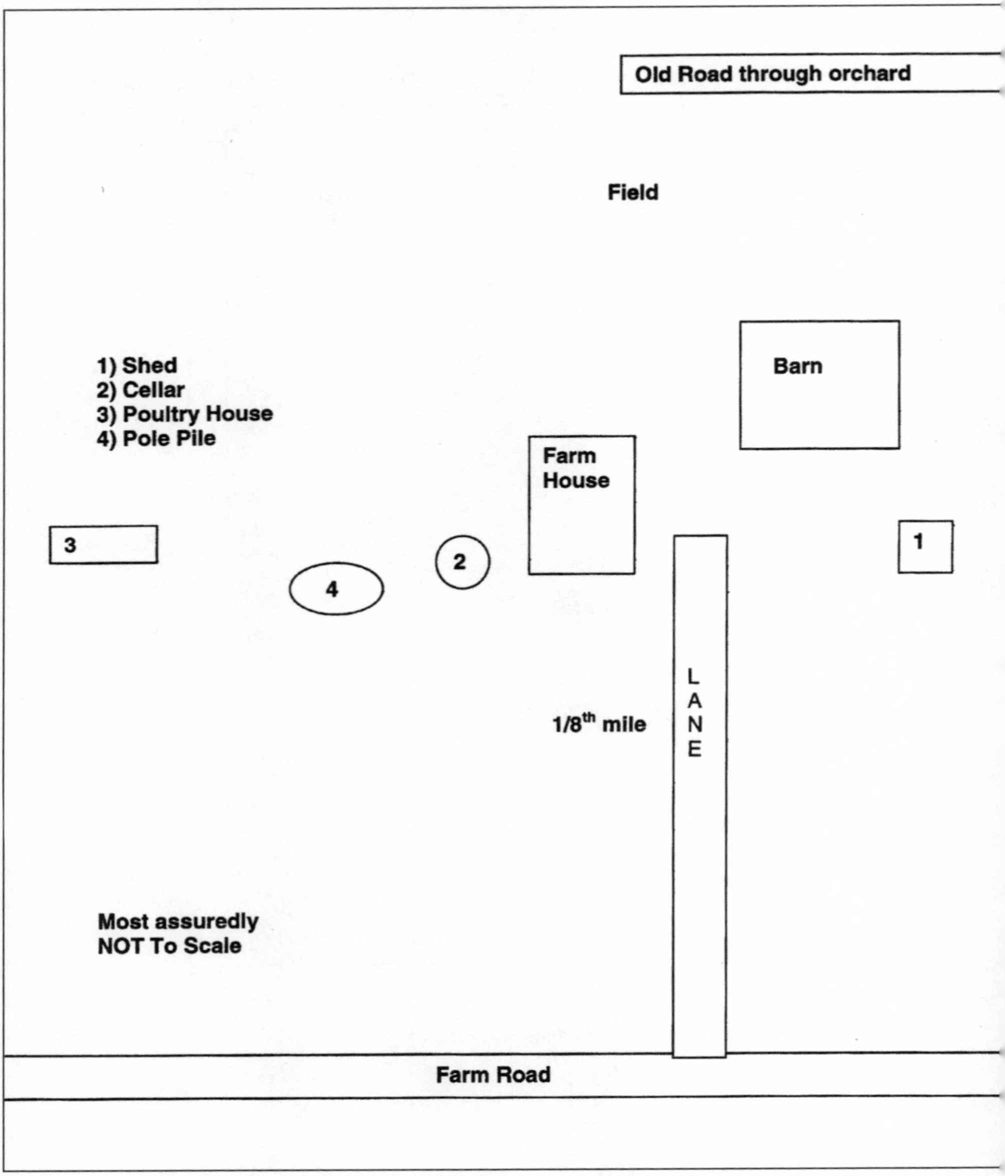

Old Road through orchard

Field

1) Shed
2) Cellar
3) Poultry House
4) Pole Pile

Barn

Farm House

3

4

2

1

L
A
N
E

1/8th mile

Most assuredly
NOT To Scale

Farm Road

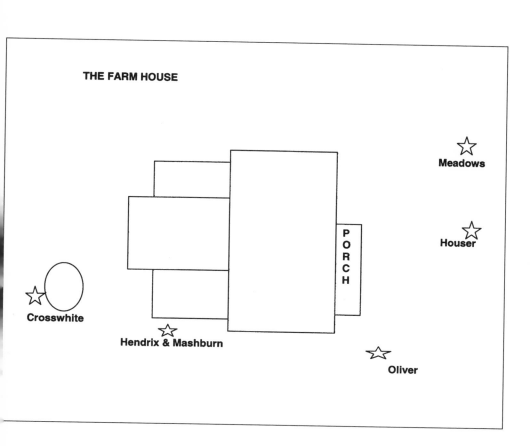

THE FARM HOUSE

Meadows

Houser

P
O
R
C
H

Crosswhite

Hendrix & Mashburn

Oliver

Greene County Jail. Courtesy of the History Museum for Springfield-Greene County.

James David Young family from A Diamond Jubilee History of Tillman County, 1901-1976. Courtesy of Tillman County Historical and Educational Society.

Marcell Hendrix family. Courtesy of Maxine Hendrix McIntyre.

Harry Young. Courtesy of the City of Springfield.

Mayor Thomas H. Gideon. Courtesy of the City of Springfield.

Marcell Hendrix. Courtesy of the City of Springfield.

Detective Bureau. Back row (from left): Owen Brown, Sid Meadows, Virgil Johnson, Grover White. Front row (from left): Lee Jones, Tony Oliver, William Bishop, Frank Pike. Courtesy of the City of Springfield.

Wiley Mashburn. Courtesy of the City of Springfield.

Charles Houser.

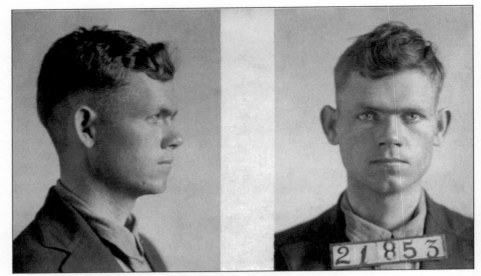

Jennings Young's mugshots from the Missouri State Prison. Courtesy of the City of Springfield.

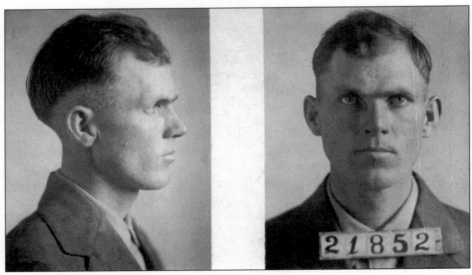

Paul Young's mugshots from the Missouri State Prison. Courtesy of the City of Springfield.

Oscar Young with the guns used by Harry and Jennings. Courtesy of the Springfield News-Leader.

Mabel Young. Courtesy of the Springfield News-Leader.

Willie Florence Young. Courtesy of the Springfield News-Leader.

Ma Young. Courtesy of the Springfield News-Leader.

Vinita and Lorena Young. Courtesy of the Springfield News-Leader.

*Tony Oliver. Courtesy of the
Springfield News-Leader.*

*Chief Ed Waddle. Courtesy of the
City of Springfield.*

*Ollie Crosswhite. Courtesy of the City of
Springfield.*

The survivors of the massacre: Brown, Bilyeu, Pike, and Johnson. Courtesy of the City of Springfield.

Tomlinson Cottage, 4710 Walker Avenue, Houston, Texas. Courtesy of the City of Springfield.

The Young farmhouse. Illustrated photograph from the Woodside pamphlet. Courtesy of the City of Springfield.

The Young farmhouse. Illustrated photograph from the Woodside pamphlet. Courtesy of the City of Springfield.

Sid Meadows. Courtesy of the City of Springfield.

Floyd Fox ambulance. Courtesy of the City of Springfield.

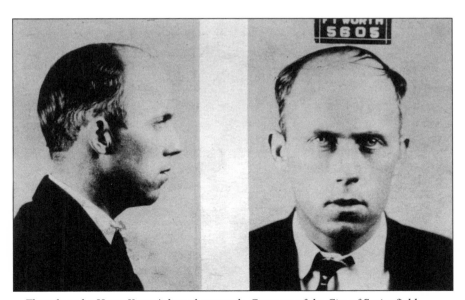

Thought to be Harry Young's last photograph. Courtesy of the City of Springfield.

Where the sheriffs fell. Courtesy of the City of Springfield.

Police String Quartet. Courtesy of the City of Springfield.

Frank Pike. Courtesy of the City of Springfield.

Downtown Springfield. Courtesy of the Local History Department, Springfield Greene County Library.

Downtown Springfield. Courtesy of the Local History Department, Springfield Greene County Library.

Downtown Springfield. Courtesy of the Local History Department, Springfield Greene County Library.

CHAPTER THIRTEEN

Deep in the Heart of Texas

"It was a lucky April shower, it was the most convenient door
I found a million dollar baby in a five and ten cent store
The rain continued for an hour, I hung around for three or four
Around a million dollar baby in a five and ten cent store."
> —Mort Dixon & Billy Rose
> *I Found A Million Dollar Baby*
> *(In a Five And Ten Cent Store)*[1]

Streetman, Texas, straddles the border of Navarro and Freestone Counties, some seventy miles south of Dallas. In 1931, the town boasted thirty-five businesses and its own newspaper. Within the city limits were 509 souls of mixed ethnicity,[2] but the town's primary *raison d'être* was to serve the needs of area farmers such as H. H. Carroll.

Sometime after noon on Sunday, but no later than one o'clock, a Ford Coupe skidded off the concrete road in front of Carroll's farmhouse, rolling over several times before coming to rest. Two men crawled out of the wreckage. Carroll offered to fetch some mules to turn the car right side up and pull it out of the field, but by the time he returned with the animals, the men were gone.

While Carroll had been hitching the mules, his daughters were watching from inside the house. They saw the strangers pull the license plate off the Ford, heave the plate into the field, then hail a small roadster. The car seemed to have passed by, but then stopped and backed up. The two men climbed in, whereupon the roadster took off, heading south. Houston was 170 miles in that direction.

Most peculiar of all, Carroll retrieved the license plate, then pulled the ruined Ford into his place. Two long guns were in the back.[3]

That's when Carroll cranked his phone and Mrs. Gaddy put him through to the Navarro County Sheriff's Department. According to the

155

Houston Chronicle, "He described the men as between 35 and 40 years old and weighing between 160 and 170 pounds. One was bald except for a little light hair. Both wore gray overcoats. One had a light colored hat and the other a dark one. The bald man had a cut on his lip and another on his head."[4]

And there the matter stayed for several hours, until Mrs. Gaddy hung up the headset for the evening, went home, and shared the day's gossip with her son. In contrast to the somnambulant Corsicana Sheriff's Department, Mrs. Gaddy's son, A. E. Gaddy Jr.,[5] had been keeping up with breaking news from Springfield, via KMOX radio out of St. Louis.[6] Gaddy Jr. connected the dots, resulting in the telegram received by Greene County Prosecutor Dan Nee, around eight o'clock Sunday evening: "Two men fitting description of Harry and Jennings Young wrecked Ford car at Streetman, Texas, today. Disappeared immediately going toward Houston. Missouri license number 363-662."[7]

The plate matched a car reported missing from a Springfield lot Saturday night. Nee wasted no time contacting the Gaddys and Navarro County. Navarro Deputy Sheriff J. M. Westbrook described the abandoned firearms: "a Remington model No. 25, 25-30 caliber, with three shots remaining in the magazine, and an automatic shotgun with one cartridge belt fired. . . . The shotgun number was U171542 and the rifle number AA7539."[8] These surely did sound like the guns Greene County was looking for.

Nee initially said Springfield would send officers to retrieve the weapons, but then thought again; it would be faster if Texas brought the guns to Springfield.[9] O. D. Sanders, special agent with the Texas & Pacific Railroad out of Fort Worth, volunteered for the assignment, reporting, "The rifle stock was broken and the shotgun barrel bent— probably from the impact of the wreck."[10]

There was new intensity now to the questioning of Willie Florence and her daughters—particularly Lorena, who had come up from Houston. The sisters were in a cell on the upper floor of the police station, a guard posted at the bottom of the stairwell "with orders to let no one go upstairs" without Waddle's permission.[11] Assistant Greene County Prosecutor James Hornbostel and E. H. Wilson, "crack detective of the Frisco railroad," served as lead interrogators. Lorena went first and made "several damaging admissions." Finishing with Lorena around one A.M., HornBostel and Wilson called in Vinita, who was reported "breaking down." As information was received, it was "rapidly relayed to Texas officers."[12]

Surely no information was relayed more rapidly than this: Harry Young had been living in Houston under the alias "Claude Walker." He had very recently married a girl named Florence Calvert. When Harry and Jennings came up to Missouri last week, the new bride stayed behind in Houston.

Early morning raids in Houston, Texas, Monday, January 4[13]:

Four A.M. A Park Place address in Houston's Golfcrest subdivision, southeast of downtown. Goodrich Rubber salesman T. T. Mackey and his wife, the former Florence Willie Young, made their home in what was described as a "trim stucco bungalow."[14] The knock on the door could not have been wholly unexpected—though perhaps not at this ungodly hour.

The raid was led by Detective Lieutenant Claude Beverly, accompanied by a team of officers armed for any eventuality. "Each wore his pistol. Some carried heavy rifles, others sawed off shotguns. Their pockets were full of shells and cartridges. Tear gas guns protruded from their overcoats."[15] There was no sign of the fugitives, but guards were posted, just in case. Florence Mackey told police her brothers were "desperate" and would never be taken alive. "I hope to God you hear they've committed suicide."[16]

Up to Magnolia Park, an apartment on Avenue J. The lady at the door admits Florence Calvert used to live here, but that's been a while ago. She and Florence knew each other from their hometown of Lovelady, north of Houston, and she'd heard Florence recently married a fellow who worked at the creamery, or maybe a dairy—but that's about all. Florence Calvert had a sister over on Avenue H; police might try there.[17]

Avenue H and Terminal Street, the residence of Joe and Lily Calvert Shaw. Lily tells police Harry had been by earlier, looking for his bride, but Florence had already left to keep a doctor's appointment.

The doctor's office was a dry hole. Florence Calvert had indeed been scheduled for minor throat surgery, but never showed.[18]

A neighbor of the Shaws reported noise in her attic. This drew attention. A riot squad "exploded gas and tear bombs in the garret, only to find it unoccupied."[19]

According to Lily Shaw, after leaving her place disappointed, Harry had taken a bus in the direction of the ship channel.[20] The ship channel was already being searched—though with nine oil refineries, and vessels going in and out, a cunning man could make himself awfully hard to find in there. Worse yet, "it was feared [Harry] might have stowed away on an outgoing vessel."[21]

Another Terminal Street address, this a small brown cottage, said to be the Claude Walker residence. Police opened the door with a passkey. No one was home, but officers found a pan sticky with bacon grease, unwashed breakfast dishes for two, and a letter addressed to Florence Calvert.[22] Women's clothing ("hose, stepins, a silk frock") was draped about the bedroom.[23] The *Chronicle* used the term "disorder" to describe the place; either Florence Calvert was a sloppy housekeeper or she had left in a hurry.

Harry's mother-in-law, it was learned, lived on Avenue I.[24] (There seems to have been an exodus of Calverts from Lovelady, all landing in Houston's Magnolia Park district.[25]) When police arrived at her place, around one o'clock Monday afternoon, Sarah Calvert said they'd just missed her son-in-law—whatever his name was today—who, of course, had been looking for her daughter. As Sarah Calvert had told Harry/Claude then, she told police now: Florence wasn't here, either. Harry had walked down to Canal Street and caught an outbound Harrisburg bus.[26]

Police tracked down the driver of the bus, but he was no help.[27] Heavily armed officers guarded every highway leading into the city. Police squads roamed "dives" and "hang outs" known to be frequented by Houston's criminal elements.[28]

Where police had been, news hounds quickly followed. At Golfcrest, Florence Willie Young Mackey's eyes were reported "red from lack of sleep"; nevertheless, she was amenable to interview.

"Clad in brilliant, flowered lounging pajamas, she stood in the door of her home and told of her family in Missouri"—though the telling seems to have been less than entirely forthright. Florence presented herself as the youngest of four children, the other three being Oscar, Jennings, and Harry. This is a consistent Young family pattern: Tell what you know is already known; otherwise, obfuscate, obfuscate, obfuscate.

Was Harry indeed recently married? That would be news to Mrs. Mackey, though he had been going out with a girl who worked in a store on Main Street. No, she didn't remember the girl's name. "The boys never came by to see me very much. They were out here a week or two before Christmas—just for a little while." Nor did she know anything about any caves at the farm in Springfield. "I hope they don't come down here and make a slaughter pen out of my house."

Having given her cooperation, the "willowy young matron" asked for reciprocity. "I sure wish there was some way my name could be kept out of the papers. You see, there's my church."[29]

Reporters quickly dubbed Florence Calvert, Harry's "million dollar baby from a five and ten cent store."[30] She was described as a twenty-five-year-old brunette who came to Houston three or four years ago from Lovelady, up near Crockett. According to the *Chronicle,* police were "taking their cue from the French detective's maxim: *Cherchez la femme*—find the woman." One of the places Texas detectives looked was the store on Main Street, where *la femme* was said to have worked as a saleslady. According to the manager, Florence had indeed been employed there, but asked for some time off after the holidays, related to the aforementioned throat procedure.[31]

Houston wasn't the only place under alert. From Streetman, the brothers could have easily doubled back to old haunts. At one o'clock Monday morning, Greene County Prosecutor Nee called police in Fort Worth, where Harry had been in custody just eight months earlier. Here's how that happened:

In January of 1931, *Fort Worth Press* employee Eddie Willard suffered the indignity of having his car stolen. On March 25, Willard was surprised to see his missing auto parked in front of the Montgomery Ward store. He notified police, who found Eddie's car with Mr. and Mrs. William Stewart in it. The Stewarts fingered Claude Walker. Police arrested "Claude," who surrendered without resistance, then released him on a $1,000 bond, whereupon he disappeared before anyone realized Claude Walker was actually fugitive Harry Young.[32] What was left of Harry's hair may have been dyed red, contributing to Fort Worth's confusion.[33]

The day after the Springfield massacre, the killers were reportedly seen driving around downtown Fort Worth. The local chief said, "The policeman who arrests either of the Young brothers will have to be quick on the trigger. Those two slayers are as tough as a boot. They proved they will kill rather than face capture. I doubt that they will ever be captured alive."[34]

In Tulsa, Police Chief Nelson J. Moore gave orders to "shoot on sight."[35] The Frederick *Leader* reported: "Close Watch Being Kept in Tillman."[36] Texas Rangers were posted along the Rio Grande, in case the brothers tried to slip over the border into Mexico.[37] In Corpus Christi, a posse was waiting "to search a steamship on its arrival there from Houston."[38]

And that afternoon, Monday, January 4, a "little fellow" calling himself Wallace rented a room on Walker Avenue in Houston, for himself and his brother. The brother, "Wallace" explained to the proprietor, was suffering from the extraction of two teeth and needed a quiet place for rest and recovery.

CHAPTER FOURTEEN

The Concrete Highway

"66 is the path of a people in flight, refugees from dust and shrinking land, from the thunder of tractors and shrinking ownership, from the desert's slow northward invasion, from the twisting winds that howl up out of Texas, from the floods that bring no richness to the land and steal what little richness is there. From all of these the people are in flight, and they come into 66 from the tributary side roads, from the wagon tracks and the rutted country roads. 66 is the mother road, the road of flight."[1]
—John Steinbeck, *The Grapes of Wrath*

The Model A from Harry Rogers' lot in Springfield was not the first car Jennings and Harry Young had stolen, but it would be the last. There was no time to switch the plate—Missouri license 363-662. The Young brothers were in a hurry.

The Ford coupe already had a circuitous history. Rogers originally sold it to his nephew, J. H. Rogers, who lived up in Bolivar, but the nephew had run into legal problems of his own. He had been jailed in Warrensburg on forgery charges, then sent to the state hospital in Nevada, whereupon J.H.'s sister, Mrs. W. C. Crawford of Louisburg, took possession of the Ford and sold it back to Uncle Harry. As day turned to night on January 2, 1932, the 1929 coupe was on the Rogers lot, 231 W. Commercial Street in Springfield, gone missing sometime before midnight.[2]

That's fact. Most of the rest is supposition. Assuming it was Harry and Jennings who stole the car off the Rogers lot (as opposed to Jesse Moore or another accomplice heisting the Ford and meeting the brothers at a predetermined point of rendezvous), we must first get them from the farm into Springfield.

It is impossible to pinpoint at what time the shooting finally ceased. Pike and Brown zigzagged out of the killing yard fully convinced the six remaining officers were dead. We will assume the same—with the

exception of Mashburn, of course, who may have regained consciousness only after Pike and Brown fled the scene. Not that the duo would
have seen him anyway; Mashburn was slumped in back of the house,
while Pike and Brown were in front, behind the cover of trees, before
running for their lives, away from the house.

It seemed beyond belief, initially, that only two men could put down
a half-dozen of the county's finest. But if, in fact, Jennings Young
could shoot fifty walnuts off a tree without changing stance, plug a
half-dollar piece from a distance of fifty yards thirty-nine out of forty
tries, keep a spool spinning with rapid fire, not to mention being barred
from turkey shoots—even allowing for some exaggeration—he and
Harry may have actually been disappointed in the final tally: Six killed,
three wounded, one officer missed altogether. And the Crosswhite kill
hadn't been clean at all. Still, it had been ten against two, and these
weren't turkeys.

Sometime after Pike and Brown fled, the Young brothers disabled
the lone police vehicle that remained in the yard[3] and stripped the dead
of their guns (an image made all the more haunting in that Mashburn
was still alive as they looted his body). Harry and Jennings then exited the premises. That much is known. What isn't known—and clearly
never will be—is just when they exited and in what direction.

The reader whose life is regulated by wristwatch may be frustrated
by the time-telling, or lack thereof, regarding the events of January 2,
1932. Pike, Brown, Virgil Johnson—none of these wore a wristwatch.
Hendrix carried a timepiece in his pocket, but the watch had to be
opened and closed. The contemporary reader wears time on his or her
wrist; Hendrix kept it in his clothing.[4]

Pike estimated, "I guess we were there under fire about a half to
three-quarters of an hour."[5] Having zigzagged to Haseltine Road, he
and Brown may have been waiting another ten or fifteen minutes
before relief came. That's the way they told it in 1932, though forty
years later, in Pike's retelling to Frank Farmer, the wait on Haseltine
Road had expanded to a half hour. In fairness, the situation surely
warped all sense of time. According to Pike, Tony Oliver complained
that Virgil Johnson must have driven to Kansas City, it was taking so
long for help to arrive—when, in Woodside's telling, at least, Virgil
arrived in Springfield like "an arrow in flight."[6] But for men under fire,
each minute must have *seemed* an eternity.

Time may have felt much different to the killers. Harry had experience with the taking of human life, up close and personal, and it was

almost certainly he who started the killing on January 2, felling Mashburn and Hendrix with the shotgun at point-blank range. Jennings, in contrast, while having a long record of crime, had no history of accompanying violence.

When the double blast from Harry's shotgun took the brothers past the point of no return, Jennings fought as if his life depended on it—which by that point, it most certainly did. It was surely Jennings who killed Houser and Meadows with clean shots through the forehead and whose rifle was the death of Oliver.

The survival of Frank Pike and Owen Brown is attributed to rapid zigzagging, but Jennings was an accomplished sportsman in a region famous for fox-hunting.[7] Harry's older brother was renowned for hunting rabbit, quail, and other small moving targets with a rifle, as opposed to the more commonly used shotgun.[8] Pike and Brown wouldn't have been much of a challenge, had Jennings actually wanted to kill them. Oliver and the other fallen officers had posed a mortal threat; in contrast, Pike and Brown were out of bullets and running away. Harry was still shooting to kill—hence Pike's shotgun wound (which, as posited by Woodside, was received in mid zigzag)—but by this point, Jennings may well have been shooting to scare off.

Once Brown and Pike were beyond firing range, we can imagine Jennings was more than a little shaken by what had just transpired and perhaps not entirely happy with baby brother for having turned him into a man-killer.

Having reached Haseltine Road, Pike and Brown flagged down the first would-be-rescuers. Among these were Springfield auto dealer Sam Herrick and his brother, Otto.[9] Sam Herrick had been at the police station when Hendrix, Oliver, and the others first left for the Young farm. According to the *Press,* "[Herrick] and several others started for the farm to see how the raid was progressing . . . and did not know that the officers had been slain until they met [Pike and Brown] on the road about a quarter of a mile from the house."[10]

In 1972, Frank Pike would remember Otto Herrick driving his car to the crest of a knoll—likely the same position used earlier by Hendrix and Oliver in their initial reconnaissance. As reported by Frank Farmer, Otto Herrick "stood on the running board of the car and peered toward the Young farmstead. With terrible urgency, Herrick meshed into reverse and accelerated with such speed that [Pike and Brown] had to leap into a ditch for safety. . . . 'Let's get out of here,' [Herrick] said. 'I saw them lying in the yard.'"[11]

This initial wave of rescuers included Officer Cecil McBride, in an automobile driven by Virgil Johnson. Virgil had been shot through the ankle,[12] but was still game. Other passengers in the same car included Ben Bilyeu and Officers Sidney Kemp and Lee Jones.

Brown was quite sure that any officers still at the house were dead. "Hell yes, they are so dead they couldn't get any deader if they were drowned."[13] As to the killers, Pike was "positive the men in the house did not get away in a car."[14] The farm lane was the only way in and out by automobile, so unless they "took off across the cornfield"[15] on foot, the desperadoes were still on the premises.

After making a right turn at the next farm road, Johnson, McBride, and company were quickly at the mouth of the lane leading north to the Young home. From the farm road, McBride saw movement up at the barn. The barn door was open. McBride could see an automobile inside the barn and someone moving in front of the car. McBride fired "two or three times," but from this distance, there was little chance of hitting anything.

Ben Bilyeu testified to the coroner's jury:

> Bilyeu: "I came back with Lee Jones, McBride, Virgil Johnson and Sidney Kemp; McBride wanted a rifle, and I had this one, I says, 'Mac. There is a rifle, but it is no account, it won't shoot, you can work it but it won't throw the cartridges out.'"[16]
> Stone: "That is the one [McBride] shot with from the road?"
> Bilyeu: "I don't know, he had that rifle, I told him it wouldn't shoot, he had it, I don't know whether he ever shot it, or not, it wouldn't shoot when I had it."

Officer McBride and the Herrick brothers looped north and east on foot, to a position north of and behind the barn. McBride told the jury: "We got in back of the barn, and someone tried to open the back barn door, he didn't open it; a police dog came out of the back of the barn, and in just a second there was another came out of the barn, come out in front of a Ford car that was in a shed."

McBride wanted to attack; Sam Herrick wouldn't hear of it. "You will never make the barn," he said. So they "laid there for sometime, twenty or thirty minutes." The "laid there" detail may be significant in wading through what appears to be tangled testimony. As McBride and the Herricks were in prone position, none too anxious to be seen themselves, it was perhaps difficult for *them* to see what was actually going on.

Woodside quotes McBride telling Otto and Sam, "We'll shoot anybody that shows his face," Otto Herrick whispering, "Hell yes. I'd shoot

Santa Claus now if he stuck his head out of one of them doors."[17]

It would have been in this interval that Lon Scott was tripping over himself as he and Lee Jones made their cautious approach from the west, finally coming upon the mortally wounded Mashburn and shouting for help. With the cry, "Come on you hometown heroes," the ambulances-turned-war-wagons started their laborious drive up the lane. Lewis Canady was behind the wheel of the Herman Lohmeyer machine:

> Canady: "I could see a man slip out of the main barn door and come part way down the incline [a wide ramp from the barn's loft to ground level], and step off the incline; there was about three or four people on the east side of the ambulance, they all saw it."
>
> Stone: "Did this man have any weapon in his hand?"
>
> Canady: "Not that I could see, if he had a rifle it was on the off side, and if he had a revolver it was under his coat; someone hollowed and he ran off in a north-east direction, all of us watched him until he had gone off down there."
>
> Back to Cecil McBride: "I heard corn stalks and weeds popping; Herrick said to me, one of them I don't know which, says, 'that is them in the corn field there.' I could hear them but I couldn't see them."

McBride sent the Herricks for help, while he tracked the presumed killers:

> "I seen they kept getting further down in the cornfield; I followed down behind this bank by this fence row . . . for two hundred, two hundred and fifty yards, and I got in a place behind some brush and a bunch of weeds, I raised up and was watching through these weeds and finally located them, they was coming to me; I went to work this rifle and found it wouldn't extract the shells, and I laid it down and got my six shooter, they was coming right straight towards me, two men, they was bent low; I was waiting for them to come right to me, I figured they was going to cross the fence there; I was under cover and I figured I had the breaks; they got in about twenty-five or thirty yards of me when this police dog [surely belonging to the Youngs] spied me, he began to growl and bark and came right towards me, and I fired the first shot, one of them said, 'oh, my God', and turned around and fell, I am confident he was hit; the other one commenced shooting at me with an automatic rifle and throwed dirt in my face, and hit a tree by the side of me; I hollowed for help and there was several answered me; I hollowed several times, I don't know how many; I hollowed and told them there was two men in the corn field,

and one was wounded, and they was headed back towards the house, that they were going in that direction. . . ."

Lewis Canady: "Shortly after that we heard a couple of shots down there, then what we took to be McBride hollowing, 'hey there', we stood and listened, he says, 'down here to me, come on down,' nobody would go . . . "

Stone: "What time was this?"

Canady: "That was five-forty-five."

McBride: "I waited there a few minutes more and hollowed again and got no answer; I went back around the fence row and back up to where they was at the house and around back of the barn; I was there trying to get a bunch to come down through the corn fields with me; it seemed like they all wanted to stay at the house."

Investigators discounted McBride's story, assuming the brothers had already fled the scene on foot, in a direction north and west—based, it seems, on the supposition that Brown and Pike would have seen the killers had they hoofed in the direction of Haseltine Station, north and east. Nevertheless, forensic evidence would indicate that Harry Young was, in fact, wounded sometime Saturday, shot through the palm of his right hand.[18] Perhaps it happened in the firefight with Oliver, Crosswhite, and the other doomed officers, but McBride's scenario seems at least equally plausible.

Getting past McBride would have put the fugitives in a northeast flight plan, which fits well with reports that two men were seen about 6:50 P.M. in the vicinity of Haseltine Station, climbing into a car driven by a third man, headed into Springfield on Mount Vernon Road.[19]

Woodside speculates the rapidly growing mob actually facilitated the escape. "Somewhere in that motley mob in all probability [and it would have been very dark by this time], three or more men who were present during the massacre milled about and lost themselves till they could get away and cheat the law."[20]

The posse would discover three stolen automobiles inside the barn. Did the first rescuers—McBride, the Herricks, et. al—arrive at the farm lane just as Harry and Jennings were ready to start one of these cars and make their getaway?

The next credible sighting is from the Missouri/Kansas/Oklahoma border town of Quapaw, Oklahoma[21]—though the details again are fuzzy, at best. According to G. B. Kinder, a Ford pulled up in front of his establishment, described as a "drug store," around 11:30 P.M. Which sounds like late hours for a drug store. Speculation: The Eighteenth Amendment was not "bone dry." The law made allowance for medicinal purposes—making "druggists" very popular. Again, that's just speculation.

As G. B. Kinder told it, a nervous looking fellow came into the store late Saturday, wearing a derby pulled down at an angle, but unable to conceal powder burns on his face that matched his hands. The customer purchased two packs of cigarettes, then went back out to the car, where two other men were waiting, and all drove away.[22]

Two other men?

Wait. In another version of Kinder's story, a woman is involved, described in the *Joplin Globe*, "as having dark, curly hair, fingernails well manicured, 5 feet 6 inches tall, weighing about 130 pounds, fair complexion and wearing a black coat with fur collar and cuffs." Kinder described the male companion as weighing about "165 pounds, 5 feet 6 inches in height, medium complexion, slightly bald, sandy red hair and wearing a dark suit." The description does seem to generally match Harry Young—particularly when accounts of red hair dye are factored in. Kinder sold the couple milk chocolates and the three of them discussed the killings in Springfield.[23] The male stranger said he had read all about it in an "extra" edition of the Springfield papers, which he'd left out in the car.[24]

Were *two* cars somehow involved in the getaway? One stopping at Kinder's at 11:00, driven by Harry and the dark-haired woman; the other at 11:30, carrying the powder-burned man (presumably Jennings) and companions? Did one of the men purchase ointment for a wounded hand?[25] Had Druggist Kinder been helping himself to some of his own medicine and gotten his details crossed?

Exactitude aside, the route and timeline work. Investigator Joe Anderson's theory: The Young brothers stopped at Kinder's in Quapaw around 11:30 Saturday night, and there was no compelling reason to believe the stolen Ford carried anyone but Harry and Jennings.[26]

Quapaw led investigators to speculate the Model A had been taken from Harry Rogers' lot around 8:30, or perhaps as late as 9:00 Saturday evening. Assuming the brothers were away from the farm around 5:45, that would give them almost three hours to get into Springfield. Perhaps they got a ride into town from the likes of Jesse Moore. The timeline would not preclude simply walking. As avid hunters, the Young brothers likely knew the landscape well enough to stay out of the glare of headlights coming in the opposite direction. For that matter, they may have just walked the railroad tracks.

And really, who would have looked for the killers coming *into*

Springfield? Marcell Hendrix or Tony Oliver might have remembered that Harry had pulled just such a stunt after murdering Mark Noe in 1929—but Hendrix and Oliver were dead. An old fox like G. C. Pike might have sniffed it out—but he was disgraced and out of office. Leaving "My Name Is Still Ed" Waddle, who was no match for the wiles of Jennings and Harry Young.

The 1929 Model A coupe was reported to be "one of the fastest models ever turned out."[27] Any image of the Young Brothers driving through the night has Jennings behind the wheel. Was Harry able to drive at all, given the wound through the palm of his right hand?[28] Steering wouldn't have been the problem; the problem would have been shifting gears. The Model A featured what was most literally a "stick-shift"—a straight metal rod coming out of the floor to the driver's immediate right.[29] Grasping the nob at the top of the stick, maneuvering to shift, would have surely been a pain-multiplier. Therefore, it seems probable Jennings did all the driving.

Which may have contributed to the accident outside Streetman. Jennings had been driving all night and through the morning, and the concrete pavement was slick from rain.

One thing is for certain, it had been a wild ride: Out of Springfield, onto Route 66—a marvel in 1932, but a roller coaster nonetheless. A driver in the steel-belted radial-era, following the urging of the sign on Interstate 44, "Take the Offramp into a Bygone Era," may well think, *This isn't so bad.* But what's left of Steinbeck's "Mother Road" has gone through multiple upgrades since the last ride of the Young brothers. The road Harry and Jennings traveled would have been considerably narrower in width, the turns sharper, the hills steeper.

West of Joplin, at the Missouri/Kansas border, a sign on the latest 66 invites the driver to turn onto "Old 66"—and it is only here, on this wild stretch of forlorn concrete ribbon, that we can begin to appreciate the achievement of Jennings Young on the first Saturday night and Sunday morning of 1932.

Having angled through the extreme southeast corner of Kansas, the brothers turned off 66 at Vinita, Oklahoma, headed south. The going was even more challenging from here. Vinita to Choteau to Muskogee to Eufala to Crowder to McAlester to Kiowa—the Young Brothers drive through the night, over a variety of surfaces: concrete, macadam, graded earth. Factor this, as well: It's dark. Black dark. The modern interstate is illuminated by multiple sources of ambient light that were non-existent in 1932. The lamps of the Model A, advanced as they were for the time, would have provided only a feeble piercing of the winter night.

Perhaps the brothers were in the vicinity of Stringtown, Oklahoma, as the sun came up, just before 7:30, crossing the Red River into Texas, making Dallas at mid-morning, turning onto the concrete highway toward Houston, their ride ending in a ditch in front of H. H. Carroll's place outside Streetman around lunchtime.

The roadster that took them a lift from the crash scene was driven by pharmaceutical salesman E. C. Hogan, who later told police, "one of the men seemed badly injured around the back, shoulder, head and hip."[30] The fellows were "so covered with mud and blood"[31] that it was difficult for Hogan to provide a positive description. While the passengers were anything but talkative, one did identify himself as Oscar Phillips of Houston. Hogan intended to rush them to medical help in Fairfield, some thirteen miles south of Streetman, but in the rush Hogan perhaps pushed the roadster beyond its endurance, as the car blew a bearing.[32] We can only imagine the exasperation of his passengers.

Isaac Levy of Corsicana was on his way to Fairfield when he came upon Hogan's stalled auto, The roadster was blocking a bridge, so Levy had little choice but to stop. He volunteered to take the injured men into Fairfield. The injured men offered to pay Levy handsomely to take them on to Houston. Levy, described as "aged,"[33] feared for a time his passengers might force the matter, effectively hijacking him, but the pair was content to get out at a Fairfield gas station, thanking Levy for his help, having decided they didn't need a doctor, after all.[34] They were later seen boarding a cotton truck headed south,[35] and were likely in Houston before Springfield got the call from Gaddy Jr.

CHAPTER FIFTEEN

Monday Mourning

"In the rain, slush and mud, two mornings after the night of tragedy at the Young farm house, sight seers were still straggling into the fenced yard, peering in the windows, begging for admission into the house and exchanging gossip of, 'I heard that—' or 'Did you know—?'"
—*The Springfield Leader,* January 4, 1932

It was a dreary, wet winter day in the Ozarks. A photo in the *Leader* captures the moment when Ollie Crosswhite was carried out of the Starne Mortuary Chapel. The angle is such that the photographer must have been situated at an upper window across the street from the funeral home. Hats are off, held to men's chests, in solemn respect. The sidewalks glisten with moisture.

The back door of a long black hearse stands open to receive the light-colored casket.[1] As hearses seem to have doubled for ambulances, this may have been the same vehicle that brought Crosswhite's corpse into town Saturday night. The windshield is at a ninety-degree angle to the hood, a flat roof extending backward the length of the vehicle, giving the effect of a large coffin with running boards about to receive a smaller one. The photo offers visual image to what was reported in the *Kansas City Star,* "a heavy mist hung over the city, adding to the air of gloom."[2]

Crosswhite's service had been lead by J. F. Sherman of Walnut Grove Baptist, described as a "white-haired, kindly-faced minister." "I knew Ollie Crosswhite as a boy," spoke Sherman, "and I knew him as a man. . . . Since his conversion he has felt near to God and he was ready."[3] We hope so.

Crosswhite's was the first of Monday's three law enforcement interments. Tony Oliver lay "in state" at the Floyd Fox Funeral Home until two o'clock, when the casket was taken in procession to Grant Avenue Baptist for eulogizing, then on to Hazelwood Cemetery for burying. Survivors Frank Pike and Owen Brown were among the pallbearers. A huge crowd was expected. As courtesy to mourners unable to squeeze into the church, the *Daily News* published the hearse's intended route, so respect could be paid from the street.[4]

The Wiley Mashburn funeral was also scheduled for two o'clock, overlapping with the Oliver farewell. Deputy Mashburn's service was held at the Alma Lohmeyer chapel, Reverend J. F. Killian officiating. This is interesting: Killian, pastor of Calvary Baptist, had married the widowed Effie Trogden Hendrix following the death of her husband, Daniel Hendrix—Marcell's father.

Reverend Killian was just back from a revival in Carterville, Missouri. While the meeting had been "successful," the exertions of soul-winning left him depleted and the evangelist was reported to be confined to his home by illness.[5] But, when the flock is attacked by wolves, the good shepherd does not stay in bed.

Nowhere in the coverage of comings and goings from the Hendrix residence is mention made of the presence of Reverend Killian and/or Marcell's stepmother. That doesn't mean Effie didn't offer support, and there may have been other factors involved, such as health. Does it say anything about step-familial relationships that Killian led the service for Mashburn, but is nowhere mentioned in accounts of the Hendrix funeral and/or the mourning leading up to it?

Maude Hendrix's Monday started at Springfield's Eastlawn Cemetery, where she selected a gravesite for her husband.[6] That sad duty complete, Mrs. Hendrix was sworn in as Sheriff Hendrix. The appointment was made by the County Court. Said one Republican leader, "We feel that the current term of office belongs to members of the Hendrix family because of their expense in making the campaign."[7]

By Missouri State law, a special election was required within thirty days to complete the term that would have naturally expired January 1, 1933. Republicans hoped Democrats would not make a race of it; surely the county owed this much to Marcell's widow.[8]

Mrs. Hendrix made no pretense of having any particular qualifications. "I don't know a lot about the work," admitted Maude, "but I'll carry on to the best of my ability."[9] On the other hand, she wanted to be clear on this: Greene County's new sheriff knew how to handle a gun.[10] Her first official act was the signing of a reissued divorce petition. The original had been in Wiley Mashburn's pocket Saturday; it was described as "blood soaked," necessitating new papers and new signatures, including that of Sheriff Maude Hendrix.[11]

Reward money was mounting, albeit with little help from the State of Missouri. The state constitution of 1875 had capped the governor's reward authority at a maximum of three hundred dollars. According to T. J. Stiles, this was "a present" from a sympathetic state legislature, dominated by ex-Confederates, to none other than Jesse James, as disincentive to his capture.[12] And in 1932, that's as far as Governor Caulfield could go: three hundred dollars per Young brother.[13] This did not, however, prevent others from contributing to the bounty. Greene County was offering five hundred dollars apiece, "dead or alive,"[14] and the Nichols Anti-Horse Thief Association was also pledging to contribute.[15]

Greene County had posted guards at the farmhouse, at a wage of two dollars apiece per day.[16] Not that there was much left to guard. The *Leader* reported:

> Soggy dirty feathers were on the porch and more in the small entrance way—someone had torn open a feather matress and the tick lay slung in a corner of what was once a living room.
>
> In the house itself the upheaval was complete, not a drawer, cupboard or closed place of any kind which had not been opened and ransacked for whatever evidence they might contain. . . .
>
> Heaped on dresser tops were things taken from the drawers: handkerchiefs, ties, a gold rimmed pair of glasses, several yards of pink muslin, a cheap empty purse and a world of stuff in such confusion that it would take hours to sort it out.
>
> The upright piano and a stove in the kitchen were about the only things which stood apparently where the family had placed them. Everything was dirty from the continued tramping in and out during the searching of the house. The odor of tear gas bombs was still disagreeably noticeable and eyes not used to it smarted upon leaving the place.

That readers might have a sense of what the place looked like *before* it was torn apart, the paper continued:

> The house was furnished in a comfortable but commonplace way, as any average farm house might be. There was little color, everything verging on a grayness, the papered walls, the rugs on the floor, the overstuffed furniture and scarfs on the piano. The beds were iron; the books were few. In the leaves of a school book of Robert L. Stephenson's Travels With A Donkey was folded a clipping cut from the Springfield Leader of the death of Rudolph Valentino and a picture of the screen idol.[17]

Among items turned up in the ransacking was merchandise reported stolen from S. C. Hoover's clothing establishment in Marshfield, east of Springfield, the 26th of October. Burglars had entered through the store's back window, taking "several suitcases or handbags, three or four men's suits, 22 pairs of men's hose, 34 pairs of ladies' hose . . . "[18] Perhaps Vinita and Lorena were wearing S. C. Hoover hosiery even as they talked to a *Daily News* reporter in the city jail.

The sisters were reported "fresh and alert Monday, despite their all-night interviews with cross-examiners." They apologized for having been less than truthful in a previous interview with the same journalist. "You wouldn't want to get your own brothers in trouble would you? No matter what they done."[19]

On the *Leader* editorial page that evening, January 4, Bixby reporter Beth Campbell would write of her experiences with Lorena and Vinita:

> I have seen the sisters of the killers, whose crime startled the nation, and watched their eyes droop as they told evident lies about their brothers' whereabouts, noted the manner in which their eyes were set close together. I have heard them disclaim knowledge of their brothers' criminal activities, knowing that the three they spoke of have served penitentiary sentences. Then I have heard the same two girls tell the truth, and apologize for the other, and call me by my first name.

Lorena, speaking in a "southern drawl," revealed her love for "sports of all kinds"—particularly swimming and horseback riding. "She plays the piano by ear a little, reads Photoplay, The Red Book, The Deliniator and Better Homes and Gardens." Lorena was also an avid fan of "picture shows," counting Norma Sherer, Greta Garbo, and William Powell among her favorite Hollywood stars. On the other hand, confessed Lorena, "I can't see what everybody's raving so about this Clark Gable for."

Lorena had attended a business college for a while and worked as a stenographer, but her bliss was staying home with the baby. Did the reporter have any news about Natalie? And would the reporter please pass this on to Lorena's mother, over at the county jail: "Tell mama to bear up and tell her I'm all right."

Turning its attention to the younger sister, the *Daily News* reported:

> Vinita, her short blonde straight hair giving her face a hoydenish look, was more sprightly than her sister. She laughed about the cold potatoes brought her for breakfast and said they had sent out for some fruit, however, and hadn't starved.[20]

She had very few friends in the farm neighborhood, she said, but knew lots of boys and girls in Springfield.

"I like to go to shows when I can go to them, but don't like to get interested and then have to stop." She reads very little, and has no talents, she declared, though she likes to sew.

The *Leader* had gained access to Vinita's senior year book. From the "autographs," Vinita was clearly a "keen" girl—perhaps contributing to her attention issues at movie theatres.

—Dear Vinita, Here's to a keen sport. Please do not forget me or the good old days at S.H.S. I have enjoyed being with you a whole lot.

—Here's to one of the 'keenest' kids I know. I hope that you won't forget me.

—I am glad you let me write in your book, because this is probably the last chance I will have to tell you that even though I don't know you very well, I can say you are a keen looking girl and I'll bet a real sport—and everyone likes a sport.

To this orgy of sporting keen-ness, her expression instructor added, "Dear Vinita, I shall always remember you as a little girl who tried to do her best."[21]

Around six o'clock that evening, Dan Nee told reporters the rifle and shotgun from the wrecked Ford in Texas had been identified. Both belonged to Oscar Young. Oscar was saying Jennings gave him the rifle as a present four years ago, before Jennings was sent off to Leavenworth.[22] Oscar had purchased the shotgun himself.

Harry had come over to Oscar's place Friday night asking to borrow the guns, so he and Jennings could go hunting. When Oscar and Mabel arrived at his mother's house on Saturday, the shotgun was standing in a corner of the downstairs living room. He and Mabel only stayed about a half-hour. Oscar said he talked with Harry, but Jennings had absented himself. There seems to have been bad blood between Oscar and Jennings, and it was speculated Jennings had seen his older brother coming and taken the rifle upstairs.

That was Oscar's story. Yes, the guns belonged to him, but he had loaned them to Harry for sporting purpose only. Yes, Oscar had been at his mother's house on Saturday, having come by to pick up a couple of mares, but he and Mabel were gone before Hendrix and Oliver arrived, and Oscar knew nothing of the shootout other than what he'd been told. Prosecutor Nee almost sounded as if he believed him, but until this got sorted out, Oscar and Mabel were staying put in the county jail.[23]

The day's most dramatic development, however, was surely a quote from Willie Florence. There was nothing reticent about Ma Young's relationship with reporters. She might appear "dazed," and even turn "hysterical" (the *Press*), "distraught and unable to answer questions directly at times" (the *Daily News*), and described as "lifting herself with difficulty from the county jail cot" (the *Leader*), but Willie Florence was going to give the papers something to write about, regardless.[24]

"Harry was a good boy," she told the *Leader,* "and the older ones always petted and pampered him, first because he was the youngest and then because he had been crazy." There were tears in her eyes as she added, "He brought me $3 for a Christmas present when he came this time."

Harry and Jennings had come to Greene County because they were homesick and wanted to see her. "We had such a nice time," she was quoted in the *Press*. "We cooked dinner and then sat around and talked. We were so glad to see each other. I thought everything was alright. I never thought anything like this would happen."

Willie Florence shared good memories from Oklahoma. "We were very nice people, and everyone commented on how nice the children were. And they always went to Sunday school and church, too."[25]

The *Daily News* reported the mother's description of one of Harry's "crazy spells," at age thirteen, when the family was living on the farm outside Ozark. "He said all of a sudden that Clarence, my soninlaw, was comin', that he knew, and when I asked him how he knew he burst out crying. He talked about how he wanted to be buried there, too, and knocked window glasses out of doors, and bent the dipper. We had to confine him six weeks."[26]

While the report offers no context as to where the morbid boy wanted to be buried, one would assume he was referring to McCauley Cemetery, where Youngs had been buried since 1903.

As to the alleged murder of Marshall Noe in 1929, Mother Young explained, "I tried to get Harry to give himself up last summer and have a trial about that shooting at Republic, 'cause he said he never done it, and there was a lot of folks who would have helped him fight it if he had a trial, but he didn't want to and left before daylight next morning."

While not admitting Harry had anything to do with the Noe killing, Willie Florence said if her boy *was* involved, it happened this way: When the constable tried to arrest Harry, the two exchanged words. Noe then hit Harry over the head with Noe's own gun. The gun fell out of Noe's hand, into the back seat, and went off in the ensuing scuffle.[27] It went off accidentally. It went off accidentally three times.

Mother Young was incensed at suggestions Harry had been drinking that fateful night in 1929. "None of my boys did. Harry was the only one who smoked. The girls don't smoke either."[28] Asked about liquor bottles reported found at the farm, she insisted, "There was no drinking at my house New Year's Eve."

"And the five little tubes of 'narcotics' they found at the house," she continued, "were just little vials of grease Paul left there when he was selling sewing machines and vacuum cleaners in Springfield."[29] As if that innuendo wasn't insulting enough, "A man came in here and asked me, 'Mrs. Young, do you smoke?' I said, 'No, I've got more respect for myself than to do anything like that.' He said, 'Now, Mrs. Young, you'd like to have a drink of whisky, wouldn't you?' I was so mad I almost slapped him."[30]

She wanted to be clear on this: Back in Oklahoma, she had been a member of the Women's Christian Temperance Union, and while she hadn't been active in recent years, she was a Baptist—"and I'm going to keep on being."[31]

Bemoaning the reported ransacking of her farmhouse, Willie Florence declared, "I don't have nothin' to live for. My home's gone. Mr. Willey said they burned my davenport I paid $135 for. The other children? They're better off than I am. If my home's gone I don't want to be here."[32]

And then the fateful utterance: "I've tried to get the boys to go right. But now if they did this, they deserve punishment. I can't bear to think of them hangin'. I hope they shoot themselves."

Resulting in the headline that would appear in Tuesday morning's *Houston Post-Dispatch:* "Mother of Killers Hopes Hunted Sons Will End Own Lives."[33]

CHAPTER SIXTEEN

The Battle of Walker Avenue

"We're dead, come on in."

—Harry Young

Reports vary as to the exact verbiage of Harry's *bon mot.*

Houston Chief of Police Percy Heard heard, "Come get us, we are dead."

Detective Lieutenant Claude Beverly thought Harry said: "We're dead—come on in."

City Detective J. H. Stinson remembered the words from the other side of the bullet-ridden bathroom door this way: "We're dead—come get us."

Housepainter/human shield A. P. Singleton offered an interesting variation: "Come on in, we've killed ourselves."

Nor is there agreement as to Harry Young's tone. Was it one final mocking of law enforcement, or simple resignation? In various accounts, the words are reported as "gasped," "shouted above the din," and having "rang out as a final gesture of defiance to the law they had so long flaunted."[1]

This much is certain: If not dead, the Young brothers were dying and Houston's finest were coming in—though not quite yet.

J. L. Tomlinson lived in "a green little cottage" at 4710 Walker Avenue, east of downtown. The "mild mannered" carpenter supplemented his income by renting out the front bedroom. On Monday, January 4, 1932, he let the room to two men who identified themselves as brothers. The "little fellow" wasn't a total stranger; Tomlinson had seen the man around the neighborhood and knew him as Claude Walker—though this night, the renter told Tomlinson's fifteen-year-old daughter to call him Wallace. Whatever. Tomlinson and his wife spent the evening with friends, playing "forty-two," returning home around ten o'clock.[2] Tomlinson would tell reporters:

When we got home, I had to look at The Chronicle before I went to bed.[3] I've been taking it for 20 years. The picture of the man on the front page struck me as familiar as soon as I opened up the paper. It looked like the man who had rented my room.

Then I got to thinking. This man I thought was Claude Walker had kept his hat on all the time—even when he was in the house. The picture in the paper was of a man without a hat. And I remembered he told Mary Ellise—that's our daughter—not to call him 'Mr. Walker.' He told her his name was 'Wallace.'

My wife and I read every word in the paper about the Young boys and what happened up in Missouri. I guess we didn't sleep much that night. I started to go get the officers, but then I thought maybe there'd be a lot of people killed right there in my home.

Yesterday morning I got up about the same time I always do to take Mary Ellise to school. As I was going out into the hall to leave, I saw the little fellow going out the front door.

'What if he's gone for good!' I said to myself.

Had Tomlinson spent the night alternating between fits of terror and counting reward money?

It would be said Harry Young went out the front door and bought a paper himself, picking up a *Houston Post-Dispatch* with this headline: "Mother of Killers Hopes Hunted Sons Will End Own Lives."[4]

It had been another long night for the Houston Police Department: A promising lead at the Sinclair Refinery focused even closer scrutiny on the ship channel and fueled fears the fugitives had successfully fled.[5] Harry and Jennings were reported seen hitching a ride to Galveston. They could be found asleep in a car on Odin Avenue. Police checked out a pool hall on Texas Avenue.

Dry leads all, frustration heaped upon frustration. Then Tomlinson showed up on Chief Percy Heard's doorstep.

Percy Heard was a veteran of many tight spots. With the city in an uproar over a series of drug store robberies, it had been Heard who caught Frank Pierce in the act and put a bullet through his temple. The *Chronicle* informed its readers, "And Heard has 'handled' such desperadoes as Ed Crowder, who held up the bank in the Heights in 1926; Bob Silver, the Fort Worth theatre bandit; Tony Corona, self-styled 'phantom bandit,' and others just as tough."[6]

Harry and Jennings were playing in a different league, now. Percy Heard wasn't likely to repeat the neighborly mistakes of Marcell Hendrix.

In relating what the *Chronicle* termed "The battle of Walker Avenue,"[7] we begin with Chief Heard, a surprisingly youthful-looking fellow, dressed for battle in a light-colored suit, topped with a wide-brimmed felt hat pulled down to the eye-line:

> This morning a party came to my house, stating that at about 1:30 yesterday he rented a room to two men and that the photograph he saw in the paper resembled one of them quite a bit, and from the way he talked it looked very much like they were the Young boys.
>
> I called my office and eight of the men came out to my house. We then planned to search this house, which was on Walker Avenue. Before doing this, I had this man [Tomlinson] go to the house and make sure that his wife had left so as not to get any innocent party hurt. We waited two blocks from the house until he did this. He came back and said the house was clear and thought these men were still in the room he had rented them.[8]

According to the *Houston Post-Dispatch,* "Three minutes later the cottage, small, painted green and surrounded by evergreens and rose bushes, was completely encircled by a ring of officers, armed with every conceivable weapon and prepared to 'shoot it out' with the men they were seeking."[9] According to the United Press, the "ring of officers," numbered over fifty men.[10]

Houston Press reporter Harry McCormick was on the scene—in fact, *in* the scene. We'll let him take up the story:

> The officers formed a semi-circle around the front lawn of the home, while others watched the back to keep the men from fleeing in that direction. Reinforcements arrived momentarily until it was certain their escape was cut off.
>
> Led by Chief Heard and Claude Beverly, a police lieutenant, a group of officers advanced on the house. . . . [11] The officers had their guns cocked. Cautiously Heard opened the door. Beverly slipped in behind it.
>
> I peered around the corner. I had no gun but wanted to leave the doorway open so that if trouble came up Heard and Beverly could retreat. I punched a porch chair against the screen to hold it back.[12]

Chief Percy Heard told reporters, "Myself and two lieutenants entered the front door, the rest of the men surrounding the house."

Among Heard's lieutenants was Claude Beverly. Like his chief,

Detective Lieutenant Beverly was no stranger to danger. In 1928, he and a partner went to the premises of "an Italian" on information the latter was operating a still. The Italian pulled a gun. Beverly's partner was shot dead. Beverly, in turn, terminated the Italian. His track record also including shooting and killing "a negro" in a raid on "a negro crap game" in 1916.[13] Beverly picked up where Heard left off:

> A hall extends through the house from front to rear. On the left side, there is a front bedroom and a rear bedroom. There is a bathroom between these two rooms, opening into each of them. On the right side, there is a living room, dining room and kitchen. The Young brothers had been occupying the front bedroom. . . .
>
> We started into the hall and met a man coming out and took him into the house with us. He turned out to be a visitor at the house. We walked into the hall together. We knocked on the front bedroom door. There was no answer.
>
> Chief Heard stayed at the front [bedroom] door and [Lieutenant George] Peyton and I went to the rear bedroom door. We opened it and tiptoed in. We went to the door which connected the bedroom with the bath. We unlatched the bathroom door.
>
> The door opened a little way and we jumped back into the hall. Three shots were fired, one coming into the hallway. Then we went to the kitchen across the hall, from which we had a view of the rear bedroom and the bathroom door.[14]

Reporter McCormick: "There was a roar of pistol fire and I saw Beverly's gun spit fire. I saw the officers retreating."

Claude Beverly: "Everything was quiet for a few minutes. Then the bathroom door opened a few inches and one of the Young brothers peeped out. I fired one time with a sawed-off shotgun. There were four more shots in the bathroom. A voice called: 'We're dead—come on in.'"

McCormick: "From the house the roar of guns came again. Then a muffled voice reached our ears, 'Come and get us,' the voice said, 'we're dead.'"

But not dead enough to suit Claude Beverly:

> I called to Stinson and told him to start firing with the tear gas. Barrett went to the bathroom window and started pouring gas into the bathroom. Stinson went to the front bedroom door and started shooting gas in there.
>
> We waited for the gas to clear up and then went into the bathroom and found the two men—one dead and the other dying.

It was Jennings dead, Harry dying, never to regain consciousness. As to the "visitor" in the hallway, that was Singleton, whose version of events cast the officers in a somewhat less heroic light:

> I had rung the door bell three times and no one would answer. I was fixing to leave when I saw about 10 policemen on foot, carrying shotguns, rifles and gas guns.
>
> 'Who are you?' one of the officers said. I told him and he said: 'Stick up your hands!'
>
> I was so surprised, and as I raised my hand, I asked the man: 'What's going on here?' But the officers were closing in on me.
>
> One cop pushed me in the front door and he, with another man, whom they kept calling 'Chief,' stuck a shotgun and pistol in my back. They walked me into the house and one of them said: 'Kick that door open.' I kicked, but the door was locked.'
>
> 'I'm an innocent guy in here and you'd better let me go before I get shot,' I pleaded with the cops.
>
> 'Keep still and you won't get shot,' they said, and kept nudging me with the barrels of the guns.
>
> "Let those hands down and I'll fix you,' the fellow with the pistol said. I was in a tight spot and knew it, so I reached higher.
>
> They said that they couldn't open the door, so the cop with the shotgun walked to the end of the hall where a door was open and just as he entered the room, two shots were fired and then a voice said: 'Come on in, we've killed ourselves.'
>
> The fellow with the shotgun ran out of the room like a shot and into another room across the hall. 'Look out, they're in there,' he said.
>
> The fellow with the pistol that they called chief nudged me with the barrel of that gun again. 'If you let those hands down I'll shoot you,' he kept saying.
>
> Finally, he went out. I followed him. There wasn't anything else to do. When I got outside I ran into a cop with a machine gun. 'Stop!' he said.
>
> I stopped. Another one ran up and put some handcuffs on my wrists and chained me to a tree, while the other one held the machine gun on me. I never have been in such a predicament.
>
> Then they started shooting tear gas in the house. They shot twice and ran out of bombs and sent to the police station for more.
>
> Finally the officer came back with more ammunition and they shot a third tear gas bomb in the front window.[15]

A synthesis of accounts: Having surrounded the cottage with well-armed officers, Heard, Beverly and George Peyton approach the front steps, only to encounter Singleton, a man in the wrong place at the wrong time. No one was going to confuse lanky Singleton with any of the Young brothers. But who's to say he might not be a confederate?

"Playing possum" had served the brothers well on Saturday. Hearing movement on Tomlinson's porch, Harry and Jennings lock the door to their bedroom and slide into the small bathroom between the front and back bedrooms, revolvers in hand, waiting.

The officers enter 4710 with great caution, using Singleton as a human shield. The living room is to their right, bedrooms to the left. The front bedroom is locked. Mindful of what happened to the last officers who put their shoulders to a locked door with the Youngs on the other side, Houston law enforcement tells Singleton to give it a swift kick. When the door does not budge, Heard stays put, his gun on Singleton, while Beverly and Peyton creep down the hall. The kitchen is to their right, another bedroom to their left. This door to this bedroom is not locked.

Beverly and Peyton venture into this rear bedroom. Still no sign of life. But inside this room is another door, surely to the bathroom. When one of the officers lifts the door's latch, gunfire explodes from the other side. This time, however, the Young brothers are without a shotgun and the only damage done by their pistols is to the door itself. Beverly and Peyton retreat across the hall into the kitchen, positioning themselves at such an angle as to have a clear view into the back bedroom to the bathroom door.

When the door peeps open again, Beverly lets go with a shotgun blast. The door closes as quickly as it was opened, followed by the sound of pistols from within. A voice calls out, "We're dead, come on in." The Houston P.D. is not inclined to take any chances. Gas is rained upon the place—into the bedrooms, through the bathroom window—for that matter, all the windows.

Reporter McCormick wrote:

> It was sometime before gas cleared so that the house could be entered. Heard attached a gas mask on his face and led the men in.
>
> I was right behind him. He pushed open the bathroom door. It would only open a few inches, the dead body of Jennings Young holding it back. The tear gas was terrific. Our eyes burned and it stung our faces like a million tiny needles. It hung in clouds.
>
> We leaned against the door and felt the body of Jennings Young

slide to the floor as the door opened. He lay in a pool of blood. Jennings was naked but for his shirt and shorts. Harry had his trousers on. They were shot in the chest and in the head.

An automatic blue steel colt and nickel plated pearl handled six gun lay side by side.

Windows were opened then and the officers groped outside to fresh air. When they took hold of Harry they found that he was still alive and rushed him to the hospital. Jennings was left to lay. He was stretched out along the floor and his arms were thrown carelessly at his side. He was shot seven times.

At 11:10 A.M., Harry Young was pronounced dead at St. John's hospital.

Given his state of undress in the final battle, it was speculated Harry had been in bed when the officers arrived. The *Chronicle* took readers inside the room at 4710 Walker Avenue: "Near the bed was his other clothing, including his black well-worn oxford shoes and his socks, the supporters attached. There was no clothing in the dresser." Exactly $201.03 was found in Harry's trousers pocket. And this homey detail: "On a stand beside the bed were a dozen oranges and apples and a frosted cocoanut cake with a cherry in the middle. The cake had not been cut."[16]

As for human-shield A.P. Singleton, police cut him loose when Tomlinson came along after the shooting was over. Tomlinson seemed to think it was kind of funny, seeing Singleton chained to the tree. Tomlinson was laughing as he vouched to Heard, "Why chief, he's my friend."[17]

To quote Percy Heard, "That's about the whole thing."[18]

CHAPTER SEVENTEEN

Extra! Extra!

"Jennings and Harry Young, hunted and desperate killers from Missouri's blue Ozarks, each blasted the life out of his brother when, like trapped rats, they were surrounded by officers in a small cottage in Houston Tuesday morning.

"Standing toe to toe in the bathroom of a house besieged by grim-faced officers and drenched with tear gas, the Missouri mass slayers each turned a stream of lead into the body of his brother."
—*Houston Post-Dispatch*, January 6, 1932

Ed Waddle was at the courthouse when he took the call from police headquarters. A radio station was reporting the Young brothers had been located and killed in Houston. The chief's initial, very understandable reaction: "I will not believe it until I know it is true."[1] And even when it was known to be true, confirmed in a telegram from Percy Heard, there was little in the way of rejoicing on Market Street.[2] The department wasn't finished burying its own dead.

At the county jail, things were a bit more exuberant, Deputy Chief Hodge saying, "That is the most welcome telegram that ever came to Springfield." Jailer Willey was relieved to hear Harry and Jennings hadn't taken any more officers with them.[3] Tuesday was a regular visiting day, but Frank Willey had already announced the jail would be closed to visitors, as he and the guards would be attending funerals.[4]

The story came over the United Press wire at 10:02, Tuesday morning, dateline Houston: "Young brothers believed slain here." Eighteen minutes later, the *Springfield Press* was on the street with the first "extra," scooping the Bixbys by some thirty-five minutes—and darn proud of it, too, attributing the victory to "systematic organization."[5] And it was, after all, a genuinely thrilling occasion:

Shouts of newsboys hawking extras echoed through the streets virtually deserted just before the lunch hour. Shopkeepers rushed to their doors to buy extras. Papers sold swiftly. People fought for the first Press editions. One newsboy reported having sold 200 in less than an hour. . . .

Newspapers were propped up on luncheon tables. Girls read them as they walked down the street. . . . Men stood along the street, heads hidden behind newspapers. A negro woman complained to her daughter that she couldn't read, but she wanted a paper anyhow, to see what they did with 'those nogood men.'

In front of the 10-cent stores idlers had temporarily discarded Hoover and the prosperity program to gather in close groups and discuss the sensational climax to the bloody killing that has kept Springfield agog with excitement.

Press staffer Nancy Nance reported reader reaction:

"Gosh, that was sure a relief to me. I've been scared stiff for fear they were hanging around here."

"I'd like to have gotten my hands on one."

"It's the best thing that could have happened."

"If they'd ever been brought here there'd have been a hemp party."[6]

"I never put no faith in these stories of 'em hanging around the neighborhood. Didn't make sense."[7]

Classes were disrupted at the teacher's college and senior high school. "Everybody's going wild" was the report from campus.[8]

The Young sisters' first clue was the shouting of newsboys on the street: "Extra! Young Brothers killed!" Officers initially told Lorena and Vinita it was just a rumor, but then the sisters heard a ruckus in the hallway and a reporter demanding access to the sisters so as to record their reaction.[9]

There wasn't much reaction to record. Lorena may have actually smiled, leading an officer to ask, "Don't you ever get serious?" Lorena snapped back, "What's the use?"[10] A reporter wondered why Vinita wasn't crying; Vinita echoed her sister, "What's the use?"[11]

Blissfully unaware of what was happening in Houston, Willie Florence shared a new crisis Tuesday morning:

The worst thing's happened. I've broke my false teeth. You see last night I took out my lower teeth and I rolled 'em up in my coat and put my coat under my head, thinkin' they'd be safe. Well this morning I woke up and threw my coat over the door and the teeth fell out and broke.

And that ain't all. Last night they put a drunk girl in there, right in the same room with us, and the liquor smelled awful and I didn't like it a bit.

But my teeth's the worst. If you see my girl Vinita, down at the city jail, tell her I broke my false teeth and I'd sure like to get 'em downtown and get 'em fixed. Don't suppose it'd do any good to tell her, tho.[12]

Then came the news from Texas. According to the *Press,* Willie Florence first learned of her boys' fate from *Press* reporter Ginger Ruark, who had pencil and paper at the ready. In contrast to her daughters, Willie Florence gave Ruark and other journalists plenty to work with. "I prayed they'd do it. I prayed they would. I hope they took time to ask God to forgive them," she sobbed. "I tried. I tried to make good boys of them. I know they did a terrible thing; they should have been punished—they had to be—but they were mine and I love them."[13]

Beth Campbell was quick to the spot, reporting Mother Young's hysteria to Bixby readers:

Lord have mercy on me. Oh, my God! Oh, my God! Why did they do it?

My God, yes, I wanted them to shoot themselves. Oh yes, I didn't want them to face a mob. But my own flesh and blood—my own flesh and blood!

What am I to do now? I can't take my own life. I'd go down to eternal torment. Daddy's in heaven. I'm glad daddy didn't ever know nothing about this.

My boys! Now that this has happened to my sons, I want God to take me home.

Willie Florence had apparently tried to put her teeth in, only to have them fall out during the interview.

Harry. My Harry. He was spoiled and then daddy died and then he was just led and pursuaded [sic]. I can't stand it.

Harry told me the night before this happened that they'd never take him alive. Where'd they get them? Houston?

Poor Florence. Poor Florence. She and Paul are the only ones down there. It will be terrible for them. Poor Vinita. She is over there in awful condition. Oh my poor children.

Perhaps it wasn't the most sensitive thing for a jailer to ask, but

Frank Willey asked anyway: "Don't you think your sons got what they deserved?" According to Beth Campbell, "She almost fell as she said wildly, 'No, no.'"[14]

Willie Florence "almost fell" because she'd been standing through the interview, "leaning heavily on reporters around her." Someone asked the jailer to bring Mother Young a chair; his response: "Let her stand"—though a chair finally was provided.[15] If Willey seems rude, consider: "As her voice stilled," reported the Associated Press, "through a partition separating her from the sheriff's home could be heard the crying of mourners about the bier of Sheriff Marcel Hendrix."[16]

Maude had been sitting in the room with her husband's coffin, opening sympathy cards and arranging flowers; "He loved red roses so," she said of Marcell. The news from Houston temporarily unnerved her, but she pulled herself together. "I'm glad they got them. I'm glad they got them before they killed someone else. But, oh—that doesn't bring Marcell back to me."[17] Then it was time to bury her husband.

The body was removed from the residence at the jail to the auditorium of the American Legion Memorial home, where it lay "in state" for mass viewing. When the Legion doors were opened at 12:30, five hundred people were outside waiting. Once inside, they approached an open gray coffin. A marine in dress uniform stood at the head of the casket;[18] the navy was represented at the foot. Behind the coffin, ten flags added to the ceremonial majesty.[19] Hendrix had been laid out in "a neat brown suit."[20] "A gold badge of office was pinned to the Sheriff's breast."[21]

By 1:30—the appointed hour to take the body on to First Baptist— an estimated two thousand souls had paid tribute. "Seen among those in procession were people from all walks of life—men in overalls, ministers, priests, lawyers, college presidents and actors. A few shed tears. Most faces were expressionless."[22] Perhaps, by Tuesday afternoon, Springfield was largely cried out.

Others had come by the residence, earlier in the day. Deputy W. Ed Smith was quoted in the January 5 *Leader* as saying, "One of the most touching tributes paid to the memory of Mr. Hendrix was this morning when a little old colored woman walked for many blocks in the heavy downpour of rain to his home. I chanced to answer her knock. There she stood, dripping wet, bent and old. She asked timidly if it would be all right for her to come in and see Mr. Hendrix. She told me how far she had walked that she might take a last look at him."[23]

Did the "little old colored woman" remember the 1906 lynching, and how Ed Waddle's daddy and other law enforcement types had not only turned a blind eye, but actually laughed, as Coker, Duncan, and Allen were "roasted" by the mob? Did the *in*decency she had witnessed in her time and place make her all the more appreciative of a law enforcement figure who was fundamentally decent?

The funeral service was, of course, conducted by Lewis M. Hale. First Baptist was filled to overflowing. Dignitaries included sheriffs from at least ten Missouri counties. Loudspeakers were set up in the church basement, and there still wasn't enough room, so mourners were standing outside in the January rain.

Marcell Hendrix was eulogized as having "died gloriously" upholding "the majesty of the law." The sheriff was likened to Admiral Lord Nelson, who famously said, "England expects every man to do his duty," and to Jesus on the cross, who "saved others; himself he could not save." For the gravesite, Pastor Hale chose Tennyson's "Crossing the Bar"[24]:

> Twilight and evening bell,
> And after that the dark!
> And may there be no sadness of farewell,
> When I embark;
> For tho' from out our bourne of Time and Place
> The flood may bear me far
> I hope to see my Pilot face to face
> When I have crossed the bar

Having crossed said bar, Marcell Hendrix went into the earth, ashes to ashes, dust to dust.

The other widows offered their reactions.

Maude Oliver: "I haven't much to say and I'm bitter toward no one, for bitterness can't correct this terrible affair. I had wanted the killers brought to justice though. What I wish to say more than anything else is something about our thanks to the many wonderful friends for their kindness and sympathy shown us in the darkest hour of our lives."

Maude Mashburn: "People here at my home read me the news in the papers. I wanted them captured but other than that I can't say much."

Augusta Houser was not available for comment. She had collapsed upon receiving news of Charlie's death and was confined to bed.

Lilly Meadows: "I am sorry that they were not taken alive. I wanted them brought back here and hanged."[25]

That afternoon, Lilly's Sid joined Marcell Hendrix in the ground of

Eastlawn Cemetery. Services were held at Fox Chapel, Reverend T. H. Wiles intoning, "We know not why the good must bend beneath affliction's grievous rod, while our prayers ascend to a faithful God."[26] Meadows had been committed to the earth a half-hour before Hendrix. It was reported that Maude Hendrix paused at Sid's grave to pay her own respects.[27]

A widows and orphans relief fund was in motion, having been officially announced Monday at the Chamber of Commerce by Arch McGregor, who himself pledged a thousand dollars.[28] The Bixby papers were already on board, publicly committing a hundred dollars to "inaugurate such a public purse." In a nice turn of phrase, the *Daily News* noted, "some of these men were wealthier in courage than in goods."[29]

Contributions were rolling in: Fifty dollars from Levy-Wolf Dry Goods, fifty dollars from Domino Macaroni, one hundred dollars from Eisenmayer Milling. In endorsing the campaign, the *Press* emphasized, "No contribution is too small to be accepted"—and as if to prove the point reported, Kucker's Studio had given a single dollar.[30] The *Press* advised readers, "The family of Sheriff Hendrix is fortunately provided for."[31] The money would go to the other, "not so fortunate" families.

The Chamber was leaving no stone unturned. Railroad employees were solicited by J. K. Gibson, lawyers by Arch Johnson. Ray Kelly was working the coal and lumber dealers. If you made a living in creamery, dairy or produce, W. P. Keitner would be talking to you. Twenty such subcommittees were formed for solicitation.[32]

While applauding the fund as a means of providing in this emergency, Reverend G. Bryant Drake of First Congregational suggested it was high time the city and county provide group insurance for officers in the event of future occurrence.[33]

As the relief fund mounted, so did claims against the Young brothers. Among items retrieved from the wreck in Streetman was a Parsons, Kansas, checkbook. A pair of bandits had robbed a Parsons drug store on November 23, relieving proprietor J. M. Stewart and fifteen customers of five hundred dollars, while a third man waited outside in a getaway car. B. A. Russell said the robbers took sixty dollars off him, along with a checkbook, and wondered if this was the same found in the wrecked Ford. Shown photographs from the "rogue's gallery," Proprietor Stewart identified the two inside men as Harry Young and Charles Floyd.[34]

In Houston, dairyman J. B. Bernier looked at a picture of Jennings and saw the man who, on December 21, jumped on the running board of Bernier's automobile, relieving Bernier of two hundred dollars in cash and eight hundred dollars in checks.[35]

Marshfield merchant Mary E. Waterman was escorted to the Young farm by Ben Bilyeu and her hometown sheriff. Yep: Two dresses—one of brown silk, the other black velvet—were among items stolen from her women's ready-to-wear shop on November 25.[36]

And stolen cars kept turning up. A Ford belonging to Roy T. Morrow of Buffalo, Missouri, heisted in November, subsequently sold in Tulsa for $150, the seller identified as Jennings Young. Horace Gardner's Ford, taken from Monett, southwest of Springfield, likewise surfaced in Oklahoma. At Medley Motors, in the glove compartment of the 1931 Ford that started the avalanche, papers were found for yet another missing auto, this belonging to Wilson Raibler of Springfield.[37]

The scope of the Young Brothers' crime ring was approaching mind-boggling proportions.

Tuesday, the fifth day of 1932, had been one of great excitement in Springfield, Missouri. But Maude Hendrix was entirely correct: Neither the end of the Young brothers nor anything else was going to bring Marcell back, the incomprehensible, incontrovertible, irrevocable reality confirmed by the *Daily News:*

> On a sequestered slope in Eastlawn cemetery here last night slept Greene county's beloved sheriff, Marcell Hendrix. As they buried him there in the late afternoon, a brisk breeze blew from over the fields which he had worked and loved and in the protection of which he died, symbol of the life which is done here and passes on to kinder climes.
>
> The grass under foot was not yet seared by winter. Skies were darkening overhead as the wind fanned billowy clouds across the heavens, but through a rift appeared a spot of brilliant blue with its promise of a happier day tomorrow.[38]

CHAPTER EIGHTEEN

Cleaning Up

"Dead in Houston, Texas, but damned around the whole wide world, Jennings and Harry Young were laid out clammy with blood on a cold hard slab in a mortuary 800 miles from Springfield, where at that very hour a widow and her fatherless brood were convulsed with tears around the bier of their dear dad—72 hours previous, a victim of the killers' guns."
—J. R. Woodside, *The Young Brothers Massacre*

Things surely were a mess at 4710 Walker Avenue. "Negroes" had been dispatched from the city jail to help with the clean up, but there were fix-it challenges here beyond the scope of mop and pail. The floors would have to be sanded and refurbished to remove bloodstains. Windows were smashed, walls and doors ruined by twelve-gauge buckshot. Carpenter Tomlinson was planning to do much of the repair work himself, with the Houston PD footing the costs.[1] The forty-year-old master of the house was described as "ashey-faced and stooped, but keeping a grim hold on himself."[2]

As if things weren't bad enough inside Tomlinson's cottage, sightseers/scavengers were wreaking havoc outside: breaking the front porch trellis to pieces, snipping greenery from the hedges, even removing loose bricks, so as to take home a "souvenir."[3]

The neighbors were being very protective of Mrs. Tomlinson: "'Why can't her name be kept out of the papers' they wanted to know. 'Besides, this is a nice neighborhood.'"[4] According to the *Chronicle,* Mrs. Tomlinson herself "sat at the window across the street, gazing misty-eyed at the strange folks who milled around her home, tramping down her hedges and flowers, peeping in the windows, filing up and down the front steps and to the side entrance in muddy boots."[5]

At the Fogle-West morgue, "scores of people" came hoping to see the remains of the Young brothers, only to be turned away at the door.

Viewing was limited to police officers and journalists. Jennings, "on a cot beside one wall," was described as covered with a pink spread to the chin, and "a sheer gauze spread that covered the face and fell in folds to the floor." Harry's "smooth-shaven face" was reported "twisted in a sardonic half smile." Gazing at the body of Harry Young/Claude Walker, a traffic officer exclaimed, "Why, that feller used to be my milkman!"[6]

The Houston coroner's jury arrived at a speedy verdict regarding cause of death: "Jennings Young, pistol wounds inflicted by Harry Young. Murder," "Harry Young, pistol wounds inflicted by Jennings Young. Murder."[7] This conclusion would produce much skepticism. J. R. Woodside reported that "Not a few old-time officers . . . are prone to disbelieve that Harry and Jennings Young fired all of the bullets reputed to have made wounds in their respective bodies."[8] Likewise, the *Houston Chronicle* was frank with its readers:

> There's a brotherhood among officers of the law; the man who kills an officer henceforth is a 'marked man.' And the two men whose bodies lay in this tiny room shot down six officers. Throughout the Southwest—to Texas rangers riding the mesquite along the Rio Grande, to policemen in scores of cities, to sheriffs and their deputies in a hundred counties, to marshals in a thousand towns—the order had gone out: 'Shoot to kill—give no quarter.'[9]

Had Harry shot Jennings and vice versa? Had Harry shot Harry and Jennings shot Jennings?[10] Or, had the "brotherhood among officers" in fact given "no quarter," adding their lead to the killing equation?[11] Consider that Houston justice/coroner Campbell Overstreet originally ruled that Harry shot Jennings *"seven times."*[12]

Not that the official verdict wasn't plenty satisfying. It seemed poetically just that Jennings had killed Harry with Wiley Mashburn's stag-handled .44 caliber Smith and Wesson. Houston's *Chronicle* noted, "Whether the Young brothers selected [Mashburn's] gun in the double killings as an ironic gesture or whether it was the pistol which lay closest at hand was a matter of speculation Wednesday."[13]

A photograph from the bathroom shows Jennings face up, eyes open in death gaze, clad in an undershirt, Mashburn's revolver in his left hand—indeed, it almost appears to have been posed that way. Hendrix's pearl-handled .44 was also found at the scene, along with a pistol thought to belong to Crosswhite.[14] Altogether, Harry and Jennings had seven pistols in their possession.

Greene County Coroner Murray Stone amended his original report.

Upon microscopic examination of shells and cartridges from the farm-house, Stone was now certain only two guns had done the killing of January 2—the very same rifle and shotgun found in the back of the car in Streetman, Texas. If anyone else had been in the house with Harry and Jennings, surmised the coroner, "it is logical to suppose that they, too, would have been shooting, with one of the Young boy's revolvers, if they had nothing else."[15] This was beginning to tidy up.

As to *le femme* being *cherzed*, Florence Calvert Young/Walker surfaced in Houston on Thursday—not that anyone particularly cared anymore, the *Chronicle* commenting, "Now that her husband lies dead, officers no longer seek the girl. Perhaps, she will soon return to her counter and thrifty housewives, fingering the garment that lays before them, will not dream of the tragedy packed in the life of the girl who smiles back at them."[16]

Houston Mayor Walter E. Monteith praised his department, saying this should serve as a lesson to criminals: They would find no refuge in his town.[17] The *Chronicle* editorialized on January 5:

> The Young boys came a long way from the Ozarks hills to get themselves killed.
>
> Every man's hand was against them on the long trek from Missouri. They belonged to the 'wild bunch' and they followed a bloody trail south from Springfield. At the end, they died like wolves, in the trap which the law always lays to catch the unwary lawless.
>
> Harry and Jennings Young were stupid: stupid in the first place to shoot down peace officers; stupid in the second place to stay in Houston when their pictures had been broadcast to the four corners of America. That is the one real advantage the enforcers of the law have in this country, the stupidity of the criminal sought.

In fairness, Harry and Jennings may not have been so stupid, necessarily—at least not in the "second place." Perhaps they had another, better plan, involving a short stop in Houston to pick up Harry's bride, then scooting on over into Mexico. Or perhaps they would have bypassed Houston altogether. And such a plan might well have worked, if not for the wreck in Streetman. Which changed everything.

At the rate they'd been going, the brothers could have been in and out of Houston by late afternoon Sunday—about the time Claude Pike was launching his raid in Bird Eye and Springfield was excited about leads from Kansas City and Iowa. Not only did the wreck slow Jennings and Harry down, and eventually alert authorities to the direction they were headed, but by the time they got into Houston, the brothers were thoroughly beat up. Harry was shot through the hand, Jennings was battered from injuries sustained in the tumbling Model A.

Adding to the pathos, having presumably gone to Houston to fetch his bride, Harry may never have actually linked up with her. If Lily Shaw is to be believed, Harry came looking for his Florence, but his Florence had absented herself. Had the bride of Harry read the papers, seen the pictures, and recoiled? How many lies had Claude/Harry told her? We know they did not spend Monday night together. Had Harry come all this way, only to have her avoid him?

According to Tomlinson, "Claude Walker" had been on the Tomlinson doorstep the previous week, inquiring about renting a room. Tomlinson's price was too high; Claude/Harry left, presumably in search of less expensive accommodation.[18] Leading us to wonder: Were Harry and his "million dollar baby" having problems *before* his fateful trip to the Ozarks? Had she kicked him out? Did this contribute to the decision to visit his mama in Missouri?

One other note that may or may not be significant. In a conversation with authors Paul and Mary Barrett, Vinita Young remembered Harry's ex-wife had moved to Texas.[19] In the frenzied post-massacre investigation, Tarrant County law enforcement announced they had good information that the ex-wife of an unnamed Young Brother, a woman currently living in the town of Joshua, Texas, had regularly been sending money to her fugitive ex-husband.[20]

What kind of mess had Frances Calvert gotten herself into?

And remember: Harry killed Constable Mark Noe just a couple of weeks after Harry's divorce from Frances Lee. If Harry was, in fact, estranged from Frances Calvert after only a few weeks of marriage, did this contribute to a mood that might have quickly turned murderous?

While we're at it, consider what Steinbeck's Muley said to Tom Joad: "I was mean like a wolf. Now I'm mean like a weasel. When you're huntin' somepin you're a hunter, an' you're strong. Can't nobody beat a hunter. But when you get hunted—that's different. Somepin happens to you. You ain't strong; maybe you're fierce, but you ain't strong. I been hunted now for a long time."[21]

Harry Young had been hunted a long time.

In the same January 6 edition of the *Chronicle,* dominated by reporting from 4710 Walker Avenue, the following appeared in a small box at the bottom of a page:

PELICAN KILLS SELF BY STANDING WITH MOUTH OPEN
Inhabitants of the Little Rock Zoo today were mourning the death of their fellow inmate, the pelican.

The bird stood with its mouth open during a rainstorm last night and was drowned.

Zoo attendants were of the opinion the pelican was despondent when he committed suicide.

One can only speculate as to the level of the Young brothers' despondency on January 5, adding credence to the official verdict of fraternal suicide. *Startling Detective* Frank Pike put it succinctly, "At last they had obeyed a wish of their mother's."

Harry and Jennings Young might be dead, but Greene County Prosecutor Dan Nee was filing murder charges against them, anyway, "Because some complications might arise."[22] Harry was posthumously looking at eight murder counts: Mark Noe, the six officers at the farm, and Jennings. Nee still wasn't "thoroughly satisfied" that only two men had done all the killing at the Young farm and wanted to keep the investigation going.[23]

An abundance of charges were being filed. Willie Florence, Vinita, Lorena, and Albert Conley each stood accused of receiving stolen automobiles. It was worse for Oscar and Mabel, both charged as "accessories before the fact" in the slaughter of January 2.[24]

Nevertheless, Springfield could begin returning to politics as usual. Mayor Gideon, who intimated that he and Chief Waddle had tried to restrain Hendrix, Oliver, and the others from going out to the farm in the first place,[25] spoke before the city council. "We've either got to have equipment or quit trying to catch hardened criminals. We just have two high-powered guns and they're old ones. Ben Bilyeu said the gun he had Saturday jammed on him and was useless."

Gideon had tried and tried to get the council to move on this, but nothing came of it—and now look what had happened. "I'm going to buy guns and equipment for the police force and charge it to the city of Springfield; if Ellis Cogley doesn't pay for it, that's no affair of mine."

Members of the council—Mr. Cogley in particular—took considerable exception to the mayor's remarks. Had Gideon ever brought such a recommendation for a vote? No, not exactly.

Asked if his newfound resolve to purchase modern weaponry was the equivalent of "locking the stable door after the horse has been stolen," Gideon had this to say:

Correct. It does seem so. Fact is, it took a wholesale slaughter of police to offset the persistent and ill-aimed criticism that has been heaped upon the police department. It is a shame that so many good men had to die to pave the way to more adequate police equipment. Not because of any sincere motive, but merely because of a desire to persecute me and discredit my administration, certain critics have hammered the police department unmercifully and wholly without reason.[26]

Thomas H. Gideon was first, last and always a politician, using the disaster as opportunity to heap abuse on his enemies.

The *Leader* also got back on the snide track, editorializing:

It has been interesting to observe how men in authority have been behaving during the massacre on the Young farm. Some—especially including some of self-assumed authority—have had to buy new and larger hats.

A fellow can't help but wondering how Jennings and Harry managed, without being seen, to get from their farm to the place on Campbell street where, so it has been reported, they got the auto in which they fled. If that is what they did they must have been awfully clever about concealing their rather cumbersome and conspicuous weapons.

That is one link in the story of their escape that never has been cleared up. Maybe, when Springfield gets a police department, such mysteries will be solved.[27]

Reverend G. Bryant Drake blamed the State of Missouri:

Our manner of handling criminals is a survival of ox-cart days. The state at one time had the bodies of the murderers under its control, and then calmly released them on society. If these men were abnormal there were scientific means of determining the fact, and a potential murderer should not have been liberated any more than a scarlet fever victim.[28]

On Wednesday, January 6, the day after her sons died in Houston, Willie Florence Haguewood Young went in front of the "sound cameras" of Movietone News, Inc. Filming took place at the Greene County Jail, under the direction of a Movietone representative from Chicago. The interviewer was none other than Willie Florence's jailer, Frank Willey. According to newspaper accounts, "at first her answers were so faint that it was necessary to take the picture over several times. She obligingly raised her voice and attempted to face the bright glare of the light about the camera as she talked."[29]

> Willey: "How did you want your boys to go?"
> Willie Florence: "I said that under the conditions I would rather they would take their own lives than be tortured by a mob."
> Willey: "Did you advise them to do what they did?"
> Willie Florence: "I advised them to do right. I always told them to do right. . . . After Saturday night when they did that awful crime, I wanted them to do just what they did."
> Willey: "Where do you want your boys buried?"
> Willie Florence: "I want them buried by their father in the McCauley cemetery. And I want to go and I want to see them. And I want all who want to go, to go."
> Willey: "Do you think there is any chance for them to get forgiveness for what they have done?"
> Willie Florence: "Oh, I don't know. I've been waiting for word from down there to see if they said anything before they died. I don't know whether they could be forgiven or not. He said, 'Whatever you asked you shall receive.'"[30]
> Willey: "What caused your boys to go wrong?"
> Willie Florence: "Bad company years ago. The boys were brought up awful good. We all went to church and Sunday school and had a nice time until their father died. Then they began to scatter, then got into bad company, and went from bad to worse—and this is the way it finished up."

According to the review in the January 6 edition of the *Springfield Leader,* "She gave a moan, buried her chin in her hands, and said no more as this statement closed the camera interview."

On the other side of the partition, Sheriff Maude Hendrix had to be pondering her future. The special election was only three weeks away. Maude would not be running unopposed, after all. Scott Curtis, who was getting high marks for his work at the Young farm, was among those already campaigning for the Democratic nomination.[31]

Of the six officers killed Saturday, January 2, 1932, Charlie Houser was last to go into the ground. Originally scheduled for Tuesday, his funeral had been moved back twenty-four hours, due to Augusta's emotional condition. She was sufficiently recovered by Wednesday to attend the memorial service at First Baptist in Springfield.

The very busy Lewis M. Hale read from First Corinthians, intoning "Now we see through a glass darkly, but then we shall see face to face," and quoted the lyric of a popular hymn, "Lord, help me to live from day to day/ in such a self-forgetful way/ that even when I kneel to pray/ my prayer may be for others." The service ended with tenor George Monteer singing "Beautiful Isle of Somewhere."[32]

Burial itself was the next day at Joplin's Mount Hope Cemetery. Charlie had gone to high school in Joplin. Joplin gravediggers were going to be kept busy for a while.

CHAPTER NINETEEN

First Person

"Survivors of the slaughter at the Young farmhouse west of here, where six Springfield officers died Saturday afternoon, pieced together an eye-witness story of the tragedy before a coroner's jury in session at the courthouse last night.

"The stories conflicted in some particulars, due no doubt to the terror and excitement which prevailed at the time, but the essential details checked."

—The Springfield Leader, January 5, 1932

The Greene County Coroner's Jury heard testimony Monday evening, continuing through Tuesday. For the sake of narrative, we will take liberties with the order of witnesses, calling first on Ben Bilyeu.

Bilyeu—pronounced "blue"—was quite the character, disavowed by Mayor Gideon in the corruption trials of 1930 and conspicuously absent from group photos in the department's 1932 *Souvenir Review.* Born and raised in the old Christian County Bald Knobber hotbed of Spokane, Bilyeu and three of his kin had been charged with murder in 1917. The case against Ben was eventually dropped, but the stain remained. In another 1932 judicial proceeding, Bilyeu was photographed as a somewhat seedy fellow, his cylindrical head topped off with an unruly garden of hair.[1]

Bilyeu: "I came to the station about four o'clock; when I came to the station, Tony Oliver said, 'we have got them bad men located, let's go.' I says, 'you mean the Young Brothers', and he said, 'yes.' I says, 'I am ready.'"

There was a slight delay in getting away. As the officers were going out the door, an insurance salesman named Duerr was coming in. Tony Oliver had previously committed to the purchase of a two-thousand-dollar life insurance policy and Duerr was here to collect the premium that would put the policy into effect. Oliver told Duerr to wait at the station; this shouldn't take long.[2]

It would be said that Oliver also took a moment to send Officer Tom Fielder out for some prime whiskey, so as to have a drink waiting when he got back.[3] Indeed, there would be persistent rumors that the officers had been imbibing *before* going out to the Young place, this contributing to the debacle. It is not incredible that Oliver and Bilyeu might have had a nip or two, but any such allegations against Hendrix are likely a slander. Not the Baptist with a badge.

Notified by Waddle of the hot lead on Harry, Hendrix and Mashburn, just back from Ash Grove with their morning catch, ran by to pick up Crosswhite, who was sitting down to his favorite meal: hamhocks and beans. Before Ollie could take a bite, Marcell and Wiley were at the door. Crosswhite had every justification for staying home and eating his dinner; it's not as if he was on the payroll. But Ollie Crosswhite would "fight a buzzsaw" and wasn't going to miss this.

Ethel Crosswhite, on the other hand, didn't need any more loss than she had already experienced. "Be careful, you'll get killed," she pleaded as her husband was going out the door. "Don't worry—no I won't." And she would always regret that Ollie never got to eat his hamhocks and beans.[4]

> Bilyeu: "We followed Hendrix out, and when we got out on 66, we took down through the orchard; we got down there where that road turns up through the orchard, and the Sheriff and Tony had a talk."
>
> Virgil Johnson: "We went out there with the Sheriff, Ollie Crosswhite, Sid Meadows, Deputy Sheriff Wiley Mashburn, and myself in the Sheriff's car; we drove up there; Tony Oliver, Charlie Houser and Ben Bilyeu was in another car, they followed us out there; just before we got out in sight of the house we all stopped. . . . "

The two-car caravan having halted, Oliver and Hendrix walked up a crest to the right of the autos for a brief reconnoiter. From this vantage point, the farmstead was a quarter mile to the west.

> Bilyeu: "The Sheriff says, 'Now Tony, we will turn up there and you boys go through this lane, and we will all get there about the same time.' Tony says, 'What will we do when we get there?' He says, 'We will bust in on them.' Oliver says, 'now we want to be careful Sheriff, these boys are killers,'and he says, 'we will bring them out of there.'"

Johnson: "The Sheriff said for Tony's car to go in on the old road back of the field there and up through the orchard with his men, and get out and come in on the north side of the house; so Tony went up the road back north of the house there; we drove on around in front of the house, we drove on around the road and drove up from the road that goes up to the house and drove up in the front yard."

With Charlie Houser at the wheel, the Oliver/Bilyeu auto negotiated what was surely a messy track east to west through the orchard, the threesome emerging from the treeline on foot, making their way across a field toward the Young farmhouse from the north. The Hendrix group continued down Haseltine Road, turned right at the first farm road, then right again into the lane leading up to the house. The front yard was enclosed by a wire fence. Hendrix parked outside the fence, the car positioned at the southeast corner facing the house. Oliver and his team arrived. Other than smoke from the chimney, there was no sign of the Young brothers or anyone else. Hendrix's was the only car in the driveway.

The house is unremarkable: white frame, two stories, the length of the place twice that of the width. The roof is peaked at approximately forty-five degrees. The front door is positioned at midpoint of the length facing east, flanked on either side by rectangular double window casings. On the floor above are two single windows. At either end of the rectangle, facing north and south, single windows are cut into both the upper and lower levels.

Seventy years later, this basic design can still be seen in old houses dotting the rural landscape of the Ozarks—the rectangular proportions of hotel pieces in the Monopoly board game. Even in 1932, however, the Young home featured some additions.

A handsome roofed porch covers the front door and south front windows. The upper story front windows are gabled. The house has been added onto in the back. A second peaked roof runs east to west, creating a blunt T-shape. Beneath this peak, a single window on the second floor and a door and window on the first create a triangular visual effect. On either side of this section, north and south, are smaller, one-room additions. The southern addition has a window facing west and a door facing south toward the farm road.

It is this door—what will be referred to as the "south-west door"—that Marcell Hendrix will kick in.[5]

As teams Hendrix and Oliver converged in the front yard, unbidden reinforcements arrived in the form of Frank Pike and Owen Brown.

Frank Pike: "I went down to the station, I was up in town; I under-
stood there was a bunch of men had left the station, and was going
out to the Harry Young place; Owen Brown walked up about that
time and asked me about it, and said he was going; I went to the station and was talking to Ed. Waddle about it, and Ed. Waddle said they
had gone out to the Harry Young place."

Owen Brown: "Well, when I came to the police station, Officer
Pike was out in front, and said there is a bunch of men gone out to
the Young farm to catch them Young boys, and says, 'do you want to
go', and I says, yes; I asked him if he had seen the chief, and he said,
'yes', and we drove on out."

Pike: "We run and got in one of the Police cars and started; we
went out the Fort Street Road; I don't know what that road is that
leads of out that way; we went out the Fort Street[6] and turned there,
anyhow, we went out to this place and drove up in the yard; Marcel
Hendrix had just got there when we drove up, he was getting out of
his car, him and Virgil Johnson, Ollie Crosswhite, Sid. Meadows,
Ben Bilyeu and Tony Oliver."

Let's be clear on this. Pike and Brown were not part of the original
party, arriving only after the others were already on the Young premises. Did Sheriff Hendrix and Chief of Detectives Oliver see the car coming up the lane and brace for the Young brothers? But it was only Frank
and Owen. Did this false alarm contribute to a fast-growing sense of
wild goose chase?

Pike and Brown were accompanied by a third party, Springfield jew-
eler R. E. Wegmen. Wegmen's movements at the farm are nowhere
mentioned. Perhaps, having just come along for the ride, Wegman had
the good sense not to get out of the car.

Owen Brown wasn't nearly the talker Frank Pike was. It was a challenge just getting his name straight—alternately listed as "Owen,"
"Oren" and "Orin." The name was, in fact, "Owen," but perhaps regional dialect was confusing to hearers, including the inquest stenographer.

Owen's son, Mickey Brown, who died in 2002, was a man of considerable prominence in Greene County, both in business and
Republican politics. Mick didn't have much light to shed on events of
January 2, 1932, for the simple reason that his dad never talked about
it.[7] Owen did offer this detail to his son: There was a method to the
Young brothers' killing. An officer would lean around a tree, take a
peek toward the house. There would be no shot. But when the officer
leaned out again, that's when the killing stroke was delivered.[8]

With the arrival of Pike and Brown, there were now two police cars in the turnaround area, one driven by Pike, the other belonging to Hendrix. (Oliver's car was still up in the orchard.) No other autos were in sight—all the more reason to suspect the house was likely empty. Imagine Generals Lyon and Sigel in 1861, converging on Wilson's Creek, but finding no sign of the enemy.

And it must always be remembered that Marcell Hendrix had already had a very long Saturday. The Ash Grove raid in itself would have been enough excitement for any *month*. Really, what were the odds on capturing Harry Young the same day? Still, this needed to be checked out.

> Pike: "Well, we all walked kind of up in front of the house, and the Sheriff tried the front door, the door was locked . . . "
>
> Johnson: " . . . we all got out, it didn't look like anybody was at home; they had a warm fire there, you could see they had a hot fire there, there was a lot of smoke, you could tell they had a hot fire; we walked around the door a time or two kicking on the door and asked them to come out, but never did get any report; they never answered; Ollie Crosswhite said he heard somebody walking around in there."[9]
>
> Brown: "When we drove up there the men had assembled out in front kind of conversing there; part of the men went to the front door to unlock it, Mr. Mashburn turned around and says, 'has any of you men got a skeleton key?'; I think Charlie Houser gave him a skeleton key . . . "
>
> Pike: "Charlie Houser who is a policeman here on the police force, he said he thought he had a skeleton key that would unlock the door . . . "
>
> Johnson: "Somebody said something about shooting in the house with this gas; the Sheriff said it would be allright, to go ahead and shoot."
>
> Brown: "And in the meantime Virgil Johnson stepped up there and shot this big gas gun in the upper story window."

At least Nathaniel Lyon brought some cannon to Wilson's Creek. The only thing stronger than a revolver in Hendrix's army was this gas contraption, so new to the police arsenal it had never been fired before. While no mention is made of specific model, the "newness" leads to speculation it was a Police Club Gas Gun, produced and promoted by Federal Laboratories of Pittsburgh: "The solid brass barrel is covered with high grade leather washers which are machined and polished to the shape of the 'Club.' The Gun holds one large Gas Shell and is easily reloaded. Strong leather thong is attached and gun has excellent safety device. Cartridges contain enough gas to disperse small mob outdoors. The gas produces temporary blindness but is harmless."[10]

It is to Virgil Johnson's credit that, having never previously fired this device, he nonetheless managed to hit the target. The canister shattered an upstairs window, releasing its presumably debilitating payload— albeit one that did not debilitate.

Virgil Johnson: "I shot in the house with the gas, and told them it would take a few minutes for the gas to take effect, and to wait a little bit and they would come out if they were in there."

As earlier stated, the first comprehensive account of the massacre was written by Springfield newspaperman J. R. Woodside, released mere months after the killing. *The Young Brothers Massacre* was sold at newsstands, sponsored by the aforementioned Federal Laboratories Inc.— self-described as "World's Oldest and Largest Manufacturers of Tear Gas Weapons." The advertiser wanted readers to know that "This story of the pitiless massacre of six officers might not have been written had the unfortunate victims used plenty of Federal Gas in the proper way. Our message to police officers is this: Don't expect a single tear gas charge to fill an entire house; use tear gas plentifully from protected points of vantage. Allow plenty of time before entering premises.

The story according to Woodside:

> "You'd better wait a minute," Johnson scolded, "before breaking in and give that gas a chance to work."
> "It'll be working alright," Hendrix returned, "by the time we get upstairs. Come on Wiley, let's you and I go to the back door and Johnson you'd better come around with another shell. We may want one in the rear if we hear them somewhere in a room or closet."

Marcell Hendrix seems to have been wholly ignorant as to the doctrine of this kind of weaponry. As the gas began to disperse upstairs, did one of the hunted (likely Jennings) simply close the door, push towels under the door jamb, containing the stuff, so that the only tears would be shed outside, induced not by gas, but by pain and rage?

> Owen Brown: "They couldn't get the front door unlocked."
> Frank Pike: "It looked like it was deserted to look at it; we walked on around and the Sheriff said we would kick in the back door; there was a back door around on the south-west side of the house the way I get it . . . "
> Brown: "Hendrix says, 'I will tell you men what you can do, you just surround the house so if they make a break you will be there handy, and we will go to the back door and break it in'; I remember

seeing Mr. Mashburn and Mr. Hendrix go around the corner of the house, and Ollie Crosswhite and myself take a position on the north side of the house, Ollie I might say was on the north-west corner, and I was at the north-east corner."

Virgil Johnson: "So we went around to the back door then, the kitchen door; I said, any kind of old key will unlock that door, it is an old lock; I took out a skeleton key and tried to unlock the door, and there was a key on the inside and couldn't get the key in there; then we took a few runs against the door, I think it was about three times, and we knocked it in."

Pike: "We went up and kicked the door, and it was locked pretty well, so we just lammed up against the door, three of us,[11] and the door flew open; Virgil Johnson was around there. I don't remember exactly where he was when this door flew open, anyhow, when the door flew open there was two shots fired, one was a shot gun."

Marcel Hendrix had, at long last, come face-to-face with Harry Young.

Johnson: "The door flew open directly, and Wiley stepped up in the door, right up in the door, he might have been one step in the door; the door didn't swing plumb back, it swung open about half way, and Wiley stepped in the door, and the Sheriff stepped right up behind him; there is a block of concrete at that back door [a step of sorts]; he was on this block there; Wiley hadn't got more than one step up there, and he had his gun out and looked like he was going to turn around, looked like he started to turn around like he was going to shoot; when he done that there was report from a shot gun it sounded like; then the flesh flew off Wiley's face all around, you could see it was a shot gun."

Pike: "The Sheriffs both went down; I felt as if I had my arm shot off, I couldn't tell."

Bilyeu: "They went up against the door three times and then knocked it loose, and when it popped there was a shot just like that, [Witness indicating][12], and Sheriff fell in, and Mashburn fell this way, [Witness indicating], his feet sticking out the door, Mashburn fell back, his hands clasped like that, [Witness indicating], he just laid there in that shape the last I saw of him; it looked to me like the whole side of his face was blown off."

Johnson: " . . . and it wasn't over three or four seconds until the second shot was fired; the Sheriff sat right backwards in the yard, it looked like he sat back in the yard, backwards there crumpled up in the door; he didn't fall in the house, but out of the house, it looked like he squatted down there; they shot some more, I don't know how many shots were fired; there were either two or three more the best I remember; they shot me in the ankle with a couple of shots; I went around to the front of the house, I don't remember where Frank was, I think he went around there too."

Coroner's Verdict: "Let the record show that the wound on the body of Marcell Hendrix was a large shot gun wound at the upper part of the right chest, part of the charge had penetrated the lung and crossed through the outer back in the muscles of the back."

Springfield enthusiast John Jones pictures the blast that killed Hendix as a locomotive-powered baseball driven through the chest.[13] The shots were heard across the highway on Route 7 by Adiline Myers, who fixed the time around four o'clock.[14]

Brown: "I heard three shots right in rapid succession, and Mr. Oliver says, 'they have got them', and I said, who do you mean. . . . and he says, 'they have got Mashburn and Hendrix.'"

Coroner's Verdict: "The wound on the body of Wiley Mashburn was also a charge from a shot gun which had passed across the front of the face from left to right, and destroyed the features of the upper part of the face."

Pike: "I went in front of the house then; I hollowed that they had got both of the Sheriffs; I got behind a tree that stood in front of the house, a small tree; Tony Oliver was at a station over toward Marcel Hendrix's car behind a tree that stood over towards the fence, it seemed like there was three trees in a row."

The trees were eight soft maples in the front yard, trunks only slightly taller and wider than the men taking refuge behind them, denuded branches in the shape of demented candelabra.

Pike: "I got behind a tree, and Sid. Meadows jumped behind a tree just in north of me; Ollie Crosswhite was [kneeling] down on his knees out on the north-east side of the house, that is the last I seen of Ollie Crosswhite because he went on around the house."

Stone: "Went around to the north?"

Pike: "Yes."

Johnson: "Then I shot the gas gun again [hitting the side of the house this time, to no apparent effect], Tony Oliver, Sid Meadows, Ollie Crosswhite and all the rest of them was around in the front yard; they were all getting behind trees, and Ollie Crosswhite was back up against the house, right up against the north-east corner; he had one of these bombs in his hand, a hand grenade; he stepped in the corner up next to the house and throwed this in there and it went off in there, you could hear it go off in there. I don't know whether it was Tony, or not, but somebody suggested about getting some more guns and ammunition, and some more help; I started off to the car; then there was I don't know how many shots, but they shot several times as I got into the car; I could see a man coming through the front room, I could see him raise his gun to his shoulder."

Stone: "Was that the north room or the south room?"

Johnson: "South room down stairs; he done like that [Witness indicating], he wouldn't get it to his shoulder until he would shoot; he shot the windshield out of the car, pretty well all out."

Dan Nee: "That was evidently a rifle?"

Johnson: "Yes, that was the first shot."

Nee: "Was that fired through a window pane also, or could you tell?"

Johnson: "Yes, it was fired through a window."

Nee: "Came through a window pane?"

Johnson: "Yes, Sir."

Interior photograph of the south front room downstairs: The piano, originally purchased by J. D. Young to grace the parlor of his new house in Oklahoma, is located to the immediate right of a double set of windows. The deadliest fire came from here. Assuming Jennings was the rifleman, we see him kneeling and firing from the window, then quickly sliding behind the piano, which would have served as an admirable ambuscade.[15]

As reported in the *Springfield Leader and Press* ten years after the fact, "Johnson dashed to the car and started the motor. A shot hit the windshield, sending criss-cross cracks through it. A charge of buckshot cleared out all the glass. But Johnson kept going."[16]

Stone: "Was this the car you came out in?"

Johnson: "No, that was the car that Frank Pike drove out, Frank Pike and Oren Brown came in. They parked the car right along by the Sheriff's car, that is the car I was getting in when they was shooting; Ben and somebody else got into the car, I don't know who the other fellow was [the aforementioned R. E. Wegman], it wasn't an officer. I backed the car out and we came on to town for help; when we left there wasn't anybody else shot except the Sheriff and Wiley Mashburn, that is the only two that was shot when we left; they was doing a lot of shooting, but nobody else was shot."

Dan Nee: "Did you actually see anyone in the house?"

Frank Pike: "No, Sir, I never saw anyone."

Nee: "You never saw anyone at any of the windows at the time they were firing?"

Pike: "No, Sir."

Nee: "You couldn't tell if the shots were coming from down stairs or the second floor of the house, could you?"

Pike: "Just what we could tell by the glass."

Nee: "They were shooting through the windows?"

Pike: "Yes, Sir."

Nee: "You think shots were fired from upstairs as well as down stairs?"

Pike: "Yes, Sir."

Nee: "These widows that were broken, is it possible they could have been hit by bullets that were fired by the officers outside?"

Pike: "Well, it could have been that we broke the windows, some of us from the outside, but there was glass flying out of the house there."

Coroner Stone: "Did you see anyone else in the building?"

Bilyeu: "I saw a man in the lower building at the same time, the man in the lower building is the man that killed Sheriff Kelly, I never recognized the man before; I managed to see the picture, and I says, there is the man that killed Sheriff Kelly—"

The headline in the next day's *Springfield Press* read, "Ben Bilyeu Says He Saw Fred In House," followed by this summary: "Fred Barker, alleged killer of Sheriff C. R. Kelly of Howell county, was linked to the massacre of six Springfield officers."[17] This was sensational. On December 19, 1931—just a couple of weeks before the massacre at the Young farm— C. Roy Kelly, former candy salesman turned county sheriff, confronted Fred Barker and Alvin Karpis at the Davidson Motor Company in West Plains. Kelly took two shots to the heart. But hardly anyone seemed to take Ben's identification seriously then, nor has anyone since.

This would not be the last time Ben Bilyeu was suspected of exaggerating, if not fabricating to a jury. And the rifleman he identified as Harry was almost certainly Jennings.

Stone: "You know all of the Young boys?"

Bilyeu: "I know all those Young boys, yes; this was Harry that shot at Virgil Johnson and I, and shot the wind-shield out; he was shooting where he aimed, he was aiming to shoot Virgil between the eyes; there was three people there in that house that I know of, there was three guns, three different calibers shooting right there together; I could tell that, I have handled lots of guns, and shot lots of them; I think Mashburn and Hendrix was both shot with a shot gun, I don't know whether I am right, or not; this report that come when the door flew open, just boom, boom, just like that."

Stone: "What was the other guns?"

Bilyeu: "A rifle fired by this Harry Young out of the window; there was some curtains, the curtains was about that far apart, [Witness indicating] he shot out the window just like that, [Witness indicating] he is the best shot I ever saw; they had two high powered rifles, they had about a 30-30 and a 25-20, and a 25-20 is what he shot at us with."

Stone: "You had gone a little east after you had gone up by the trees then?"

Bilyeu: "Yes, Sir."

Stone: "Where did you go from there?"

Bilyeu: "Tony Oliver says, 'boys, go bring some more help', and Virgil Johnson says, 'let's go', when we went to the car that is when Harry Young cut down on us."

Stone: "It was you and Virgil Johnson in this car?"

Bilyeu: "Yes."

Stone: "You are the only ones that went back?"

Bilyeu: "No, there is another fellow that runs a store up there on Campbell, I don't know what his name is."

Brown: " . . . so Mr. Crosswhite was kneeling down at the side of the house; he had taken this bomb out of his pocket and set it off, and threw it through the window glass in the north door."

Crosswhite's "bomb" seems to have been a gas grenade that had little if any effect on the battle.

Like Johnson and Pike, Owen Brown never saw the faces of the enemy, but he told Dan Nee, "they was shooting through the lace curtains and the window glass, I was standing right at the corner of the house facing Houser, when Houser was shot part of this curtain came out of the window."

Brown: "Well, when [Crosswhite] done that he went on back of the house on the west side; right at the north-east corner of the house there is a tree there, I hadn't more than stepped behind it and there was a shot fired out of the front window on the north side, that hit Mr. Houser, and he fell right there by the tree."

Pike: "Charlie Houser walked right out somewhere in front of the house; they shot him and he fell right there."

Coroner's Verdict: "The wound on the body of Charles Houser was a bullet wound on the forehead, passing directly through and out the back."

Brown: "I decided I would get out in the front where I might do some good; I climbed over a fence back of me and went across this garden and come back in behind Mr. Meadows, behind a tree right back of him; he says, 'you will get yourself killed.' He cautioned me about running around out there in plain sight; just then another shot was fired, and Tony hollowed and says, 'they have got Crosswhite.'"

Greene County Prosecuter, Dan Nee: "Did you see Crosswhite when he was killed?"

Ben Bilyeu: "I never saw him when he was killed, I saw him before that."

Nee: "Did you see him out behind the cellar?"

Bilyeu: "No, I didn't see him behind the cellar, I saw him at the west side of the house, coming around the house."

Frank Pike: "Then somebody hollowed, I don't know who it was, that they had got Crosswhite."

Nee: "Did you hear any shots back of the house?"

Pike: "I heard some shots back there."

Of the massacre's unanswered questions, none is more puzzling than the end of Ollie Crosswhite. Having come around the north side of the house, he was running for cover behind the cellar—and it would have been good cover, too: raised earth surrounded by a short retaining wall. We image the veteran officer positioning himself for a one-man assault on the buzz saw, but before he could reach the cellar, the rifleman opened fire and Ollie went down.

It is likely here that Oliver hollered, "They have got Crosswhite!"— but the rifle had not, as initially assumed, delivered the killing blow. The 25-20 tore through Crosswhite's hat, but the coroner concluded this bullet did no damage to Crosswhite himself. The surprising autopsy result: Crosswhite was killed at close range, with a shotgun blast to the back of the head.

The story according to Woodside: "The killer with the rifle went to the dining room window and upon a chair he fired bullet after bullet at Crosswhite to keep him still, while the killer with the shot gun sneaked out the kitchen door and up behind the Deputy to shoot point blank at two-feet range the charge that struck their old time enemy and sent him sprawling to his death."

Maybe. But when? The January 5 *Leader* reported that Coroner Stone and Prosecutor Nee were inclined to believe Crosswhite "may have met his death after the Young brothers started running from the house"—Harry and Jennings having either killed or run off all the others. Likewise, Woodside places the above-quoted action as the last of the killings. This would mean, however, that Crosswhite essentially did nothing while his fellow officers were being cut down, which, from what we know of Ollie Crosswhite, seems improbable.

Another possiblity comes to mind. Ollie had been through a lot in recent weeks. Perhaps behind the cellar, one rifle shot having already ripped through his hat, the veteran lawman thought of Ethel, incapacitated by grief at the fate of their eldest son. What would become of Ollie's family if he got himself killed out here? Did the combination of physical and emotional forces effectively paralyze him? For that matter, the first shot may have caused him to stumble, hit his head on the retaining wall and lose consciousness, not to mention other possible concussion/incapacitation scenarios.

Brown was quoted in the January 4 edition of the *Press,* saying that Houser went down "less than ten seconds" after Meadows was dropped—yet another reason to put Crosswhite at the end. But there is the report of Tony Oliver shouting, "They got Crosswhite!" And, if Harry and Jennings were indeed blasting away at Pike and Brown as the latter duo was running away, what was Ollie doing? If Ollie was killed after Frank and Owen reached Haseltine Road, why didn't they report another barrage of gunfire? Surely, at least the shotgun blast would have been audible.

Now, if Harry had tried to slip out the kitchen door to finish off Crosswhite, Tony Oliver would have been in position to see him and shout a warning; but there was another door facing west, at the house's northwest corner, out of the sight lines of the officers. It's at least possible that after Jennings squeezed off the shot that went through Crosswhite's hat, big brother crossed the room and started firing out the front window in the direction of Houser, Meadows, et. al; meanwhile Harry snuck out this northwest door, perhaps with the intention of flanking the other officers, perhaps to make sure Crosswhite stayed down—and finding Crosswhite still alive, finished him off.

Eyewitness testimony and a photo published in *St. Louis Post-Dispatch* suggest that at some point, Hendrix's body was dragged inside and a barricade constructed to prevent entry through the kitchen. A pole was wedged between the door and kitchen table, the latter braced against the wall opposite, the pole supported at midpoint by a straight back wooden chair.[18] If Harry and Jennings had time to drag

Marcell in and construct a barricade, then trying to make linear sense of this takes on an air of futility. For that matter, one can appreciate why Woodside was reluctant to give up on the idea of a third party inside the house.

Bottom line: We'll put Ollie here, without much confidence either way.

> Coroner's Verdict: "The wound on the body of Ollie Crosswhite was a shot gun wound which ranged about two inches above the right ear, the full charge including a thick felt wad had entered the brain."
>
> Frank Pike: "In the house the rifles was making a popping sound when they shot, more like a cap pistol than anything I know of; when somebody hollowed that Crosswhite was shot, Tony Oliver hollowed out, 'they are going to kill us all', Tony was only a few feet from me there then, all of us was shooting, shots was firing all around us all the time; Owen Brown had been around on the north side of the house; he went north a little ways, and then got back around there towards the front, come back in behind a tree; I says, 'I am going to get behind a big tree'; the barn sits the best I remember north-east of the house; I was there a little while longer, and Tony hollowed that they had shot him, he says, 'they have got me', and right then someone hollowed, I think it was Sid. Meadows, he hollowed that Crosswhite was shot: Sid. was standing behind a tree sideways; they shot him and he fell."

Brown would add this detail in a newspaper account: Meadows fell with "one of his hands in his pocket, the other gripped to his gun."[19] The hand in the pocket may have been groping for extra bullets; if so, Jennings sent him one.

Forty years later, Pike would tell Frank Farmer, "I heard two sounds like cracking walnuts with a hammer. It was bullets hitting Sid in the head. I heard that before I heard the report of the weapons in the house."[20]

> Coroner's Verdict: "The wound on Sidney Meadows was a bullet wound on the forehead, there was a large wound at the entrance, and a small wound where part of the bullet had come out; this bullet had been split coming into contact with the skull; a large fragment of this bullet was recovered from inside the head."
>
> Brown: "Just then I heard another shot and Mr. Meadows fell, and when he fell Mr. Oliver made some remark, I don't remember just what it was, and just right then he hollowed and says, 'I am hit', I looked at him, I had my back to him, I looked around over my shoul-

der at him; he throwed the rifle up and shot again, I think he shot once and then the gun snapped on an empty shell the next time."

Pike: "When Sid. fell I seen Brown coming around then from the north part of the house, he got behind a tree up towards the front; then Tony kept shooting, he kept hollowing they had shot him, but he kept shooting, Tony says to me, 'you had better run for it, they are going to kill us all,' I seen he was pretty well gone, he was staggering, I says, 'Tony get behind that car', and Tony went down; I don't know, I think he was shot the second time, I don't know for sure."

Brown: "Then he reached back and got his revolver and emptied his revolver on the house; he kept hollowing, 'I am hit, I am hit, I am hit' and kind of backing up a little bit, so he turned right out back in behind the car, and he hollowed 'I am hit' again, they hit him when he turned around to go to this car; he walked around behind this car and his knees began to wobble; he went to his knees once, and he got up and went a little ways and then he fell flat."

Coroner's Verdict: "The wounds on the body of Tony Oliver consisted of two penetrating wounds, one entering in the left shoulder blade, coming out on the front of the chest on the right side; the other one passed through the right shoulder; the body also showed about fifteen scattered marks from shot on the left side, these however did not penetrate."

J. R. Woodside images the shotgun blasting away at Oliver's soft maple, producing a shower of splinter; his flesh burning from the bird shot, Tony Oliver steps back to protect his eyes, making himself vulnerable to the rifle, whereupon "he pitched forward on his side upon a small pile of horse-shoes and other scraps of iron. There he lay in torture, scuffing with his feet and pawing with his hands, not for seconds only, but for minutes, many of them in all probability. The brave Chief did not die painlessly and quickly."[21]

Pike: "When [Oliver] 'went down me and this Oren Brown was shooting at the window lights, that is about all we could do, we couldn't see anybody to shoot at; then these fellows hollowed out the window and says, 'throw down your guns and come in here, we are going to kill you if you don't', I says, 'I am not throwing down any gun'; I didn't have any chance to see them; Oren Brown says, 'I am out of cartridges, let's run for it'; we started to run, they shot at us so far as they could see us down towards the barn and over the fence."

Brown: "Officer Pike turned to me and says, 'We are the only ones left, what will we do?', just then this fellow in the house says, 'come on out of there, I am going to kill both of you', I said we wasn't coming out; I said, 'Frank, you had better make the barn and take chances, they will kill you where you are standing'; Frank made that barn, and when he started they started shooting at him, they never hit him; I figured if we didn't get over there everyone of us would be killed; we cut across this pasture; it wasn't but a few minutes until Otto Herrick, Virgil Johnson and Lee Jones and another fellow or two [came along]; I explained to them what had happened, and cautioned them about getting up there; Officer Johnson said he was feeling kind of sick, and I told him he had better go to town; I went on up there, I was gone from the house maybe ten minutes."

Prosecuter Nee: "In your judgement those men made their escape during the time you were gone?"

Brown: "Yes, that is what I think, they made their get-a-way then."

Coroner Stone: "Then you came back to town?"

Pike: "We went to the road [Haseltine Road, east of the house] . . . we was figuring on help coming right away; when we got down to the road, we had been down at the road quite a few minutes, I would say ten or fifteen minutes . . . "

The story according to Frank Farmer: "They kept apprehensive eyes on the foreboding house looming against the gray January skyline, half expecting an army of outlaws to burst forth with guns still blazing."[22]

Pike: "When here come a bunch of fellows, I don't know just who all. I warned them, I says, if you go up there don't go in a hundred yards of the house because they have shot these men up there; I told them they were all dead. I thought they was all dead; one of them took me to the station; I don't remember where Orin Brown went after that, whether he came on in with some of the other boys, or where he went. I have told this story the best I can remember everything."

CHAPTER TWENTY

Criminology

"In this country the method of selecting policemen is without doubt the least likely to produce the most necessary qualifications. Recently some of the larger cities have started training schools, as have most of the state police forces in the states where such organizations exist, but as a rule, in the smaller cities, the policeman is appointed, given a uniform, a badge, a billy and a gun, and then sent out with an older policeman to learn the limits of his beat."
> —1932 Souvenir Review of the Department of Police,
> City of Springfield, Missouri

The big city St. Louis Post-Dispatch bemoaned, "What's Wrong With The Ozarks?" Springfield seemed a "strange place for the butchery of Saturday afternoon"; the hill country "a planet removed from Chicago's gangsterism." Yet, noted the paper, "this is not the hill country's first appearance in the criminal news." Citing the recent example of Jake Fleagle, St. Louis speculated, "How many Fleagles, first and last, retire to the Ozarks when police pursuit is too hot may only be conjectured."

Admitting the hills were a great place to hide, the Post-Dispatch nevertheless laid the root of the problem squarely at the feet of prohibition. "Moonshine has come to be an important business, a far too powerful business of the Ozarks." "Resolutely shutting its eyes to the facts," the region remained steadfastly "dry" in sentiment, sending staunch prohibitionists to the state legislature.

"Sooner or later," opined the paper, "the people of the Ozarks will rid themselves of the law-imposed lawlessness that now casts its viscous shadow over their lovely land."[1]

It's no wonder some in the Ozarks saw that as a cheap shot. The Youngs, after all, were in the stolen car business, not bootlegging. But by January 1932, America was inclined to see everything through the prism of prohibition.

That said, there can be no doubt that national prohibition did indeed strain the resources of local law enforcement—particularly in places where it was taken seriously. According to the Springfield Police Department's 1932 Souvenir Review, "Since Mr. Volstead gained the spotlight and dedicated the entire country to his beliefs, prohibition cases frown aridly on perhaps sixty per cent of the docket sheet."

As evidence of the creativity of the prohibition criminal, the Souvenir Review continued:

> And among other things, prohibition has produced a few chemists and inventors. Hot water bottles are used when booze is to be transported; and one defendant once uncorked the vials of his inventive genius and poured forth a mixture that amazed the court and watered the lips of the spectators. At his house five bottles were found and each bottle contained a different color of the 'what have you' that makes the bootleg business pay. There was red booze, blue booze, pink booze, green booze and the inevitable white booze. The grand jury labored manfully over this individual. But the secret of the test tubes was never known. It was locked in the brain of the defendant who was securely locked in jail. And thus ended an era when men might have said: "I'll take mine blue today."

While "moonshine" played no direct role in the tragedy at the Young farm, it must always be remembered that, by late Saturday afternoon, Marcell Hendrix had already had a very long and stressful day, starting with the 4 a.m. raid on bootleggers in Ash Grove. Perhaps the editorial in the St. Louis Post-Dispatch wasn't such a cheap shot, after all.

As rebuttal to the St. Louis paper, Walter Cralle, head of the sociology department at Springfield's Southwest Missouri State Teacher's College, shot back via Springfield's *Sunday News & Leader:*

> There was nothing essentially Ozarkian about the tragic killings just outside Springfield last Saturday, nor about any crime committed in this region. To be sure, the Ozarks, with virtually every other rural community, is facing the fact that its machinery for apprehending criminals has not kept up with the criminal's facilities for committing crime and getting away with it.
>
> It used to be in rural communities in the old days that when a hen house was robbed or a ham stolen, the thief was within a radius of 10

or 12 miles. The modes of transportation would not allow him to be farther away than that before daylight. Nowadays it's different. A concrete ribbon across the nation and speedy cars make it so.[2]

To illustrate the effectiveness of rural law enforcement in dealing with problems in the hen house, we offer this article from the weekly Ash Grove Commonwealth, January 7, 1932, printed adjacent to the horrifying news from Springfield:

CHICKEN THIEF GOES TO PEN WITHOUT DELAY
Arrested on Monday, Pleaded Guilty Tuesday and Was Taken to Jefferson City Pronto

L. C. Small of near Everton missed eight buff orpington hens and two turkeys on Thursday morning of last week. On investigating it was found that similar fowls had been sold at Ash Grove by George Scritchfield of that place. Scritchfield was arrested on Monday at Ash Grove, brought here by Sheriff Killingsworth that night, pleaded guilty in preliminary before Justice Hobbs Tuesday morning and again at a special term of circuit court convened by Judge Hendricks Tuesday afternoon, was sentenced to two years in the penitentiary, and within the hour was on his way to Jefferson City in charge of the sheriff, to begin his term.[3]

This was justice swift and sure, in response to crime within a rural sheriff's expected competency. The Young Brothers and Pretty Boy Floyd were another matter.

Professor Cralle contrasted the resources of a "courageous but untrained" sheriff, lacking proper weaponry, relying on his family automobile, "which may be old and slow," with that of the thoroughly modern criminal, "equipped with his machine gun and high powered car and experienced in his racket." The state-imposed term limit for sheriffs—four years and out—was but one example of "backward laws" hampering enforcement. About the time a sheriff was learning how to do the job, he was shown the door. In contrast, the only term limit on criminals was the capacity of law enforcement to apprehend them.

Law enforcement was well aware of the problem. Ed Waddle contributed an essay to the aforementioned Souvenir Review, titled "Modern Crime":

The advance in technical knowledge and mechanical skill is quickly used by the modern crook. The detection of crime must, therefore, keep pace with the opportunities to deceive and cheat.[4]

With our present-day means of fast communication, it is possible for the criminal to place great distances between himself and the scene of the crime in a very short space of time. With police forces disconnected, each interested in its own problems, it is a surprising thing that so many are ever caught.

Regarding the issue of disconnectedness, consider: H. H. Carroll phoned the Navarro County Sheriff's department early Sunday afternoon to report the overturned automobile with long guns in the back— but there was no connecting of the dots. If Gaddy Jr. hadn't taken it upon himself to contact Springfield, the huge clue might have been entirely for naught, with a very different ending to the story.

Greene County Deputy Sheriff R. E. Hodge was bitter that Fort Worth hadn't made an earlier connection of finger whirls. As previously noted, Fort Worth police had arrested Harry Young on auto theft charges in March of 1931. If, instead of accepting the "Claude Walker" alias and letting him loose on bond, Fort Worth had sent the suspect's fingerprints to the Bureau of Identification in Washington D.C., Washington D.C. could have notified Greene County that Mark Noe's killer was in custody in Fort Worth. Hodge contended that "This neglect cost the lives of six officers as well as the suicide of two desperadoes."[5]

For that matter, Scott Curtis had sent Harry's "photograph and description" to Houston police in June of 1931. Shortly thereafter, Harry was in fact arrested for speeding in Houston, but was again routinely processed through the revolving door of the justice system without detection as a wanted cop killer.[6]

This narrative has made multiple reference to J. R. Woodside's booklet, *The Young Brothers Massacre*. Published in 1932, sold in newsstands under the sponsorship of a tear gas manufacturer, the Springfield journalist's account reads as the purplest of prose: "Out in the yard, Detective Johnson sped for the front as Chief Oliver yelled, 'Boys, they got the Sheriff and Wiley. Damn their dirty souls, empty your guns in every window.'"[7]

But behind the colorful narrative style ("Kill the damn curs"), there were lessons to be learned. Gary Ponder, curator of the Ralph Foster Museum on the College of the Ozarks, terms the Woodside pamphlet "the first SWAT manual"[8]—an object lesson in how *not* to storm a building.

Woodside consulted a metropolitan "expert," who wished to remain anonymous. The consultant pointed straight at the officers' "lack of caution"—"the cause of more deaths in law enforcement circles than any other contributing factor. Bravery is always to be applauded, but lack of caution should not be condoned." However, in the expert's opinion, even if Hendrix and Oliver had been more cautious, there were "many odds against them."

> They had no armored car to protect them, they had no bullet-proof shields or vests, they had no sub-machine guns or automatic rifles, they had no gas masks, they had no smoke screens, they had no sickening gas, they had little tear gas; in fact, they had very little that would be considered useful in such raids by metropolitan police. They had a world of valor then, but it doesn't do them or their families any good now.[9]

More problems, per "expert" analysis:

- From the Young farmhouse, "one can see in all directions from considerable distance"—reducing odds on the element of surprise. Remember, in denying she had called from Etta Smith's place to tip her sons, Willie Florence said the boys already expected the police to show up at any time. It's possible, perhaps even probable, Jennings and Harry saw the officers coming.
- Once on the property, officers should have thoroughly searched the barn and other outbuildings. Had the team opened the barn door, they would have found three automobiles within, alerting them to the likelihood someone was indeed at home.
- Turning their attention to the house, officers should have been stationed in a prone position, "far enough apart to permit not flank or enfilade fire to injure more than one of them at a time."
- Chivalry has no place in criminal apprehension. The sisters could have been used as negotiators, imploring their brothers to come out with their hands up. This, if you will recall, was suggested by Officer Lee Jones before he was sent off to cut Oscar Lowe's hair.
- If gas is employed, use lots of it, then give it time to work.

But where was Marcell Hendrix supposed to learn tactics of enfilade? And he only had two tear gas shells at his disposal. So Hendrix and Mashburn put their shoulders to the back door, and the turkey shoot commenced.

Reviewing this manuscript, Officer Kirk Manlove of the Springfield Police Department suggests both Woodside's "expert" and I have underestimated Hendrix's grasp of tactics. In chapter two, we noted that Hendrix split his forces, sending Oliver in from the north, Hendrix himself leading the charge from the south. Manlove:

> "Splitting of Forces," while certainly a military consideration, is typically not a factor in law enforcement tactics. It's my guess Hendrix's concern, as you touched on, was escape. I believe the sheriff probably wanted "eyes on" both front and rear doors as early as possible for as great a distance as possible, a tactic still in use and a "must" when knocking on the front door of a "wanted" person. Too often, they will run out of the back door at a knock on the front. We usually send two to the back, two to the front. Sometimes this is even coordinated by radio to a degree where we don't even see each other even when standing at the same house. In fact, Hendrix had probably employed this method dozens of times with success and may have even used it on the bootleggers earlier in the day.

It is a mistake to underestimate the capabilities of Marcell Hendrix.

Woodside's "expert" closed with another hymn to gas, noting how well it worked in Houston, surely pleasing the sponsor to no end. Lest Woodside's readers miss the point, the following was printed in big bold letters:

EXTRA!
Young Brothers Captured
By Federal Tear Gas

The Last Ride of the Young Brothers

"If anything ever happens to me, the last thing I want is to be taken back to Springfield."

—Harry Young, as quoted by his sister, Florence Mackey[1]

The final fiasco could have been avoided. Willie Florence's daughter in Houston, Florence Mackey, argued persuasively that Harry and Jennings wouldn't want to be buried in the Ozarks. "It's lots better that you remember them as you last saw them," pleaded Florence, via long-distance telephone.

The two newest widows were said to be of one mind with Florence on the matter, as were Gladys and Mary Ellen, who had driven from Frederick to Springfield. Yes, Mrs. Mackey assured her mother, if the brothers were interred in Texas soil, someone could sing, "Rock Of Ages" and the boys would be "put away nice." Willie Florence said she couldn't ask for more, "But I'd sure love to have seen them."[2]

But then presiding judge of the Greene County Court, R. A. Young (no relation), announced the thousand-dollar county reward would not be paid unless the bodies were brought back for positive identification.[3] Not that there was any doubt; Deputy Sheriff Hodge said the picture in the *Leader* was proof enough for him. The man with the revolvers by his head was clearly Jennings Young and Jennings was very dead.[4] But with the ruling of the court, the sad circus began.

It is curious, however. As Greene County Assistant Prosecutor Charles Chandler told reporters, no one could compel the Youngs to bring the bodies back to Greene County.[5] And since no one in the Young family was going to get a dime of any reward money, it's hard to see the incentive.[6]

But while Missouri couldn't force the issue and Texas law gave the wives final say, when Springfield mortician W. L. Starne showed up at

Houston's Fogel-West Undertaking Company with a paper signed by Willie Florence, the tussle over the corpses went into high gear.[7]

W. L. Starne operated what was likely the least successful of Springfield's six funeral parlors.[8] He was beset by personal problems and a somewhat quarrelsome temperament, but no one could say Starne wasn't a go-getter. Hearing news of the Young brothers' deaths in Houston, Starne went straight to the grieving mother's cell,[9] emerging with the signed document, which stated, "I, Mrs. Willie Florence Young, the mother, or Mrs. J. D. Young, do authorize the bodies of Jennings and Harry Young to be turned over to W. L. Starne, undertaker of Springfield, Mo., to be returned to Springfield and buried in McCauley chapel cemetery near Ozark, Mo."[10]

Starne's political connections may have helped open cell doors. On the night of the failed mayoral recall election, when an effigy of Edson K. Bixby was toted around the public square, it was a Starne ambulance that did the toting.[11]

The undertaker and assistant Rex Rainey arrived in Houston at daybreak Thursday. It took all day to untangle things. Sometime that afternoon, Fogle-West received a note signed by the Florences (Mackey and Calvert-Walker-Young) and Jenning's wife (the former Bessie Smith, we presume), acceding to Mother Young's wishes. The bodies were removed from morgue to hearse around 7 P.M., placed on cots in the back of the vehicle, sans coffin or box of any kind.[12]

Cash in the amount of $269.72 was also entrusted to Starne. The money had been found among the brothers' personal effects and was to be turned over to Willie Florence. The Houston PD was hanging on to other items from the crime scene, including clothing, a watch, and the seven pistols.[13]

Willie Florence might be pleased her sons were coming home for burial, but the rest of the family was horrified—with good reason. Harry and Jennings had denied Greene County the satisfaction of a public execution. Even Marcell Hendrix's boy, Merl, was saying it was too bad they killed themselves; Harry and Jennings should have been hung in the public square.[14] With emotions at fever pitch, who was to say what an angry mob might do to the corpses?

Vinita and Lorena were aghast, Vinita quoted, "Do you suppose—do you think—. They wouldn't mutilate the bodies would they? They wouldn't let them do that, would they?" Bottom line, according to Vinita: "They should have left them in Texas, buried them there, and had it over with," adding, "I don't want to see them buried by my father, either."[15]

Willie Florence's judgement might be clouded by "a strange blending of grief and elation at the manner in which two of her sons cheated the gallows," and Starne might have his own reasons, but Willie Florence's daughters saw nothing but more trouble and heartache for a family that had already experienced quite enough of both.

Ma Young was clear as to her funereal wishes. The boys would be buried in McCauley Cemetery, next to their father. A friend would prepare "a nice spray of flowers." Willie Florence wanted "Brother Hale" from First Baptist to "pray a good prayer." (Lewis M. Hale told reporters he would respect a grieving mother's wishes.) And, of course, someone would sing "Rock of Ages"—the hymn that had soothed Harry during his "fits" at age thirteen. Mother Young was less certain about what Bible verses should be read, saying "I know a lot of Scripture but I just can't think—it's so hard for me to think these days."[16]

Starne was suggesting a Friday service at his mortuary chapel in Springfield. Deputy Sheriff Hodge said the Youngs could have a funeral on Friday if they wanted—but that didn't mean Willie Florence would be attending. As far as Hodge was concerned, she wasn't going anywhere—and that included McCauley Cemetery: "I don't see that we owe them anything."[17]

Another sign of the growing ugliness was a feature story in Thursday's *Springfield Leader* headline:

VINITA YOUNG GIDDY SEEKER OF 'HIGH LIFE'
Love Letters of Slayers' Sister Reveal
Amazing Contrasts of Character

How a 'sweet little girl' changed in four years to a woman of the underworld, living riotously in an endless round of flirtations, casual and serious, was gleaned today from the love letters of Vinita Young, 22, blonde sister of the most ruthless killers Southwest Missouri has ever known.

After such a salacious buildup, the letters—purloined along with the previously mentioned high school yearbook—are something of a letdown. This missive from "Buddy" is typical:

Say ole dear, we're going to have to be disappointed again tomorrow night. We are working tonight and tomorrow night too. I suppose you will be all mad at me again and I don't blame you but it just can't be helped. You know I told you how it would be and as you know I'm a poor boy and must work and make the shekels. Maybe I can take you home some other Tuesday night tho. But say Vinita I don't see why you keep wanting to see me after I've disappointed you so much. Looks like you would get sore at me and tell me to go to — or something. Most girls would. Anyway I'm not worth it ole dear. Just the same it's sweet of you and makes me feel good.

While that may be pathetic, it hardly seems to justify the paper's bottom-line conclusion: "In any event, her letters reveal, the downfall of this one-time friend of the brightest cleanest young folk of Springfield has been thorough, devastatingly complete."

Also found among Vinita's belongings was a "frayed and yellow" newspaper sermon cut out of *The Ozark Countryman:*

Poor old mother! Your daughter is having a 'grand time.' Sure she is, but how? Out every night on some lonesome road with the car parked. Most of the popularity of these days is born of promiscuous love. 'My little girl is different!' That is what they all say; that is what they all think and feel. Don't take my word. Go and see. The sight is awaiting you any night on earth you see fit to go out and investigate.

"What prompted the preservation of that clipping?" inquired the *Leader.* "Whether it was a gesture by Mother Young, in a vain effort to warn her child, or the act of a young girl trying to justify her downfall, no will know."

Nor will any know how the newspaper could have justified what it was doing to a young girl. There is nothing in Vinita's letters that is half as reprehensible as this exercise in journalistic voyeurism.[18]

The paper might have balanced its coverage by noting that, in order to make ends meet, Vinita had worked a variety of odd jobs, including an egg-drying assembly line, where she cracked and separated the product.[19] Maybe she deserved some fun.

The *Leader* did concede, "Perhaps Vinita Young never had a chance. Her brother Harry was branded as a murderer soon after she left high school. Her home, more than once, had yielded stolen goods. Another brother could tell her stories of 'the big house' at Jefferson City and the sordid loathsome things that land men there."

Vinita, however, managed to keep a certain sense of humor. She was thinking of running an ad in the newspaper: "Slightly used farm for sale reasonably cheap. Might be used as a souvenir."[20]

E. A. Greenshaw of the *Springfield Press* described Vinita as a "small, blonde girl," who seemed, "even younger than she is." Little sister did have some good memories of Harry, who had "been home several times in the past two years."[21]

"I think he talked to me about things much more than he did to mother," she continued. "He was just like a kid when he used to come home. One day not so long ago we were upstairs going through some old trunks of father's and looking at old pictures, and Harry said, 'Gee, I hate to come back home because every time I do, I want to stay. For a little, I'd just go on in and give myself up.'"

Vinita had urged Harry to do just that. "Oh, how I wish now he had."

Like sister Lorena, Vinita was being held on the charge of receiving stolen goods. Vinita admitted Paul had given her a Ford sedan last summer, but she didn't know if it was stolen or not; either way, she and her mother had since sold it to an used car agency in Springfield—one of three dealers Harry regularly did business with.

Lorena was described as "a pretty, frail looking young woman, who speaks with precision, using excellent English and bearing herself with poise." Her house had served as the family hub in Houston. "Paul, Jennings and Harry all used to come to my house often—they loved to play with my baby." Lorena professed to be deeply offended that Jennings would have used her to fence a stolen car: "I didn't think Jennings would do this to me."

While having no wish to see the faces of her dead brothers, Lorena told Greenshaw, "I'll go to the funeral out of the sisterly love I still bear them." The reporter asked an interesting follow-up question: *Was the car you and Albert drove up from Texas itself stolen?* Lorena thought Albert had purchased it from a man named Cook, but she wasn't really sure.

Greenshaw said of Lorena that "As she looks straight at a questioner with her large eyes, she makes her answers sound convincing."

Oscar's wife, Mabel, was back home with her kids, released on a bond of $5,000—though not without complaining to reporters regarding Greene County's lead prosecutor: "Nee can get tougher with a woman than any man can and still be called a gentleman. I've been third-degreed in a way which comes up to what I've seen in the movies."[22]

Oscar, who, like Mabel, had been charged as an accessory to murder before the fact, could have been cut loose, too, on the same terms, but Mabel's bail had been posted by her side of the family. As the Conns were unable or unwilling to post a like sum for their son-in-law, Oscar stayed in jail. [23]

The killing weapons having been returned to Springfield, someone had the idea of reuniting them with their owner for a photo opportunity. On the front page of the January 7 *Leader,* Oscar is pictured in a winter jacket worn over white shirt and overalls, seated warily on a wooden chair, stocks of the rifle and shotgun on the floor, the respective barrels in either hand. Oscar is a hard-looking man, lean like a wolf. (For those viewing the photograph seven decades later, the movie *Fargo*—specifically the killer who puts Steve Buscemi in the woodchipper—may come to mind.) But it must be remembered that Oscar never had been and never would be convicted of anything.

With all other bodies—dead and alive—accounted for, focus shifted to the whereabouts of Paul Young. Was the thirty-seven-year-old ex-con, as reported, drunk and roaming 66 west of Springfield, perhaps in "an old model Ford touring car," watching for the hearse bearing his brothers?[24] Or did he remain in Houston, with designs on the life of J. L. Tomlinson?

A radio station reported the carpenter was already dead. No. Tomlinson was still alive, but had received a threatening letter—"Pick your grave for I will get you"—signed, "Paul Young."[25]

Houston police seriously doubted Paul Young would have signed his name to a death threat, nevertheless, a "blanket order" had been issued "to be on the lookout for a blue sedan," which Paul was thought to be driving.[26] He finally surrendered Friday morning, in Houston, accompanied by an attorney named Heidingsfelder.

Paul adamantly denied any involvement in the Springfield slayings. These last couple of years, he'd been living at a boarding house on LaBranch. The owner of the place, Mrs. Jesse R. Martin, would swear Paul had been at her dinner table Saturday evening.

Attorney Heidingsfelder: "Young says that he didn't see his brothers when they came back to Houston Monday, but that if he had, he would have helped them in any way possible."

And, no, Heidengsfelder's client hadn't sent the threatening letter to Tomlinson. Police were inclined to believe him. Inspector W. F. Kessler said, "Young argued that if he were going to kill a man, he wouldn't write him a letter about it beforehand."[27]

A photograph from the January 8 edition of the *The Houston*

Chronicle: Paul has inherited his father's male-pattern baldness. This is a man experienced at looking into police cameras. His gaze is steely, eyes fierce, lips pursed tight. Still, there is a certain brutal handsomeness. And one can't quite shake the homey detail that once upon a time, between prison terms, he had tried to make a living selling vacuum sweepers. (Hold the pathos. It seems Paul stole the vacuum sweepers off a freight car.[28])

Dan Nee told Houston it would be better if Texas kept Paul, for the time being, as there was a real risk of mob violence if he were brought back to Springfield.[29] And while Paul might be cleared of the Springfield slayings, stolen car charges kept accruing, the latest belonging to Mrs. Ed H. Lang of Sherman Street in Houston.[30]

Starne and Rex Rainey were decribed as making "excellent time" Friday, reaching the Texas/Oklahoma border around noon.[31] The hearse made a pit stop on the Texas side of the Red River, as reported in the *Denison Daily Herald:*

> Having followed the less traveled route through the city, the large Springfield funeral coach eased into H. E. Coggin's filling station on the outskirts of Denison, for servicing before entering Oklahoma.
>
> At the request of the Young brothers' mother, the funeral coach curtains were closely drawn and none was permitted to peek into the gloomy compartment where the bodies of the desperadoes lay. Driving the vehicle was a Mr. Starnes [sic], Springfield undertaker, and his assistant, who were obviously wearied by a dash to Houston and the return.
>
> When the coach rolled into the station, the drivers quietly asked for gasoline without betraying the identity of the cargo. At the station was Mr. Coggin and G. J. Stafford who noticing the Springfield license plates asked that by chance were the bodies of the Young brothers in the coach. Somewhat reluctantly at first, the undertakers admitted they were.
>
> The undertakers willingly answered questions asked about the tragedy and otherwise appeared decidedly agreeable; but on one point they were unyielding—in denying the curious even a peep into the dark enclosure containing the bodies of the two killers.
>
> Exhibition of the bodies would bring hundreds of dollars, the filling station attendants were told, but eager eyes must satisfy themselves with a glimpse at the drab exterior of the giant hearse in which the Young brothers are going home to a heart-broken mother.
>
> Their machine serviced, the drivers eased back onto the highway,

where a stream of automobiles had been plying back and forth with the occupants scarcely noticing what to them was just a funeral coach. The black machine faded in the distance toward the free bridge—the Young brothers were going home![32]

By three o'clock, the hearse was through McAlester; two hours later, Starne and Rainey were in Muskogee, stopping long enough to eat and shave.[33] At Vinita, Oklahoma, the hearse was halted at the request of the Springfield Police Department. Springfield wasn't ready for this circus to come to town.[34] Not that Starne was complaining, having heard that a band of thugs was on its way from Springfield with the express purpose of intercepting the hearse and molesting the bodies.[35]

The *Daily News* was frank with readers regarding "a vague fear that if the burial arrangements were known a crowd of friends seeking to avenge the death of the six officers might attempt to steal the bodies and mutilate them."[36] The Springfield widows tried to help calm the situation, issuing a collective statement:

> With deep appreciation to the public for its sympathy expressed to us in our recent bereavement, we earnestly request that there be no demonstration when the bodies of Harry and Jennings Young are returned. Nothing will bring back our husbands to us. A demonstration of vengeance against the two dead men would only bring further hours of terror to the community. It would revive the reality of agonies we suffered on learning of the loss of our loved ones.
>
> Therefore, it is our sincere request to the citizens of Springfield and Greene county that the bodies of Harry and Jennings Young be permitted to be buried quietly and peaceably.[37]

Prosecutor Nee: "The eyes of the United States are on Greene county. We must conduct ourselves in such a way that the good name of our county will not be disgraced."[38]

Highway 66 was crowded with carloads of people waiting to see the hearse and what would happen when it crossed the line into Greene County. Police and American Legion volunteers were also out on 66, "prepared to keep order should the necessity arise."[39]

Others waited at McCauley Cemetery in Christian County. The graveyard was described as in derelict condition: "weeds and grass, waist high, almost obliterate the graves."[40] A large hole was freshly dug, sufficient for two coffins.[41] With rumors abounding that the burial was to take place Sunday afternoon or evening—Monday morning at the latest[42]— some hardy souls spent the night at McCauley, "under the weird outlines of a new moon."[43] A bonfire provided warmth and light. One spectator, asked if he was a member of the Young family or perhaps a guard, said, "No, I'm here to see and be seen—just like everyone else."[44]

The prisoners—Willie Florence, Oscar, Vinita, Lorena, and Albert—were moved out of Springfield, to other jails in undisclosed locations. Afterward, it was revealed Vinita and Lorena had been held in Lebanon, fifty miles east of Springfield;[45] the sisters rated it a "darn good jail."[46] The *Leader* reported the relocations as "a precautionary measure to prevent any possible violence against them should the bodies be returned and sentiment fired up again."[47]

W. L. Starne caused a ruckus Saturday, appearing in Springfield with an empty hearse, announcing Harry and Jennings had already been buried in Oklahoma.[48] While Starne may have been a practiced liar, he seems to have fooled no one.

Chief Waddle issued this statement: "The whereabouts of the Young brothers are known only by a few persons, officers and members of the family, but there's one thing certain—they're dead."[49]

The bodies were, in fact, in Pittsburg, Kansas, having first been taken to the J. J. Gees Undertaking Company, then hidden in a private garage.[50] Greene County had no intention of permitting the corpses to cross the county line.

Governor Caulfield was in Springfield Saturday for a community memorial service, attended by over fifteen hundred people jammed into the Landers Theatre. While the governor was the featured speaker, it must have been hard to follow Judge Warren L. White's introduction:

> We have lived through a terrible tragedy that has struck us with the force of a tornado. The lightning has been the flash of the gunfire; the thunder has been the boom of the deadly weapons; the hail has been the lead and steel; the raindrops have been the tears of the loved ones. In this moment of terror we have sought to answer brutality with brutality, and death with death, so that the mantle of civilization which we have developed to cover the best that is in us has slipped a little."[51]

When it was his turn, Governor Caulfield said all the right things, including this bit of eloquence: "As that fire swept the farmyard they were looking out upon the frontier of civilization, battling to protect all that our civilization stands for."

Dan Nee took a classical turn: "As the Spartans inscribed in the side of the mountain, in memory of the three hundred who died at Thermopyle, *Tell Sparta, traveler, her dead kept faith with them,* so we can say, *Tell them, citizens of Greene county, your officers kept faith with you.*"

Mayor Gideon sat with the governor and others on the Landers' platform, but if Springfield's chief executive added his own oratory, it is not recorded.

Finally, on Wednesday, January 13, Starne, having gone back to Kansas and "prepared the bodies for burial,"[52] drove the "giant hearse" to the county line, twenty miles west of Springfield. Prosecutor Nee took charge and verified that, yes, the remains were those of Jennings and Harry Young, and they were, indeed, dead. Whereupon the hearse was turned around, destination Fairview Cemetery in Joplin, just west of downtown.

The sun was shining on a nice January day in the Ozarks. Some fifty persons were on hand, including fifteen family members of the deceased; the remainder composed primarily of law enforcement officials—none of whom were from Joplin. Local police weren't happy about having the cop killers buried in their town, either, the Joplin chief saying, "I wasn't going to have any of my boys hurt for no good reason."[53] Owen Brown was present; Frank Pike wasn't.

The *Press* described the opening scene to the final act:

> Vinita and Lorena Young arrived at the cemetery first, brought in an auto with Lester Scott and Chester Brumley, motorcycle officers, and Ben Vanhook driver. As they came up the winding drive into the peaceful sunny cemetery where bare trees stood guard above old graves, a second car entered the gates, carrying Prosecutor Dan M. Nee and his assistant, James Hornbostel. Closely following them was a car with the three members of the county court, Judges Sam Moore, R. A. Young and J. W. Nicholson; [Virgil] Johnson and Detective Lee Jones. John Burger, federal investigator, followed with an assistant.
>
> Then came the hearse with its double load, and close behind it the car bearing Deputy Sheriff R. E. Hodge, H. D. Linker, fingerprint expert, and the wailing mother. Her cries could be heard in a rising crescendo as the car in which she rode turned in at the cemetery gates and she grew hysterical as she neared the open graves where officers and newspaper men waited.[54]

Undertaker Starne asked Springfield officers to carry the gray velour coffins from hearse to hole. When Springfield officers refused, the task fell on employees of the cemetery, who wished to remain anonymous.[55]

"In place over the yawning graves," the caskets were opened. Harry was dressed in a blue suit, Jennings in gray.[56] The bullet wound in Harry's forehead "appeared only as a slight abrasion." In keeping with modern scientific method (perhaps, also, as an "in-your-face" to Fort Worth, per the complaint of Deputy Hodge in the preceding chapter), the deceased were fingerprinted. Redundant identification complete, the *Leader* reported:

> All present except the family, which was still waiting at the car, crowded up to see the dead men's faces.
>
> Some faces filled with disgust, others manifested only curiosity, but all peered at the faces closely. Men mumbled that they "deserved what they got," and one said to the sky, "They don't look so bad. I wonder what made them do it?"

Then it was the family's turn. According to the *Leader,* "A slight undercurrent of jeering could be heard after the family filed toward the grave." Someone remarked, "I wish I were the devil. If I were I'd be getting my pitchfork sharpened for those two."

The *Press* reported, "No flowers banked the mound of raw, newly-turned earth at the graves' edges. No words of praise were spoken. No mourning veils waved. The mother and sisters were in simple-print dresses which they had donned in their jail cells before daybreak Wednesday. The young wife of Harry, married only a short time, who had made the long trip from Houston, was quietly attired."

Whether she knew the deceased as Claude Walker, Harry Young, or both, the blue-suited corpse with the abrasion in its forehead had belonged to her husband, and Florence Calvert What's-Her-Name joined in "wails of mourning" with the mother-in-law she had probably never met before.

The *Leader's* Beth Campbell[57] had long-since seized on the story's feminine side. Reporting from the cemetery, she wrote:

> The whole group of women was well dressed—Mrs. Young in a black suede coat and black felt hat with bands of green and orange, a necklace of gold and carnelian beads, and a figured white scarf pinned about her throat—the same scarf she has worn at every appearance since the fatal night of January 2.

Mrs. Mackey, who came up from Houston following her brothers' death and has taken charge of affairs at the Young farm here, appeared in a black coat with caracul trim and a black hat and looked extremely well. The two younger sisters, Lorena and Vinita, are both considered pretty girls. Lorena wore a cream colored pony coat, belted in brown, and a brown hat; Vinita a black coat and hat, and very large-mesh black hose.

Vinita and Lorena were also accessoried in handcuffs, joined to each other at the wrists.

A *Press* photographer started taking pictures of the bodies. Starne reacted angrily; Young brother-in-law Albert Conley also made a move perceived as threatening, whereupon the photographer "hastily handed his camera to a companion, who took to his heels with it," even as Starne was shouting, "I'll break your camera! I'll break every plate in it!"[58] The undertaker then ordered everyone but the family to leave. No one did.[59]

Willie Florence lay her head on Harry's chest, then kissed his face, "Goodbye Harry, boy, good boy." With Starne pushing the crowd back, she screamed, "'Don't take them from me. Don't let them take them away. Oh, my boys! My poor, poor boys!' She slumped again and officers had to hold her on her feet."[60] By this point, the only "dry-eyed" person in the family was Vinita.[61]

The service itself was a disappointment. Neither Lewis M. Hale nor any other clergy was present to officiate. There was no singing of "The Old Rugged Cross" or any other hymn. It was left to W. L. Starne to intone, "The Lord giveth and the Lord taketh away."[62] The service's lone flourish: Starne "sprinkled rose petals over each casket as it was lowered into the earth."[63]

The bodies went into the ground around 10:30.[64] The prisoners were promptly whisked back to their appointed places of incarceration in Springfield. Albert's "dapper appearance" had given way to shabbiness, "including several days growth of beard"—but he "remained cheerful even so."[65]

Vinita and Lorena were reported in "good spirits, laughing and wisecracking." A jailer provided "sponge, warm water and soap" and the sisters cleaned their shared cell "to the brightness of new money." The ladies spread out their personal belongings—"bedding, dishes, foodstuffs, movie-magazines, several changes of clothing, and considerable supplies of cosmetics." They asked for a calendar, to keep track of time, and told a reporter, "We're important people now!"[66]

Back in Joplin, that afternoon a "steady stream" of curious souls came through the cemetery to look at the graves, which were marked by three sprays of flowers from senders who wished to remain anonymous.[67] An assistant sexton was posted through the night to guard against desecration.[68]

That very evening, a big benefit show was held at Springfield's Fox-Plaza theatre, all proceeds going to the widows and orphans fund. The revue started with professional roller skating. "Goo Goo" Rutledge pleased the capacity crowd with "hillbilly ballads." In an act billed as "The Boy With Happy Feet," Jerry Goring performed "an expert bit of soft shoe work." Maxine Steinert "crooned" the blues; Ted Trapp's quartet drew cheers; there was a men's glee club, and a novelty tap dance act—and much, much more. Called for "several encores" was "the police string quartet," composed of Harrison Pearson, Ralph Sutter, the aforementioned "Goo Goo" Rutledge (in this act, "Patrolman Rutlege")—and Frank Pike.[69] No wonder the Startling Detective didn't attend the funeral in Joplin. He had been practicing!

If Pretty Boy Floyd had in any way been involved with the Young brothers, perhaps it was in their honor that precisely twenty-four hours after they went into the ground, 10:30 A.M. Thursday, he withdrew three thousand dollars from the First State Bank of Castle, Oklahoma— without a withdrawal slip, of course.[70]

CHAPTER TWENTY-TWO

Augusta Houser's Blues

"The bodies of the Youngs have been buried and now let's bury the example they left behind them. In fact, just so far as possible, let's bury all memories of the Youngs and think of things more constructive."
—*The Springfield Press*, January 14, 1932

The Springfield Press, January 16, 1932
DRASTIC POLICE SHAKEUP IF DURST NAMED MAYOR

"There is no reason why Springfield shouldn't have a modern, efficient police force," Harry D. Durst, candidate for mayor, told members of the Young Men's Business Club Friday night.

"If I am elected mayor of Springfield I will give the citizens a chief of police and a force of officers of whom they will be proud," he declared.

"In the past some of our mayors, it is regrettable to note, have gone into office only for the money. The position is an honorable one, which any one should be proud to hold."

The Springfield Leader, January 20, 1932
LORENA, VINITA CHANGED

The Young sisters, Lorena and Vinita, who gloried in the publicity they received for several days after the peace officer slaying, have gone into almost absolute seclusion and now profess "to hate newspapermen."

The Springfield Leader, January 21, 1932
GIDEON MAKES SHIRT-TEARING PLEA TO COPS

Retention of the police force is the "big plank" in Mayor Thomas H. Gideon's platform for reelection, he told some 25 officers in a brief but vigorous speech at police headquarters last night.

"And here is something I want you fellows to get and get straight," he continued, "none of you will get by with any shirking. I'm going to fire every policeman who doesn't get out and tear his shirt off working for me."

The Springfield Leader, January 22, 1932
'SURE I MARRIED CHARLIE HOUSER'

A grief-stricken woman with pleading eyes answered an unasked question this morning when she choked out between sobs, the words, "Charlie—my husband."

She was Mrs. Charles Lee Houser, widow of the police patrol driver who went to his death with five other officers at the hands of the Young brothers. She was a distraught Mrs. Houser, because yesterday Fred Houser, brother of slain Charles, filed a motion for a citation in probate court, referring to her all the way through as Augusta Sutton and asking that she prove she was married to Charles Houser.

"Of course, I was married," she declared when she was more articulate and composed. "But now I can't find my papers to prove it."

"To think," she continued, "that we took Fred and his wife in our home last summer. Their baby was born at our house, and I helped take care of it. Then he tries to do something like this. You'd think if he didn't have any respect for me, he'd have enough respect for Charlie not to bring shame on his head before he has been dead three weeks."

Mrs. Augusta Sutton Houser said this morning that she could not imagine what Fred Houser's purpose in the action was. She said that the property of her husband in Joplin was worth very little, and that she'd die before she'd let Fred have the car.[1]

The Springfield Press, January 27, 1932
SCOTT CURTIS VOTED SHERIFF IN CLOSE RACE

Scott Curtis, Democrat, defeated Mrs. Maude Hendrix, Republican, for the office of sheriff Tuesday by a margin of 34 votes in what was perhaps the most spirited special election ever known in Greene County.

A woman candidate for sheriff was a novelty adding zest to the race.

Maude had carried the rural vote by a wide margin, but Curtis' heavy majority in the city of Springfield put him just over the top. As a Democrat replacing a Republican, Curtis would, of course, be bringing in a new team of deputies.[2]

But if there was disappointment on the residence side of the jail, on the other side of the partition, Oscar Young could take some satisfaction in that charges against his missus had been dropped.[3]

Also in the news on January 27, Funeral Director W. L. Starne was in court seeking a divorce. According to the *Press*, "He declared he thought his wife had treated him 'unjustly' because she insisted on clerking in a downtown store instead of staying home and keeping house. 'I did as much of the housework as she did,' charged the undertaker." As if this wasn't bad enough, she nagged about him going fishing.

The final straw, so said Starne. He dreamt his wife was cutting his throat, then woke up to find her side of the bed empty. Mrs. Starne was downstairs with the lights off. In her version, "Then he said, 'Blankety blank, I'm going to leave this blankety blank place,' and he left."

The *Press,* usually more sedate than the Bixby papers, reported the Starne melodrama with particular relish. It was their photographer, after all, who'd been roughed up by Starne at the gravesite in Joplin. The *Press* had reprimanded him then, "The undertaking profession, as a whole, will hardly endorse Mr. Starne's spectacular hostility and people generally are likely to wonder, 'what ails him, anyhow?'"[4] Now readers could be given the answer—in headlines.

It was alleged that Starne had initiated divorce proceedings in order to marry a woman named Katherine Young—no relation to the massacre Youngs, apparently. Mrs. Starne, "a grey-haired woman of 51" (nine years older than W. L.), "dressed in a green coat with fur collar and a black straw hat," told the court, "He is still my husband in the sight of God and if God can forgive him, I can." The petition for divorce was denied, though Starne declared, "I'll never go back" and was reported considering a trip to Arkansas or Reno to try his luck there.[5]

W. L. Starne was having a tough time all around. Having brought Harry and Jennings as far as Greene County, then duly depositing them in the ground at Joplin, the mortician put in a claim for a four-hundred-dollar slice of the thousand-dollar county reward money. Starne had, after all, traveled 1,903 miles to Houston and back, expending $288.20 out of his own pocket, and was counting on the reward fund for compensation.[6] Judge Sam A. Moore of the Greene County Court was not impressed, noting the county had certainly not asked Starne to go to Houston.[7]

But who *would* receive the proffered reward? J. L. Tomlinson, who tipped the Houston PD to his renters and got his house shot up on account of it, certainly had a legitimate claim. Tomlinson, H. H. Carroll, and the Gaddys would all file reward claims with the Greene

County Court.[8] The county judges, however, seemed more inclined to reward the Texas officers who had been in on the capture and kill, as a matter of "moral obligation."[9] According to the *Houston Chronicle,* "[Chief] Heard was skeptical about the money. He preferred to 'wait till we get it' to decide on the cut to be made.'"[10]

Heard's caution was wise. There is no record of the Greene County Court ever expending any of the reward money.[11]

By the end of January, twenty cars had been impounded in Springfield, all thought to be stolen. Local law enforcement had about decided Albert, Lorena and Vinita were not nearly as unwitting as was first let on.[12]

On February 3, hundreds of spectators were on hand as Willie Florence Young was brought into the Greene County Courthouse for a preliminary hearing on the charge of receiving stolen goods—specifically, merchandise from the October 29 looting of Hoover Mercantile in Marshfield. To wit, "one pair of shoes the value of $7.50, one hand bag of the value of $10, one suit case of the value of $2.00, one suit of men's clothes of the value of $27.50, twenty pair of men's socks in the value of $10.00, five men's shirts of the value of $5.00, two neck ties of the value of $2.00, one belt of the value of $.50, one suit of underware (sic) of the value of $1.00 and five pair of ladies stockings in the value of $7.50, all of the total value of $63.00."[13]

Her children, Florence and Oscar, were on hand for moral support, the latter having been released from jail on $10,000 bond.[14] On this occasion of his mother's court appearance, Oscar was wearing overalls. No one was likely to accuse him of stealing overalls.

Ma Young's defense: She never had possession of the merchandise, and even if she did, she didn't know the merchandise was stolen. "Mrs. Young's face was partially hidden by a drooping hat brim. She appeared worn and dejected. She was wearing a silk crepe dress, white scarf and a black coat trimmed with fur."[15]

A revealing moment as to Depression-era economics: Proprietor Hoover identified a pair of shoes as stolen. On cross-examination, Willie Florence's lawyer asked, "It's possible you sold this pair of shoes, isn't it?" The retailer's answer: 'No sir. The way things have been lately, we haven't sold much of anything."[16]

On February 9, Pretty Boy Floyd was reported seen on the Springfield public square. It was said he went into a cigar store for "drinks and smokes."[17] Floyd would meet his end in October of 1934, flushed out from behind an Ohio corncrib, gunned down by Federal agents and local police. Pretty Boy himself had a brother, Sheriff E. W. Floyd of Oklahoma, who years later would tell Frank Farmer, "Young man, nobody can help who his brother is."[18]

On February 20, Paul Young, free on a $500 bond, was arrested again, this time at sister Florence Mackey's home in Houston. Authorities linked him to at least fifteen stolen automobiles. Ma Young was herself in Houston, also embroiled in new trouble. She'd sold a hot car to the Montgomery Auto Exchange in Springfield; Montgomery, in turn, sold the Ford—whose rightful owner was Mattie Sims of Houston—to W. E. Handley.[19] Authorities were offering Paul a deal: No charges would be brought against his mother if he would plead guilty and swear his mother had no idea the car was stolen (one must finally ask if Willie Florence was hopelessly gullible or a genuine co-conspirator).[20]

Also on February 20, the Springfield Chamber of Commerce began distributing the first of the relief funds, which had topped the eleven-thousand-dollar mark. Mrs. Oliver, Mrs. Crosswhite, Mrs. Meadows, and Mrs. Mashburn were beneficiaries of the public largesse. Mrs. Hendrix, said to be well provided for, asked not to be included, and Mrs. Houser's marital status was still under review. Each of the widows was to receive $40 per month, with an additional $7.50 per dependent child.[21]

Unable to produce documentary evidence of her marriage to Charlie, Augusta "Dinky" "Mutt" "Dynamite" Sutton and/or Houser would forever be shut out of the distribution.[22]

Nowhere was the money more urgently needed than the Crosswhite home. Under the formula, Ethel Crosswhite and her five younger children were to receive $87.50 a month. Ethel's first born would be receiving room and board courtesy of the State of Oregon. On February 20, Keith Crosswhite was sentenced to life in prison for the murder of Amos Helm. His partner in crime—the preacher's kid—had done the actual killing, but Oregon law held Keith equally responsible. At least the Springfield boys weren't going to hang.[23]

On March 1 the Lindbergh baby was kidnapped, and all other matters, including the massacre in Springfield, were immediately displaced in public consciousness.

Any alliance between editor Edson K. Bixby and Pastor Lewis M. Hale was shattered by a remarkable March 6 editorial, "Prohibition, Hoover and the Lindgergh Baby":

> The News and Leader is convinced that prohibition not only con-
> tributed to the kidnapping of Charles Augustus Lindbergh Jr., but

should be held responsible for the epidemic of crime that terrorizes our land.

Prohibition has bred a disrespect and a contempt for law. The criminally inclined observe the leaders of their communities and the nation scoffing at the law that prohibition leaders have repeatedly proclaimed as sacred and a hallowed portion of our constitution. If 'good men and women' may sneer at law, why not they? If law means so little why observe or fear it?

Reverend Hale shot back:

I hate the liquor business. . . . And I won't let the editor of the News and Leader, or the editor of any paper on this earth, browbeat me into silence by trying to hold me responsible for all the crime that is on this earth today.

Every man has a right to think as he pleases. . . . But I deny him the right to bring the stench of all the evil of the world and try to dump it at the door of men and women who for generations have fought for humanity and righteousness.

In the name of God, in the name of Frances E. Willard, in the name of millions of godly mothers who have fought to put this demon out of the earth—this demon that has robbed more mothers of their sons, thousands upon thousands, than ever gangsters have robbed mothers of—I resent this charge.[24]

Springfield held its quadrennial city primary on March 22. The two top mayoral vote-getters, Harry Durst and Earl Turner, moved on to the general election. The Queen City of the Ozarks wouldn't have Thomas H. Gideon to kick around any more. The incumbent finished a distant fourth in a field of six.

Results in, Gideon made an appearance at the police station, where he was greeted by Ed Waddle. Edson K. Bixby had long waited for a moment like this, his paper reporting the scene:

"We'll take her together, just like we went in together, won't we, big boy?" the chief asked Gideon, extending his right hand.

"Sure we will!" Gideon snapped back, grasping the puffy hand.

"We'll just say that 53 cops laid down on the job," Waddle commented.

"Oh yeah?" yelled an officer, far back in the crowd. "We can't see it that way. I'm tellin' the mayor right before you, it was the way you treated people when they came down here on business that have got our feet on the ground."

Cries of approval were sent out in chorus when the officer stopped speaking.[25]

On April 5, 1932, five members of the Young family stood before Federal Judge Albert Reeves for sentencing. Paul received four years at Leavenworth; Albert Conley got four months in the Henry County jail; Lorena, Vinita, and Willie Florence were each placed on a year's probation.

Of Mother Young's sentence, Judge Reeves had this to say: "Under the Missouri statutes, a mother who gives her son ordinary shelter cannot be named as an accessory. I am persuaded that Mrs. Young already has been punished enough."[26]

April 5 was a general election day, Harry D. Durst triumphant. The mayor-elect named Paul Frey as his police chief, the first volley in a new purge. Of course, Ed Waddle was gone, along with Virgil Johnson, Frank Pike, and Ben Bilyeu, who was on the payroll, after all, listed a "plainclothesman."[27]

In the last week of April, Bilyeu and his son Lloyd went on trial in federal court, accused of conspiring with bootleggers. Star witness Mabel Johnson, "grotesquely attired in a long lacy black evening dress,"[28] testified that Ben Bilyeu and Mayor Gideon had joined her for a party of home-brew last summer. Another reveler said the mayor identified himself as "Jack Wilson."

Ben strenuously denied the accusations, presenting himself as a teetotaler. He was not believed, sentenced to two years at Leavenworth.[29]

The Bilyeu verdict was poor consolation to federal prosecutors, who had once again failed to land the big fish. Gideon's 1930 conviction had been overturned. An appellate court ruled the trial was tainted by a prosecution questionairre on which prospective jurors were asked their opinions regarding prohibition.[30] Gideon II went to the jury on April 20, 1932. After deliberating through the night, the "twelve farmers chosen at random" were "hopelessly deadlocked." Unable to reach a verdict, the jurors were finally dismissed by Judge Albert Reeves.[31]

Thomas H. Gideon was a survivor. He would even win another local election, this time as a magistrate judge in 1946. It would be said, "The old judge calls 'em as he sees 'em."[32] In 1958, he was gearing up for one more race, having secured the Republican nomination to represent Greene County's second district in the state legislature, when a heart condition forced his withdrawal. He died February 12, 1959.[33]

Back to 1932. On May 16, the State of Missouri dropped all charges inst Oscar Young.[34] Oscar eventually gave up on farming, taking employment with O'Reilly Hospital in Springfield, located on what would later be the campus of Evangel College.[35] He died in 1974—having been accused of many things, convicted of none—and was buried at Brookline Cemetery beside Mabel, who had passed away in 1968.

On the first Tuesday of November, 1932, Franklin Delano Roosevelt was elected president of the United States, assuring the end of prohibition.

The Springfield News & Leader, January 1, 1933
ONCE MAD COUNTY QUICKLY FORGETS MASSACRE OF SIX
Year's Time Heals Community's Remorse. Young Survivors Grope For Existence On "Haunted Farm

When the four o'clock whistles blow Monday afternoon, it will have been exactly one year since the firing of the opening gun in Greene county's bloodiest peace-time slaying.

One year ago tomorrow night, on January 2, six city and county peace officers lay dead in morgues here. . . . The entire community was in a state of bedlam.

But today—just twelve months later—the tragedy is almost forgotten by all save the victims' survivors. The brutality and sensation of a crime that held the attention of the entire world for the time being is now little more than a fleeting memory.

The Young farm has been for sale. . . . In addition to encountering a low market for farm land, Mrs. Young has found that it is difficult to sell a place with such a hideous history. A Springfield physician holds a mortgage on the place that might have been foreclosed long ago, but he has taken no action, apparently hoping the widow may be fortunate enough to sell.

Mrs. Young told a reporter that "me and my family have had enough of that there pube-licity, and ain't a-wantin' no more." Vinita, who professes to "love reporters like a fly loves vinegar," was as arrogant as ever.

Not an animal, an implement or anything that suggests industry is seen on the place. In fact, the casual observer might easily think the farm was deserted. Some of the window panes shattered in the gun fight have not been replaced, and the holes are stuffed with old blankets.

Mrs. Young's existence, she tells her intimate acquaintances, depends on contributions from her children . . . For a time after the killing, caretakers charged the curious a 25-cent admission fee, and some revenue came from that source. Resentful neighbors threatened violence a time or two over that, and the practice was soon abandoned. However, visitors are still solicited for 20 cents, as a charge for pointing out the exact spots where the dead officers were found. But visitors are so few and far between that it is not a very profitable show. Some of those who did pay marveled at Mrs. Young's business like attitude while exhibiting the places where her sons' victims fell.

In that very same edition of the paper, on the same *page* in fact, readers learned that Greene County was suing the estate of Marcell Hendrix in the amount of $8,752. To quickly summarize a sad business: In 1929, the state legislature put a cap on how much a sheriff could earn in fees.[36] The new law was sufficiently confusing that the state Supreme Court was trying to decide what it meant even as Hendrix made his ill-fated raid.[37] Greene County eventually determined that Marcell and his immediate successor, Maude, had overcharged. The case would be settled in June of 1933, in the amount of $1,033.[38]

The *Springfield Press* sold its last paper in May of 1933, merging with the *Daily News & Leader.* Edson K. Bixby had won again, acquiring Will Rogers' column in the package.[39]

In June, the United States Senate eliminated the gold standard, "permitting payment of all contracts in legal tender money." While not everyone was happy, the ghost of William Jennings Bryan could rest in peace.

Springfield Leader and Press, January 2, 1942
OFFICERS HERE RECALL TRAGIC DAY DECADE AGO WHEN DESPERATE YOUNG BROTHERS KILLED SIX MEN

Three of the officers' widows still live in Springfield. They are Mrs. Tony Oliver, Mrs. Wiley Mashburn and Mrs. Ollie Crosswhite. Mrs. Marcell Hendrix lives near Brookline.

Mrs. Augusta Houser is believed to have married and is said to be living in Chicago. Whereabouts of Mrs. Sidney Meadows are unknown.

Of the officers, Pike is a police scout driver; Johnson is a Greene county jailer; Brown is assistant supervisor of industry at the state prison. . . . Bilyeu is guard on the county road gang. Wegman is believed to be operating a jewelry store at Kansas City.

Mrs. J. D. Young, mother of Harry and Jennings, operates a section of an apartment house here. She is 76 years old and was seriously ill several months ago.

Motherly and with her gray-streaked hair swept up to a knot on top f her head, she recalls the infamous massacre sadly. "We just couldn't do a thing with Harry and Jennings," she said.

She's bitter toward two of the raiding officers, however. "Ollie Crosswhite and Wiley Mashburn had treated Harry and Jennings awful," she says. "The boys hated them. Why, if Marcel Hendrix had of taken a couple of men with him who had common sense, Harry and Jennings would have given up. They were shooting at Mashburn and Crosswhite. Goodness me, the boys grew up almost within a stones throw of Marcell."

Never mind that Willie Florence had herself, once upon a time, implored Ollie Crosswhite to intervene and save Harry from the corrupt influence of Roscoe Tutor—this before Harry had been convicted of anything, much less committed murder. *Whatever* Harry did, it was always someone else's fault, right up to and including executing Ollie Crosswhite at close range with a shotgun blast to the back of the head.

Willie Florence Haguewood Young died, August 25, 1945, and was buried beside her husband at McCauley Cemetery in Christian County. The next grave over, J. M. Young is "Resting In Hope Of A Glorious Resurrection." James David and Willie Florence share a more modest hope, their stone diary reading, simply, "At Rest."

CHAPTER TWENTY-THREE

Housepainting

I don't have no sympathy for the Young brothers
But I do extend my sympathy to their mother.
We hear their mother pray down in the house cell.
While her two sons make their way down to HELL.

—Coda E. Blair
The Springfield News & Leader
January 10, 1932[1]

Seventy-plus years after what was and (depending on how you count September 11, 2001) still is the single deadliest peace-time law enforcement disaster in United States history, four houses in the heartland stand as unwitting . . . (What was the word used in the 1932 newspapers?) . . . *Curios.*

Most notorious, of course, is the old Young place off Haseltine Road, east of Springfield, Missouri. While some of the outbuildings are gone, the huge barn appears largely unchanged from 1932. The house itself has undergone additions and renovations; nevertheless, the twin-gabled home-cum-fortress will be immediately recognizable to any who have studied pictures from the night of January 2, 1932.

Though one might be deceived in the following respect: The night photography casts a wicked shadow that would not be supposed from viewing the place on a pleasant spring day in the Ozarks.

On a pleasant spring day in the Ozarks, we imagine the home as J. D. Young saw it in 1918: an entirely comfortable place to live and raise a family. The current residents are nice people, who let me look around the yard and didn't even charge a quarter.

Also evocative is an old path off Haseltine Road, disappearing into what's left of the orchards—presumably the same rut Oliver, Houser, and Bilyeu traveled the late afternoon of January 2, 1932. A gate prevents entry, marked by a sign, "No Trespassing/Survivors Will Be Shot."

The second house actually post-dates the 1932 police massacre, but is significant, nonetheless. After her husband was killed on the job and she lost the election to complete his term of office by thirty-four votes, Maude Hendrix first relocated to a small house on Scott Street in Springfield, where she stayed just long enough for Maxine to complete the school year, then moved back to the family farm, southwest of Brookline.

Living at the jail, Maude had become accustomed to brick. Now she cleaned out a large chicken coop to serve as a temporary dwelling place, tore down the old frame farmhouse and replaced it with a sturdy new brick home.

Daughter Maxine, now an octogenarian, remembers the return to Brookline. She knows her memory may be playing tricks on her, but recalls there were electrical storms practically every night—and she was terrified of electrical storms.[2]

And we imagine her dad, putting his shoulder to the door of the farmhouse just up the road, struck by lightning emitted from the barrel of a twelve-gauge shotgun.

Maude Hendrix died in 1952, having lived out her widowhood on the farm, where she lifted feed sacks with her own back and on a cold winter's night might be found attending the birth of a lamb.[3]

For the third house, we go to Houston, Texas. From the new downtown ballpark, drive east on McKinney, through a rundown industrial corridor, to the Eastwood intersection. On the morning of January 5, 1932, Heard, Beverly, and other officers parked their autos here, approaching Walker Avenue on foot.

The news accounts termed the place a "cottage" and I suppose that still fits. It's a small one-story structure, with a wide porch that must have looked friendly enough, once upon a time. The exterior is still green, though a lighter shade than imaged in the black and white photographs of 1932. After J. L. Tomlison repaired the bullet holes, did his friend, A. P. Singleton, do the painting?

I have come a long way and want to snap a photo myself. A nice lady is sweeping the sidewalk in front of 4710. The neighborhood may not be what it once was, but she's doing her part to keep it clean. Assuming her to be the current resident, I ask permission to point and shoot. She seems puzzled—as I surely would be in her place. I attempt a short explanation.

I have the sense that English is not her first language, but her eyes widen when I come to the part about two mass murderers dying in a hail of gunfire. I want to ask if I can go inside to take a picture of her bathroom, but decide that would be pressing my luck.

From Houston, we angle north and west, past what's left of Streetman, Texas (not much), through Dallas/Fort Worth, then Wichita Falls; over the Red River, we're into Oklahoma, and quickly come to Frederick. A mile and a half east of town, just past the vo-tech on Highway 5, is the former home of J. D. Young and family, built by their own hands in 1911. That the white-frame cube has stood all these years, through dustbowl and tornadoes, is testament to the quality of *pater* Young's workmanship and character.

Looking at the flat earth north of the house, extending to the horizon, I think of something Holly Gladys wrote in *The Diamond Jubilee History of Tillman County:* "Quanah Parker and his people always camped behind our house near the well when they went to Quanah, Texas, from Cache. Mama always cried when she saw them coming because Quanah wanted Brother Paul. He said he'd make Paul rich if Daddy would give Paul to him."

Quanah Parker was the offspring of a Comanche chief who mated with a white woman who had herself been taken captive as a child, then was recaptured as an adult, this time by white soldiers. Parker was among the holdouts from the 1867 Medicine Lodge Creek Treaty, finally surrendering in 1875 and taking his people on to the reservation. Unlike other famous warrior chiefs, who found reservation life the equivalent of a death sentence, Quanah prospered, leasing grazing rights to Texans and investing his earnings in the Acme and Pacific Railroad. A town in Texas was named for him, his stature such that Parker accompanied President Roosevelt and "Coyote Catcher" Abernathy on their famous hunt.[4]

Is that how it started? Paul Young hearing that Quanah Parker wanted him, Willie Florence crying for fear the half-breed might just take him, Paul not crying at all? While Paul's spartan father and older brothers were breaking their backs on this hard land, here was the proud, untamed Quanah Parker, riding at the head of his people, moving back and forth across the prairie on his own terms, suggesting Paul might come with him. Quanah Parker had fought the law—first in saying no to the reservation, then in actual battle at places such as Adobe Walls— and was honored! Meanwhile Paul's father played by the rules and had a pittance to show for it.

Is that what happened? What had been a code of honor for Parker translated into criminality by Paul, who infected Jennings, who infected

Harry, who killed Mark Noe and with Jennings slaughtered Marcell Hendrix and Tony Oliver and Wiley Mashburn and Ollie Crosswhite and Sid Meadows and Charlie Houser and then each other; that which started with a boy's romantic imagining in Oklahoma ending in a Houston bathroom by way of the Ozarks, where at the millenium, Highway 65 zips tourist buses south of Springfield, past the old Young farmstead in Christian County, en route to Branson for musical comedy, including "Branson's First Show": "The Baldnobbers."

An Ode to Men in White Hats:

They are living all in life
    In this world
As the flowers among the thistles
    Turn and swirl
    But the sickles cut them down.

Onward still and faltering not
    In their duty
As the flower gives fragrance
    With all its beauty
    But the sickles cut them down.

All so sudden, all so shocking
    Yet it comes to them
As the flower is wilted in ruin
    This is the death of man
    For the sickles cut them down

They are gone but their deeds
    Do not die
As neither does the seed from the
    Flower ever die
    When the sickles cut them down.

Yes, the flower of life was taken away
But the thistles cannot thrive
For the flower does as those brave men
Leaving the seed of hope, courage and honor
To the thousands of mourning lives.
    Even tho' the sickles cut them down.

—Mary V. Hawks, "The Sickles Cut Them Down,"
The Springfield News & Leader, January 10, 1932

Notes

Chapter 1

1. *Startling Detective Adventures Magazine* was pulp non-fiction, a product of Fawcett Publications in Robbinsdale, Minnesota. The Springfield Police Department keeps this copy of *Startling Detective* under glass. The cover is missing and the exact date is undetermined, though Pretty Boy Floyd was still alive at the time of the writing.

2. Frank Farmer, "Shootout!" *Springfield News & Leader,* January 9, 1972.

3. "Frankenstein Is a Thriller," *Springfield Press,* January 4, 1932.

4. According to a 1951 unpublished master's thesis by Dean Frank Rea, "A History of the *Springfield (Mo.) Leader and Press,* 1867-1950," Edson K. Bixby, owner/editor of the *News & Leader,* insisted his writers employ pseudonyms. George Olds sometimes wrote as Edward Eddy, but in this case the lead author may have been Frank Rhodes. The thesis is located in the local history archives at the Springfield-Green County Library.

5. "Ollie Crosswhite 'Afraid of Nothing' His Friends Recall," *Springfield Daily News,* January 4, 1932.

6. Michael Wallis, *Route 66, the Mother Road* (St. Martin's Press, 1990).

7. "Shaving Assignment Saves Jones' Life," *Springfield Leader,* January 4, 1932.

8. Scott's extended first person narrative is found in the January 5 edition of the *Springfield Press,* headlined "Lon Scott Writes of Rescue of Bodies in Young Farm Yard." The piece was prefaced, "The drama of the rescue of the bodies of the five dead and one wounded officer at the Young home will always seem unimportant to me. What is important about it all is the lack of preparation for such emergencies in Greene County. All of us must admit it was a shameful disgrace to let six wounded and dying men lay on the cold ground at the Young home for seeming eternity in broad daylight."

9. Edward Eddy, "Wall of Invisible Terror Keeps Men from Rushing on House of Horror," *Springfield Sunday News & Leader,* January 3, 1932. In a story printed in the *Houston Chronicle* ("Trio Crawls into Death Yard to Hunt for Bodies") of the same date, the Associated Press estimated a half hour elapsed from the time rescuers first arrived at the scene to the mass assault of "home town heroes."

10. The Rhodes account is pieced together from the *Springfield Sunday News & Leader* ("Six Officers Slain by Fugitives Who Escape Trap at Mother's Home") and St. Louis *Post-Dispatch* ("6 Officers Slain, 3 Shot Attempting Arrest Near Springfield, Mo."), both dated January 3, 1932: "Wall of Invisible Terror Keeps Men from Rushing on House of Horror."

11. Quotes in this and the preceding paragraph are from the pseudonymous "Edward Eddy's" coverage at the farm, as printed in the *Springfield Sunday News & Leader,* January 3, 1932.

12. Mary Shelley, *Frankenstein* (New York: Books, Inc., nd).

Chapter 2

1. "Youngs' Kinfolk Hesitantly Tell What They Know," *Springfield Daily News,* January 4, 1932. The paper seemed skeptical: "he was trying to leave the impression he didn't care to associate with the Young boys." Albert also "declared he did not see 'a drop to drink' at the Young farm house . . . although officers found many bottles in the place."

2. "Youngs Tried to Sell Stolen Car in Aurora," *Springfield Leader,* January 7, 1932.

3. The Model A was first offered to the public in November of 1927 at an introductory price of $385, raised in mid-1928 to $480. Brinkley, *Wheels for the World: Henry Ford, His Company, and a Century of Progress* (New York: Viking Penguin, 2003), 358.

4. The Clyde Medley ad is headed "Year End Sale: Every Car Reduced," *Springfield Press,* December 26, 1931.

5. Sometime in the summer of 1931, one of the Young brothers, probably Harry, brought a 1930 Buick sedan in to the Cowden-Buick agency in Springfield for repairs. The car with Texas plates was towed behind Willie Florence's Willys-Knight club sedan. Thad Batey described the customer as having a "gruff, cross manner." When Batey lifted the hood to check the motor number, the fellow said he didn't have time to get the car fixed after all and drove away. "Young's Dealing With Stolen Car Brought to Light," *Springfield Daily News,* January 5, 1932.

6. "Full, Graphic History of Massacre at Young Farm," *Springfield Sunday News & Leader,* January 10, 1932.

7. Also taken into custody at the Smith home was Albert Conley. Under

other circumstances, the out-of-work ambulance driver would be described as dapper, red-cheeked, and good-humored. In initial interrogation, Albert told police he had come into Springfield with his wife and sister-in-law around 3:00, raising the possibility Albert spent the morning and lunch hour at the farm before coming into town for the haircut, planning to rendezvous with the others back at Etta Smith's. But it is difficult to give credence to anything Albert had to say. For that matter, if he in fact got his hair cut at all on Saturday, the barber was never publicly identified. In a variation on the story, Monday's *Leader* reported Willie Florence was to meet the girls back at Etta Smith's, instead of being picked up at the square. Albert's story is found in "Youngs' Kinfolk," *Daily News,* January 4, 1932.

8. The January 4 *Springfield Press* ("Young Brothers' Kin") reported Willie Florence "reluctantly admitted that she called through the telephone exchange at Brookline to her farm home and 'tipped' her sons of the arrests of their two sisters." The warning is quoted in "Trail of Slayers Leads to Texas: Six of Family Held," *Daily News,* January 4, 1932.

9. "'Oh God, Oh God!' Mother of Young Boys Cries, When Told They Were Slain Here," *Houston Chronicle,* January 5, 1932.

10. J. R. Woodside, a reporter for the *Springfield Press,* put together the first comprehensive account of the massacre in 1932, *The Young Brother's Massacre.* He addressed the telephone controversy in chapter seven, stating categorically, "Mrs. Young Did Not Telephone."

11. "Mother of Killers Hopes Hunted Sons Will End Own Lives," *Houston Post-Dispatch,* January 5, 1932.

12. "'Oh God, Oh God!'" *Houston Chronicle,* January 5, 1932.

13. "Oren Brown Tells Story," *Springfield Press,* January 4. Another "grip"—a.k.a. carpet bag—was open downstairs, this containing, "not the clothing of a farmer, but that of a modishly dressed man."

14. "Trace Movements of Young Family in Prolonged Grilling," *Springfield Leader,* January 4, 1932.

15. "Young Brothers' Kin," *Springfield Press,* January 4, 1932.

16. Ibid.

17. Darrell Schulz, "Springfield's Crime of the Century," *Gateway Heritage,* Spring 2003. Schulz says the girls "came into the station house looking stylish, attactive, and mad as hell."

18. "Officers Recall Tragic Day Decade Ago When Desperate Young Brothers Killed 6 Men," *Springfield Leader and* Press, January 2, 1942.

19. Ibid.

20. Frank Farmer, "Shootout!" *Springfield News & Leader,* January 9, 1972.

21. Sunrise was 7:27.

22. Robert Flanders, "The Haseltine Orchards Historic Area," *OzarksWatch,* Vol IX, No. 1, 1996.

23. A wonderful resource: William Garrett Piston & Richard W. Hatcher III, *Wilson's Creek: The Second Battle of the Civil War and the Men Who Fought It* (Chapel Hill: The University of North Carolina Press, 2000).

Chapter 3

1. Harold Bell Wright, *The Shepherd of the Hills* (New York: Grosset and Dunlap, 1907), 31.

2. Jonathan Fairbanks and Clyde Edwin Tuck, *Past And Present Of Greene County, Missouri* (Indianapolis: A. W. Bowen & Company, 1915). Tuck was a newspaperman, Fairbanks the long time superintendent of Springfield Public Schools. Fairbanks and Tuck begin with Greene County's "prehistoric races."

3. I have also seen it "Eleanor," but "Elender" seems to be the dominant spelling.

4. Source material for the Youngs depends heavily on census records and a biographical sketch by Scott Rawson, published in *History & Families of Christian County,* Christian County Museum & Historical Society, Inc., Turner Publishing Company, 1998.

5. Irene Redfearn, *Greene County, Missouri, Tax Assessors' List, 1851 & 1856* (Springfield: Ozarks Genealogical Society, 1988), 247. The 1856 records were extracted by Redfearn.

6. *Christian County: Its First 100 Years* (Ozark, Mo: Christian County Centennial, Inc., 1959), 60.

7. Katherine Lederer, "Indian Annie" *OzarksWatch,* Vol. XI, No. 3, 4, 1998. The Ann Young material is taken from this and census records. Where the Lederer material seems at variance with the census, I have gone with the latter.

8. Elmo Ingenthron, *Borderland Rebellion* (Branson, Mo.: The Ozarks Mountaineer, 1980), 90. "Borderland Rebellion," by Elmo Ingenthron, (c) 1980. Used by permission of *The Ozarks Mountaineer,* Kirbyville, Missouri.

9. Like Wilson's Creek in Southwest Missouri, Pea Ridge, located just west of Bentonville, Arkansas, makes for a wonderful battlefield visit, offering a spectacular vista from the ridge itself.

10. Ingenthron, *Borderland Rebellion,* 207.

11. Ibid, 286.

12. Ibid, 286.

13. *Pictorial and Geneological Record of Greene County, Missouri: Together with Biographies of Prominent Men of Other Portions of the State, Both Living and Dead* (Chicago: Goodspeed Brothers, 1893), 276-280.

14. Ibid.

15. The Battle of Gettysburg was fought July 1-3, 1863; Vicksburg surrendered on the 4th of July.

16. *A Diamond Jubilee History Of Tillman County, 1901-1976* (Tillman County Historical Society, 1976), 712. *A Diamond Jubliee History of Tillman County, 1901-1976*, (c) 1976. Used by permission of the Tillman County Historical and Educational Society, Frederick, Oklahoma.

17. Ingenthron, *Borderland Rebellion,* 123.

18. Woodside, *Young Brothers Massacre,* 7.

19. Ingenthron, *Borderland Rebellion,*. 305.

20. Richard O'Conner, *Wild Bill Hickok* (Longmeadow *Press*, 1987), 87.

21. "Local Items," *Missouri Weekly Patriot,* August 10, 1865. In the same edition of the *Missouri Weekly Patriot* an interesting note gives further evidence of the war's depopulating effect in the Ozarks: "Several families passed through our city a few days since on their return to their homes in Stone county, in this State, from which they were driven by the enemies of the Government. This is an indication that peace is again restored to our once happy border counties, and we hope to see them again filled up by industrious mechanics and farmers, and other elements which represent the different callings of life."

22. R. I. Holcombe, ed., *History of Greene County, Missouri* (St. Louis: Perkins & Horner Publishers and Western Historical Company, 1883), 497-500.

23. Ibid, 489.

24. Woodside, *Young Brothers Massacre,* 7.

25. Ibid.

26. Maxine Wilson, "Christian County, Missouri Marriages, 1878-1891" (1988), 37. To order, write to: Maxine Wilson, Route 5, Box 328, Ozark, MO, 65721.

27. Woodside, *Young Brothers Massacre,* 7.

28. Ibid, 9.

29. Mary Hartman and Elmo Ingethron, *Bald Knobbers: Vigilantes on the Ozarks Frontier* (Gretna, La.: Pelican Publishing Company, 1996). The specific quote regarding Pastor Simmons is found on page 166. The triple hanging is related in chapter 15, "The Final Price."

30. Charles Morrow Wilson, *The Commoner* (New York: Doubleday &

Company, Inc., 1970), 193. Wilson employs a phrase I find delicious, referring to Bryan as "evangelist and agrarian entertainer."

Chapter 4

1. Material on Frederick and Tillman County is gleaned from assorted articles in *A Diamond Jubilee History Of Tillman County, 1901-1976,* including Carolyn Maxwell's "A Brief History of Tillman County Before Statehood." The Tillman County Museum in Frederick is a wonderful stop, part of a Pioneer Village across from the historic County Courthouse. And if you're looking for a place for breakfast, let me heartily recommend ID's, just south of the Courthouse.

2. There is not an exact known birth date for Harry Young. Contributing to the Tillman County *Diamond Jubilee History,* Harry's sister, Holly Gladys, would write, "The spring of 1904 we went back to Nixa, Missouri, for the sake of Mama's health. Brother Lyman Harry 'Dutch' was born back there. In the fall we returned [to Oklahoma]."

3. "'Oh God, Oh God!'" *Houston Chronicle,* January 5, 1932.

4. William Faulkner, *Light In August,* 14.

5. *Oklahoma Writer's Program,* Works Projects Administration, © 1941, the University of Oklahoma, 382.

6. Beth Campbell, "Boys Badness Proves Puzzle to Mrs. Young," *Springfield Leader,* January 8, 1932.

7. Greene County Draft Records, available at the Springfield-Greene County Library Center.

8. Paul W. and Mary H. Barrett, *Young Brothers Massacre* (Columbia: University of Missouri Press, 1988), 25. *Young Brothers Massacre* by Paul W. Barrett and Mary H. Barrett, by permission of the University of Missouri Press. Copyright (c) 1988 by the Curators of the University of Missouri.

9. Ibid, 5.

10. Recorder of Deeds, Tillman County, Oklahoma.

11. The church would be destroyed by fire in 1931 and residents of Frederick would remember the sound of the great bell crashing to earth.

12. Campbell, "Boys Badness," *Leader.*

13. *The Grapes of Wrath* (New York: Viking Penguin, 1967): 89. *The Grapes of Wrath,* by John Steinbeck, copyright 1939, renewed (c) 1967 by John Steinbeck. Used by permission of Viking Penguin, a division of Penguin Group (USA) Inc.

14. Campbell, "Boys Badness," *Leader.*

Chapter 5

1. Frank Farmer, "Shootout," *Springfield News & Leader,* January 9, 1972.

2. Woodside, *The Young Brothers Massacre,* 47. The *Springfield Press* of Monday, January 4, 1932, quotes Waddle as estimating Johnson arrived at the station at 5:00, seemingly lending credence to the assertion in the Farmer article that Virgil had some trouble getting into town.

3. Farmer, "Shootout!" *News & Leader,* January 9, 1972.

4. "Families Spend Agonizing Hours Waiting Definite News of Slain Officers," *Sunday News & Leader,* January 3, 1932.

5. Ibid.

6. Maxine Hendrix McIntyre, interview with the author, April 12, 2002.

7. The Sheriff's office was located on the second floor of the courthouse. City offices, including the mayor's, occupied the third floor.

8. "Chief Waddle Is Kept Busy," *Springfield Press,* January 4, 1932.

9. "Six Officers Slain By Fugitives Who Escape Trap at Mother's Home," *Springfield Sunday News & Leader,* January 3 and *Springfield Press,* January 4. According to the *Press,* the Pickwick Express Company had flown a plane down from Kansas City to aid in the search.

10. *1932 Souvenir Review of the Department of Police, City of Springfield, Missouri.*

11. Grand Jury Report, from "The Police to Blame, But Not the Sheriff," *Springfield Daily Leader,* May 24, 1906.

12. Farmer, "Shootout!" *News & Leader.*

13. "Mashburn Eight Year Officer," *Springfield Daily News & Leader,* January 3, 1932

14. "Many Grief-Torn Scan Ambulances for Their Loved," *Springfield Daily News & Leader,* January 3, 1932.

15. Ibid. The January 4 *Springfield Daily News* (Curious Citizens Buzz Excitement at Headquarters") quoted one spectator, "who had just seen the body of Ollie Crosswhite, 'He was shot right through here—a great big hole,' he said, pointing to the side of his head.'"

16. Woodside, *The Young Brothers Massacre,* 51.

17. Ibid.

18. "Lead Rescuers at Young Farm," *Springfield Press,* January 4, 1932.

19. "Sisters Effort to Sell 'Hot' Car Caused Killing," *Springfield Sunday News & Leader,* January 3, 1932.

20. "Bandits' Mother Held By Police, Grows Hysterical," *Springfield Sunday News & Leader,* January 3, 1932.

21. "Ash Grove Pays Church Tribute to Six Officers," *Springfield Leader,* January 4, 1932.

22. "Nine Arrested in Booze Raids," *Springfield Press,* January 2, 1932.

23. Ibid.

24. Ibid.

25. William L. Bande and Harry T. Brundidge, *The Inside Story of the Kidnapping & Murder of Baby Lloyd Keet* (Springfield: Webster Publishing Company, 1918). E. Hultsch, *Authentic Story of Claud Piersol, the Kidnapper* (Springfield: Hultsch Publishing,). Piersol served nineteen of the thirty-five years, released in May 1938.

26. Faithhorn Company, *Honor Roll of Greene County, Missouri: An Illustrated Historical Biography Complied from Private and Public Authentic Records* (Chicago: Faithhorn Company and George Robb Collins, 1919).

27. "Nine Arrested," *Springfield Press,* January 2, 1932.

28. "Liquor Roundup Near Ash Grove," *Springfield Sunday Daily News & Leader,* January 3, 1932.

29. "Nine Arrested," *Springfield Press,* January 2, 1932.

30. Ibid.

31. "Mashburn's Last Photo," *Springfield Press,* January 4, 1932.

32. "Nine Arrested," *Press,* January 2, 1932.

33. Ibid.

34. "Curious Citizens Buzz," *Daily News,* January 4, 1932. Hendrix had quipped, "This reward cost me a lot of money."

Chapter 6

1. Reprinted by permission from *Missouri: A Guide to the "Show Me" State,* © 1998 by the Missiouri Historical Society Press, St. Louis, Missouri. Workers of the Writers' Program of the Works Projects Administration in the State of Missouri, Duell, Sloan, and Pearce. © 1941 by the Missouri State Highway Department, 330.

2. "Death to Colorful Thomas H. Gideon," *Springfield Leader-Press,* February 13, 1959. In an April 6, 1951 "Citizen of the Week" article for the Springfield newsletter, *Bias,* Ethel Strainchamps writes that Gideon had been a "gun-toting lawyer in Bristow, Oklahoma."

3. "Never Saw Foster Till He Testified, Gordon Says," *Springfield Leader,* October 11, 1930.

4. *Missouri, the Center State, Volume 3,* 739.

5. Material on the Gideons is taken from biographical sketches in Fairbanks and Tuck, *Past and Present of Greene County, Missouri.*

6. In *Bias* mazazine, April 6, 1951 ("Citizen of the Week" by Strainchamps), Gideon's middle name is given as "Harrison."

7. "Gideon to Use Ax on City Heads: Hints He Will Name His Own Police Chief," *Springfield Leader,* March 21, 1928

8. Ibid.

9. According to the *1932 Souvenir Review,* the "total strength of the

department" was fifty-six, including the chief, assistant chief, an identification expert, a traffic sergeant, four desk sergeants, the chief's secretary, twenty-nine patrolmen, seven detectives, an eight-member motorcycle squad, Police Matron Margarite Hull, a process server and a janitor.

10. The terminations were published in "19 Cops Fired as Gideon Takes Office," *Springfield Daily News,* April 17, 1928; the hirings were reported in the next day's edition, "18 New Men Assigned to Police Post as Mayor Completes His Shakeup," April 18, 1928.

11. "The Police Massacre," *Springfield Daily News,* April 18, 1928.

12. William M. Redding, foreword to *Tom's Town,* J. B. Lippincott Company, 1947, foreword copyright 1986 by the Curators of the University of Missouri, University of Missouri Press, Columbia, Missouri.

13. "Mayor Gets Oath and Repeats Vow of 'Enforcement,'" *Springfield Daily News,* April 17, 1928.

14. Fairbanks and Tuck, *Past and Present of Greene County, Missouri,* 691.

15. Ibid, 692. For more on pre-prohibition politics, see G. K. Renner's fine article in the July 1968 edition of the *Missouri Historical Review,* "Prohibition Comes To Missouri, 1910-1919."

16. Jonathan Daniels, *The Time Between the Wars* (New York: Doubleday & Company Inc., 1966), 12.

17. Ernest Gordon, *The Wrecking of the 18th Amendment* (Francestown, N.H.: The Alcohol Information Press, 1943).

18. Norman H. Clark, *The Dry Years* (Seattle: University of Washington Press, 1965), 158.

19. "Pike Will Be Next Chief of Police," *Springfield Leader,* April 8, 1928.

20. Ibid.

21. Sometimes spelled "Dob."

22. "Officer Slain, Two Women Shot By Crazed Man on Rampage Here," *Springfield Daily News,* June 19, 1928.

23. "Witness Paints Cops as Cowards at Adams Trial," *Springfield Daily News,* July 18, 1928.

24. Both Mrs. Whalin and Miss St. Clair succumbed to their wounds.

25. It would later be reported ("Chief Tony Oliver Finds Adventure in Service Here," *Springfield Press,* April 16, 1930) that DeArmond was regarded as the "best shot on the force." Hit in the chest while reaching for the light switch, DeArmond "vainly reached for his gun but died before it could be unsheathed."

26. "Tony Oliver Noted for Fearlessness," *Springfield Sunday News & Leader,* January 3, 1932.

27. "Witness Paints," *Daily News,* July 18, 1928.

28. "Adams Is Sentenced to Death on Gallows," *Springfield Daily News,* July 20, 1928.

29. "Adams' Own Story of His Life and Crimes," *Springfield Daily News,* July 22, 1928.

30. Material on the Bixby newspaper family is found in "A History of the Springfield (Mo) Leader and Press, 1867-1950," a Master's Thesis by Dean Frank Rea, June 1951.

31. "A Happy New Year!" *Springfield Leader,* January 1, 1932.

32. "Gideon Defiant as Taxpayer Hints Recall," *Springfield Daily News,* July 31, 1928. The meeting was held at Broadway Methodist Episcopal Church.

33. This was not going to play well with God-fearing folk in Springfield. The Federal raid coincided with a revival at Campbell Avenue Methodist Episcopal. According to the November 5, 1928, edition of the *Leader* ("Dancing, Cards Are Seen Evil by Evangelist"), Reverend Norman Guice "bitterly denounced dancing, card playing, gossip and profanity." Guice contended social card playing leads to gambling. As for "modern dance": "The positions are bad and the immodest dress that the women wear to dances is bad."

34. Pike's report was in "Pike Applauds Police Record," *Springfield Leader,* November 2, 1928.

35. One hundred twenty supporters affixed their names to Hendrix's political ad, including his mother in law, Ida Brown.

36. Note and family photographs courtesy of Maxine Hendrix McIntyre.

37. Fairbanks and Tuck, *Past and Present of Greene County, Missouri,* 1504.

38. "Dan Hendrix Dies," *Springfield Republican,* February 4, 1917.

39. "Dan Hendrix Funeral Is Largely Attended," *Springfield Republican,* February 8, 1917.

40. Membership records of Brookline Baptist Church.

41. "Hendrix Reared Near Scene of His Last Grim Drama," *Springfield Sunday News & Leader,* January 3, 1932.

42. Constitution of the State of Missouri, Article 9, Section 10, as recorded in the *Revised Statutes of the State of Missouri, 1929.*

43. "G.O.P. Landslide Victims Write Own 'Obituaries,'" *Springfield Leader,* November 7, 1928.

44. "'Scott Curtis For President,'" *Springfield Leader,* November 9, 1928. The photograph appeared in the *Springfield Sunday News & Leader,* November 11, 1928.

45. The bond was registered with the Circuit Court of Greene County,

December 18, 1928. Ten co-signers included Marcell's brother, Lillard, and his brother-in-law, Al Bischoff.

46. "Spies to Be Away as City Toasts 1929!" *Springfield News,* December 31, 1928.

47. Willey biographical material is from "Veteran: F. M. Willey," *Springfield Daily News,* January 1, 1929.

48. Greene County Criminal Court Case #92696.

49. Maxine Hendrix McIntyre, interview with the author, April 12, 2002.

50. "Three New Posts Created by Pike on Police Force," *Springfield Daily News,* January 2, 1929.

51. "Drafted for Service," *Springfield Press,* March 4, 1929. The paper was unabashedly pro-Hoover, declaring: "Just as Mr. Hoover is president of ALL the people in the nation, The Press is a newspaper for ALL the people in the territory it serves."

Chapter 7

1. The Gibsons sold a total of 208 acres. The remaining eighty were purchased by Willie Florence's relative M. C. Haguewood in the price of $8,000. As gleaned from the Christian County Recorders Officer, the bulk of the Young acreage was in Section 28, Township 27, Range 21, bordering the Ozark-Galena Highway.

2. "Young Brothers Had First Clash with Law in Robberies at Ozark," *Springfield Daily News,* January 9, 1932.

3. Robert Flanders, "The Haseltine Orchards Historic Area," *OzarksWatch,* Vol IX, No. 1, 1996. Ira Haseltine arrived in the Ozarks with the Atlantic and Pacific Railroad, come from Vermont via Wisconsin. Ira had been a founding member of the Republican Party. The staunch Unionist named his sons Lincoln Abraham, Sumner Charles, Seward, and Louis Kossouth—the latter in honor of a Hungarian Revolutionary.

4. Orville Young, telephone interview with the author, March 28, 2002.

5. "Young Brothers Had First Clash," *Daily News,* January 9, 1932.

6. Ibid.

7. Paul W. and Mary H. Barrett, *Young Brothers Massacre* (Columbia: University of Missouri Press, 1988), 11.

8. *The Grapes of Wrath,* 201.

9. "Robbers Captured," Christian County, Mo., *Republican,* December 27, 1918. Paul and Jennings asked for a change of venue from the court of Circuit Judge Fred Stewart, so the case was heard by the Honorable C. A. Skinker of Missouri's eighteenth judicial district. Once Stewart was off the case, Paul and Jennings entered a plea of guilty.

10. These records were made available through the Springfield Police

Department and are maintained at the historic "Calaboose," located at Market and College Streets, behind the lot where Police Headquarters used to be.

11. "Mother feels Youngs Will Be Captured," *Springfield Press,* January 4, 1932.

12. "Mother of Killers Hopes Hunted Sons Will End Own Lives," *Houston Post-Dispatch,* January 5, 1932.

13. "Young Brothers Had First Clash," *Daily News,* January 9, 1932.

14. "Praise 'Jim' Young," *Springfield Press,* January 8, 1932.

15. "Youngs' Father Fine Character, Friends Recall," *Springfield Leader,* January 7, 1932.

16. Fairbanks and Tuck, *Past and Present of Greene County, Missouri,* 1622.

17. Lucille Morris Upton, "The Good Old Days," *Springfield Leader and Press,* November 26, 1967. See also "Landmark Is Worth Only $1," *Springfield Leader and Press,* August 20, 1958.

18. "Youngs' Father," *Leader,* January 7, 1932.

19. Seventy years later, the pastoral setting of McCauley cemetery is unmarred, surely appearing much as it did in 1921, with the exception of the golden arches of McDonalds peeking just over the eastern horizon.

20. In the January 8, 1932, article, "Praise 'Jim' Young," the *Press* reported that "due to a confusion in dates" Paul and Jennings "arrived a day late."

21. *The Grapes of Wrath,* 3-4.

22. Jonathan Daniels, *The Time Between the Wars* (New York: Doubleday and Company, 1966), 146.

23. Missouri State Penitentiary Records.

24. In their fine book, *Young Brother's Massacre,* Paul and Mary Barrett offer an entire chapter, "Paul On a Career Path of His Own," including details of Paul's incarcerations, marriages, college experience, etc.

25. "Three Arrests in Connection with Robbery," *Springfield Leader,* April 14, 1924.

26. "Brothers Started Early on Trail of Crime that Led to Grim Death," *Springfield Daily News,* April 7, 1932.

27. "Three Charged with Robbery," *Springfield Republican,* April 15, 1924.

28. Lawrence County Circuit Court Record, Case #3913.

29. Greene County Criminal Court Record, Book 26, 619.

30. "Two Arrested for Robbing Oil Station," *Springfield Leader,* February 7, 1927.

31. "Brothers Started Early," *Daily News,* January 7, 1932.

32. Greene County Marriage Records, Recorder's Office.

33. Greene County Circuit Court Record, Case # 8706.

34. Greene County Circuit Court Record, Case #8705.

35. Greene County Circuit Court Record, Case #8704.

36. "Murder Suspect's Mother Prays that He'll Escape," *Springfield Leader,* June 6, 1929.

37. Greene County Circuit Court Record, Case #8707.

38. "Prison Recalls Young as 'Good,'" *Springfield Daily News,* January 4, 1932.

39. "Young's Life in Prison," *Springfield Leader,* January 6, 1932.

40. Ibid.

41. Ibid.

42. The September 26, 1928, date was reported in "Three Young Brothers Served Terms in State Penitentiary," *Springfield Press,* January 4, 1932. The state records are a little confusing. The *Press* reported this as seven-twelfths merit time. The December 27, 1928, date and additional ninety-two days of merit time are gleaned from the state prison records.

43. *The Grapes of Wrath,* 56.

44. "Suspect's Mother Stunned at News; Visited on Sunday," *Springfield Leader,* June 3, 1929.

45. "Oh God, Oh God!" *Houston Chronicle,* January 5, 1932.

Chapter 8

1. The railroad marketed the area as "The Land of the Big Red Apple," attracting, among others, Laura Ingalls and Alonzo Wilder, whose operation was located in Mansfield, forty miles east of Springfield, on the Memphis line.

2. Republic was briefly in the national news in 1998, sued by the American Civil Liberties Union for incorporating the Greek symbol "icthus"—the outline of a fish—into the town logo. Among groups decrying a perceived endorsement of the Christian religion were Ozark-area witches.

3. Republic, Mo., *Monitor,* June 6, 1929.

4. "Hunt Officer's Killer," *Springfield Leader,* June 3, 1929.

5. Greene County Circuit Court Case #92997.

6. "Republic City Official Found Murdered," *Springfield Press,* June 3, 1929.

7. According to Missouri State Penitentiary records, Oval was eighteen when sentenced to two years, starting April 9, 1927. #31387 was discharged one year later, April 9, 1928.

8. Missouri State Penitentiary Records, located at the State Archives in Jefferson City.

9. "Republic City Official," *Press,* June 3, 1929; "Fail Find Mark Noe's Murderer," *Press,* January 4, 1932.

10. "Republic City Official," *Press,* June 3, 1929.

11. *Startling Detective Adventures Magazine.* The April 1930 edition of *Writer's Digest* described *Startling Detective Adventures:* "They are making a play for true mystery stories illustrated with actual photographs from life. . . . The April issue contains eight true features about crime including 'My Seventeen Years Among Prison Rioters,' 'How I Captured Topeka's Girl Bandit,' and 'The Clueless Crime.' Looks like a fine opportunity for a shrewd writer to interview some successful detectives and go in for collaboration. (In such cases, unless of the two collaborators is unusually famous, the split is 60-40 with the writer getting the major receipts.) *Startling Detective Adventures* also contains two serials, and two detective adventure stories. All yarns must lend themselves adequately to illustration." The *Writer's Digest* article was titled, "The 17 Detective Magazines," and can be accessed in its entirety on the *Black Mask Magazine* Web site: www.blackmaskmagazine.com/bm_13.hmtl.

12. "Hunt Officer's Killer," *Leader,* June 3, 1929.

13. "On Murderer's Trail in Kansas!" *Springfield Leader,* June 6, 1929.

14. "$500 Reward for Noe's Slayer," *Springfield Leader,* June 4, 1929. "Fail Find Mark Noe's Murderer," *Press,* June 4, 1929.

15. "Suspect's Mother Stunned at News," *Springfield Leader,* June 3, 1929.

16. Ibid.

17. "Murder Suspect's Mother Prays that He'll Escape," *Springfield Leader,* June 6, 1929.

18. Ibid.

19. "Hunt Officer's Killer," *Leader,* June 3, 1929.

20. "$500 Reward," *Leader,* June 4, 1929. The charge was finally dismissed on June 7, 1930. According to the *Press* of the same date, Oval had been out on bail "since a few weeks after the killing."

21. Very fragile back copies of the *Monitor* are lovingly kept at the Republic Historical Society on Main Street, usually open on Saturdays—though a nice guy like Billy O'Neal may let you in during the week.

Chapter 9

1. "Adams Kills Himself to Cheat Gallows," *Springfield Daily News,* September 10, 1929. The type of poison—bichloride of mercury—was identified in the September 16 *Leader.* Meada would reappear on the front page in February of 1930. She and Nate C. Faulkner were found guilty of armed robbery, having relieved Mr. and Mrs. C. O. McCain of a diamond

ring worth eight hundred dollars. Meada was sentenced to ten year in prison, her "underworld lover" to thirteen.

2. "Chief Pike Requests Quick Trial," *Springfield Press,* October 12, 1929.

3. *Springfield Daily News,* October 14, 1929.

4. Wayne C. Bartee, *A History of the First Baptist Church, Springfield, Missouri, 1852-1977,* 49.

5. Ibid, 47.

6. "Regime of Gideon Flayed in Sermon," *Springfield Daily News,* October 14, 1929.

7. "Arrest Seven in Rum Raids Here After Frequent 'Buys,'" *Springfield Daily News,* October 17, 1929. "Federal Agents Raid Another Still Here, Hold Operator!" *Springfield Daily News,* October 18, 1929.

8. "The News And Leader Have No Candidate," *Springfield Leader,* October 14, 1929. It would be difficult, however, to imagine a paper more invested in an outcome. An election-day (Oct. 18) editorial declared, "The welfare and honor of Springfield hangs in the balance today. An unscrupulous political machine, making every use of power in its control, scoffing at every election law, is fighting to continue its grip upon the city's throat."

9. "Gideon Keeps Office By Majority Of 887," *Springfield Daily News,* October 19, 1929. The paper attributed Gideon's victory to the strength of his "machine."

10. "Chief Pike Is Praised; Carried On Shoulders," *Springfield Press,* October 19, 1929.

11. "Pike's Fate Is Ready For Jurors," *Springfield Leader,* November 21, 1929.

12. "Pike Suspended As Police Chief: Mayor Names Waddle Chief As Pike Goes," *Springfield Leader,* December 19, 1929. According to Gail DeGeorge, who coordinates the Springfield Police Department's small museum at the historic "Calaboose," Pike spent some of the interim time between stepping down as chief and deportation to Leavenworth superintending the Springfield Police Department's Bureau of Investigation.

13. "Pike Begins Year's Sentence," *Springfield Leader,* April 11, 1930. The Sunnyland was so named because the Frisco railway route, with one terminus in Kansas City, ran through Springfield on to Memphis, Birmingham, and into Florida. The latter is gleaned from the January 6, 1932, *Springfield Press,* where in yet another indication of hard times, it was reported Sunnyland trains 107 & 108 were being discontinued until business improved.

14. "'I'm Sorry' Pike Says Simply As He Bids Officers Goodbye," *Springfield Leader,* April 11, 1930.

15. Missouri State Penitentiary Records, #36212.

16. "Gideon Devoting Much Time To 'Good Will' Tours In Ozarks," *Springfield Daily News,* September 21, 1930.

17. Redding, *Tom's Town,* 292.

18. "Pike, Convicted, Kept Police Star Gideon Admits," *Springfield Leader,* October 11, 1930.

19. "Extra! Gideon Guilty: An Inside Story Of How It Was Done," *Springfield Leader,* October 17, 1930.

20. "Sentence Gideon To Two-Year Term In Federal Prison," *Springfield Daily News,* October 18, 1930.

21. Fleagle material taken from an article by Gerald H. Pipes, "To Hill Folks, Outlaw Was 'Nice Walter Cook," *Springfield News-Leader,* September 27, 1959.

22. "Hiding In The Ozarks," *Springfield Leader,* October 16, 1930.

Chapter 10

1. Photo Courtesy of the History Museum for Springfield-Greene County. A greatly enlarged copy hangs on a wall above a booth at Cheddar's restaurant in Springfield.

2. "Break Is Graphic Proof That New Jail Is Needed," *Springfield Leader,* January 28, 1931.

3. Grand Jury Report, September 19, 1931. The same Grand Jury heard a complaint from Attorney Albert C. Hayward that Springfield remained a moral cesspool, tolerating three "notorious resorts" in the vicinity of Campbell Avenue and Phelps Street. The trio of establishments were "used and operated as dens of vices" including "fornication" and "the making, drinking and disposing of intoxicants of various kinds."

4. Floyd M. Sullivan, "Willey Says County Could Remodel Jail," *Springfield Press,* May 21, 1931.

5. Photo appeared in the January 28, 1931 *Springfield Press.*

6. "Find Trail Of Fleeing Bad Men!" *Springfield Leader,* January 28, 1931.

7. Robert Winter, *Mean Men: The Sons of Ma Barker,* 44. The following is said of "Jelly Beans": "Young men out for a a good time. Good dancers, good drinkers and just a little bit rowdy."

8. A photo of the Marmon was published in the January 28, 1931, *Leader* with construction worker Constant Bossi pointing at the bullet-splashed windshield.

9. "Capture Alleged Kidnaper Who Figured In Jail Delivery," *Springfield Daily News,* January 29, 1931. The kidnapping charge was eventually dropped, but the jailbreak earned Michaels two years in

Jefferson City—see Greene County Circuit Court Record, Criminal, Book 29, 27.

10. "Capture Alleged Kidnaper," *Daily News,* January 29, 1931.

11. "Alvin Bass Taken To Jefferson City To Begin 25-Year Term," *Springfield Press,* February 11, 1931.

12. Ibid.

13. Greene County Circuit Court Record, Criminal, Book 28, 594.

14. Prison term reported in "Search Ships At Sea For Desperado: Members Oglesby Band," January 5, 1932, *Springfield Daily News.*

15. "Last of Jail Breakers Is Caught," *Springfield Leader,* April 2, 1931.

16. Greene County Circuit Court Record, Criminal, Book 29, 45.

17. "Brothers Started Early," *Springfield Daily News,* January 7, 1932. Curtis termed Hendrix "Magnificently fearless."

18. "Two Girls Held For Auto Theft Tipped Sheriff," *Springfield Daily News,* January 3, 1932.

Chapter 11

1. Photo and clipping courtesy of Maxine Hendrix McIntyre.

2. "Sheriff Ignored Premonition That He Was Facing Death," *Springfield Sunday News & Leader,* January 3, 1932.

3. Ibid.

4. "Gloom Hangs Over County Court House," *Springfield Leader,* January 4, 1932.

5. This, according to Vinita Young, as told to Paul and Mary Barrett, *Young Brothers Massacre,* 57.

6. Oliver's candidacy was announced in "Tony Oliver For Sheriff," February 24, 1931, *Springfield Press.* Tony and Maude had five children. The oldest, Opal, was married and living in Sedalia, Missouri. Helen, William, and the fourteen-year-old twins, Fay and Ray, were still at home, 1224 North Sherman Avenue, though Helen was a married woman, now—Mrs. Lavine. According to Frank Farmer, in his January 9, 1972, retrospective in the *Springfield Sunday News & Leader,* Bill Oliver later served as Greene County deputy sheriff under Glenn Hendrix.

7. "Killings Remove Three Aspirants For Sheriffs Place," St. Louis *Globe Democrat,* January 4, 1932.

8. The Adams case wasn't Tony Oliver's first brush with death. The *Sunday News & Leader* ("Tony Oliver Noted For Fearlessness") reported January 3 that "he missed being stabbed to death many years ago by only a hair's breath. He had arrested a man and was taking him to the patrol wagon when the prisoner's wife made for him with a knife. Another officer shouted a warning, and Oliver dodged and missed the blow."

9. The Christmas profiles of the massacre victims and families are compiled from post-massacre coverage in the three Springfield newspapers and the *1932 Souvenir Review of the Department of Police, City of Springfield, Missouri.*

10. "'Sure I Married Charlie Houser'" *Springfield Leader,* January 22, 1932.

11. "Tragedy Stalks Houser Family, Brother Left," *Springfield Sunday News & Leader,* January 3, 1932. The Housers' address was given as 1010 W. Dale.

12. For the sake of later reference, please note the fuzziness of detail.

13. "'Sure I Married,'" *Leader,* January 22, 1932.

14. "'Even His Prisoners Liked Him,' Charlie Houser's Brother Says," *Springfield Daily News,* January 4, 1932.

15. An excerpt from page 3: "Mayor Gideon has made a splendid record as the city's chief officer, and it is the sincere hope of his many friends and admirers that he may continue to give to the City of Springfield the same progressive leadership for many years to come."

16. "Meadows Knew Of Perils In Work But Ignored Them, Family Tells," *Springfield Sunday News & Leader,* January 3, 1932.

17. Farmer, "Shootout!" *Sunday News & Leader,* January 9, 1972.

18. Barrett and Barrett, *Young Brothers Massacre,* 52.

19. "Families Of Four Dead In Massacre Face Destitution," *Springfield Daily News,* January 4, 1932. It was reported that part of Crosswhite's problem in finding work was the high insurance premium that went with his "dangerous occupation."

20. *The Revised Statutes of the State of Missouri,* 1929, Chapter 73, Article 2, Section 11516.

21. "Families Of Four Dead In Massacre Face Destitution," *Springfield Daily News,* January 4, 1932.

22. "Crosswhite's Son Collapses In Jail Cell," *Springfield Press,* January 4, 1932.

23. "One Terrible Task Faced Crosswhite; Son Faced Count," *Springfield Daily News,* January 4, 1932. News of Helms' death had been phoned in to the police station; Crosswhite was summoned. "Crosswhite hung up the phone and sat staring at the wall for several minutes."

24. Maxine Hendrix McIntyre, interview with the author, April 12, 2002. Hendrix' daughter, Maxine McIntyre, remembered Mashburn as a jolly man, always smiling, with a "nice word."

25. "Mashburn Eight Years Officer," *Springfield Sunday News & Leader,* January 3, 1932.

26. Ibid.

27. Barrett and Barrett, *Young Brothers Massacre,* 48.

28. According to the *County Directory of Greene County, Missouri, 1932,* Oscar was living on forty acres rented from J. P. Pfaff.

29. Mark Sullivan, "Low Prices May Force Money Issue Forward As Main Point Of Campaign," *Springfield Sunday News & Leader,* January 3, 1932. According to Sullivan, economic forecasters had been so often wrong the past two years that "Their errors have been collected by a cynic into a book called, derisively, 'Oh, Yeah!'" Sullivan evoked the name of William Jennings Bryan: *Give silver a chance.*

30. Whereas other sources identify Oscar as a farmer, the January 4 *Daily News* ("Trail Of Slayers Leads To Texas: Find Stolen Autos") gives his occupation as "printer."

31. Orville Young, telephone interview with the author, March 28, 2002.

Chapter 12

1. The transcript of the Coroner's Inquest may be found at the Greene County Archives in Springfield, Missouri. It begins: "AT AN INQUEST; taken before Doctor Murray C. Stone, Coroner of Greene County, Missouri, at the Greene County Court Room, Springfield, Greene County, Missouri, on the 4th day of January, A.D. 1932, to inquire into the causes of death of Wiley Mashburn, Marcel Hendrix, Ollie Crosswhite, Sidney Meadows, Charles Houser and Toney [sic] Oliver, the following proceedings where had to-wit."

2. A hardware store just south of the public square, at 313-315 South Avenue to be exact.

3. "Trail Of Slayers Leads To Texas: City At Fever Heat," *Springfield Daily News,* January 4, 1932.

4. "Keep Vigil at Young's Farm," *Springfield Press,* January 4, 1932. "Black coffee played its usual part," the report continued. "The guards were given plenty of it all night long. They were also served sandwiches."

5. Farmer, "Shootout!" *Springfield News & Leader,* January 9, 1972.

6. "Police Station Is Made Center of Wild Throng," *Springfield Sunday News & Leader,* January 3, 1932. The guardsmen had been ordered to duty by Governor Caulfield.

7. "Keep Vigil," *Springfield Press,* January 4, 1932.

8. Dallas *Times-Herald,* January 3, 1932.

9. "Trail of Slayers Leads to Texas: Guards Huddle Together," *Springfield Daily News,* January 4, 1932.

10. "Trail Of Slayers Leads To Texas: City At Fever Heat," *Springfield Daily News,* January 4, 1932.

11. This was Roy "Doobie" Walker, quoted by his daughter, Shirley Walker Garton, as told to Bradley Allen Garten, authors of *The Brookline Shoot-Out,* A&J Printing, Nixa, Mo. Copyright by Bradley Allen Garton, 1996.

12. "Secret Passages in House, Belief," *Springfield Sunday News & Leader*, January 3, 1932.

13. "Curious Citizens Buzz," *Springfield Daily News*, January 4, 1932. In contrast, a posse led by Grover White reported finding several caves, each one searched thoroughly, "without trace or footsteps."

14. "Police Station," *Springfield Sunday News & Leader*, January 3, 1932. A story reported here and repeated many other places: Waddle was heard getting gruff with the governor, "This is no playhouse. Get a move on," which must have somehow released nervous tension, as the "the office rang with laughter."

15. "Harry Young Called From Kansas City? Jailer Left Puzzled," *Springfield Leader,* January 4, 1932.

16. "Families Spend Agonizing Hours Waiting Definite News Of Slain Officers," *Springfield Sunday News & Leader*, January 3, 1932. The "half-mad with grief" quote is taken from another article in the same edition, "Officers Fall Dead In Yard As Bullets Pour From House," which is itself a continuation of the Page 1 Super-headline, "SIX OFFICERS SLAIN BY FUGITIVES WHO ESCAPE TRAP AT MOTHER'S HOME."

17. The January 4, 1932, *Press* ("Willey Stopped Fire Started At Home Of Youngs") credited Willey with stamping out a fire that might otherwise have consumed the body of Sheriff Hendrix. Willey was accompanied by ex-serviceman Amos Brewer, a jail "trusty" who joined the hunt for the killers. Brewer was quoted, in the January 7, 1932, *Leader* ("Freedom For Trusty Who Helped in Hunt to Be Asked Friday"), "I went through the Argonne, I oughtn't to mind this. Besides, I'd do anything for Mr. Hendrix."

18. "Sorrowed Prisoners Ignore Opportunity For Jail Break," *Springfield Daily News,* January 4, 1932. The article continued: "The attitude of the prisoners was a source of comfort to Merl and Glenn Hendrix, youthful sons of the sheriff. 'They certainly showed a deep respect for dad,' commented Merl, who today despite his keen sorrow was helping Jailer Willey."

19. "Nab Oscar Young For Questioning; Wife Taken, Too," *Springfield Daily News,* January 4, 1932. The same edition of the paper included a first person account of the massacre by Frank Pike, who, while admitting he hadn't actually seen any of the killers, volunteered his "opinion" that "Oscar Young was there."

20. Ibid.

21. "Trace Movements of Young Family in Prolonged Grilling," *Springfield Leader,* January 4, 1932. The formal charge against Oscar and Mabel would be that of "accessory before the fact"; this was reported in the January 5 *Springfield Leader*: "Charges On Six Drawn By Nee."

22. Hull had been with the force since 1914, the department's first commissioned female officer, with responsibility for prisoners of her gender.

23. "Sisters Effort To Sell 'Hot' Car Caused Killing," *Springfield Sunday News & Leader,* January 3, 1932.

24. Nancy Nance, "Youngest Member Of Young Clan Visits In Springfield," *Springfield Press,* January 4, 1932. It may say something about the tension in the Young family that Natalie declared she liked being at Etta's better than out at the farm.

25. "Trail of Killers of Six Officers Leads to Texas," St. Louis *Post-Dispatch,* January 4, 1932.

26. "Awed Thousands Struggle for View of House of Horror Where Six Fell," *Springfield Daily News,* January 4, 1932.

27. "Trail of Slayers Leads to Texas: Pursue Fleeing Car," *Springfield Daily News,* January 4, 1932.

28. "Thousands From Many States Gather at Scene of Murders," *Springfield Press,* January 4, 1932.

29. "Where Three Trapped Fugitives Killed Six Officers of the Law," St. Louis *Post-Dispatch,* January 4, 1932.

30. "Awed Thousands Struggle For View of House of Horror Where Six Fell," *Springfield Daily News,* January 4, 1932.

31. Ibid. One of the planes was piloted by Jim Shipp of Springfield, the other had been flown down from Kansas City, courtesy of Pickwick Express.

32. Ibid.

33. "Thousands From Many States Gather at Scene of Murders," *Springfield Press,* January 4, 1932.

34. "Awed Thousands," *Springfield Daily News,* January 4, 1932.

35. "Killer Trail Leads to Texas; Search Centers at Houston," *Springfield Daily News,* January 4, 1932.

36. "Trail of Slayers Leaders to Texas: City at Fever Heat," *Springfield Daily News,* January 4, 1932.

37. Ginger Ruark, "Murderers Escape As Citizens Hastily Form Posses to Give Chase," *Springfield Press,* January 4, 1932.

38. "Trail of Slayers Leads to Texas: Posse Storms Home," *Springfield Daily News,* January 4, 1932.

39. This and the following clergy accounts are found in "Agitated

Congregations Join Ministers In Prayers For Officers' Families,"
Springfield Daily News, January 4, 1932.

40. Ibid.

41. Wayne C. Bartee, "A History of the First Baptist Church, Springfield, Missouri, 1852-1977."

42. Given the nature of the blast, this seems improbable.

43. "Frank Pike Tells His Story of How Companions Toppled," *Springfield News & Leader,* January 3, 1932.

44. "Pike Tells of Shooting," *Springfield Press,* January 4, 1932.

45. "Frank Pike Describes Bravery of Companions as They Fell," *Springfield Daily News,* January 4, 1932. Frank Pike's newspaper account is often at radical variance with his testimony before the Coroner's Jury, which will be examined later.

46. J. R. Woodside, *Young Brothers Massacre.* Nothing in the Coroner's Jury testimony of Johnson, Brown, and Bilyeu would seem to validate Pike's claim to have been at the kitchen door. Indeed, Woodside's source seems to be Brown, per reporting in the January 4, 1932, *Springfield Press.*

47. The January 3, 1932, edition of the *New York Times* ("Six Officers Killed By Desperate Band") reported a "terrific battle" waged for "two hours." Harry was described as "one of the most dangerous men in this section since the days of the James brothers and the Younger boys."

48. Edward Eddy, "The Very Idea," *Springfield Leader,* January 6, 1932.

49. Jeffrey S. King, *The Life and Death of Pretty Boy Floyd* (Kent, Ohio: The Kent State University Press, 1998). Juanita Baird Ash was seriously wounded in the gunfire, but survived, sentenced along with Rose to three years in the Kentucky State Prison. An appeals court reversed the sentence and the sisters were released after serving ten months.

50. "Ohio Police Attempt to Connect Murderer With Slayers Here," *Springfield Daily News,* January 4, 1932.

51. "Trail of Slayers Leads to Texas: Seek Notorious Killer," *Springfield Daily News,* January 4, 1932.

52. "Many Oklahoma Towns Join Search For Youngs," *Springfield Press,* January 4, 1932.

53. Floyd, convicted of a St. Louis robbery in the first degree, was sentenced to five years in the Missouri State Pen. According to prison records, he was received on December 18, 1925, and discharged March 7, 1929. He had not been a model prisoner, receiving demerits for having dope in his possession (October 18, 1927) and striking a guard (May 15, 1928).

54. "Kansas City Man Identifies Young at His Tire Shop," *Springfield*

Daily News, January 4, 1932. It was also reported, "Floyd carries two machine guns in his automobile, one of them demountable, and that he wears a steel jacket for protection."

55. "Search Ships At Sea For Desperado: Iowa Sees Them," *Springfield Daily News*, January 5, 1932.

56. "Police Keep Watch Here," *Kansas City Star,* January 4, 1932. Kansas City law enforcement, which knew a thing or two about gangsters, doubted that Harry would seek refuge in their city. According to Detective Sergeant Thomas Higgins, at least fifty area officers knew Harry by sight, therefore "it would be foolish for Young to come here to hide and that nothing he ever had done would indicate he was foolish." It strikes me as possible the quote was mangled, and Higgins was actually referring to Floyd.

57. "Search Ships At Sea For Desperado: Iowa Sees Them," *Springfield Daily News,* January 5, 1932.

58. "Trail of Slayers Leads to Texas: Find Bed of Straw," *Springfield Daily News*, January 4, 1932. Another Oklahoma report, this one from a Miami jailer, had "three men answering description of the Young brothers walking west on the highway between Seneca, Mo. and Miami as he was going to work about 5:30 o'clock this morning."

59. "Awed Thousands," *Springfield Daily News*, January 4, 1932. Turkey shoot detail offered in the *Press,* January 4, 1932: "Young Noted For His Marksmanship, Police Here Say."

60. "Oscar Young, Brother of Killers, Confesses He Owned Guns Found in Texas," *Springfield Daily News*, January 5, 1932.

61. "Barber Believes He Shaved Harry Here Last Friday," *Springfield Daily News*, January 5, 1932. John Conley, who cut hair at the Ozark Barber Shop, 413 St. Louis Street in Springfield, said Harry was "quite a talkative person," with "about a week's growth of beard" and in need of a haircut. Given Harry's hair pattern and what is usually described as a sullen demeanor, there is reason to doubt the barber's story.

62. "Trail of Slayers Leads to Texas: Six of Family Held," *Springfield Daily News*, January 4, 1932.

63. "Search Ships At Sea For Desperado: Members Oglesby Band," *Springfield Daily News*, January 5, 1932.

64. Woodside, *Young Brothers Massacre,* 55.

65. Woodside, *Young Brothers Massacre,* 56.

66. "Murder House Reveals Scene of Wild Disarray," *Springfield Leader,* January 4, 1932.

67. Beth Campbell, "The Very Idea," *Springfield Leader,* January 4, 1932.

68. "Into Every Clue," *Kansas City Star,* January 4, 1932.

69. "Trail of Slayers Leads to Texas: Motorcar Stolen From Near Here; Guns Left Behind," *Springfield Daily News*, January 4, 1932.

70. "Killer Trail Leads to Texas; Search Centers at Houston," *Springfield Press*, January 4, 1932.

71. "Trail of Slayers Leads to Texas: Pursue Fleeing Car," *Springfield Daily News*, January 4, 1932.

72. "Search Ships At Sea For Desperado: Moore Is Grilled," *Springfield Daily News*, January 5, 1932. The January 4, 1932 *Press* ("Jesse Moore Is Questioned") quoted Jesse as saying he'd spent the evening in Pleasant Hope, north of Springfield.

73. "Secret Passages," *Springfield Sunday News & Leader*, January 3, 1932.

74. "Pike Freed From Federal Prison," *Springfield Leader,* December 20, 1930.

75. Arthur Paul Moser, *A Directory of Towns, Villages and Hamlets of Missouri* (Point Lookout, Missouri: Lyons Memorial Library, 1979). Bird Eye was located in Greene County Section 30, Township 31 North, Range 22 West.

76. "Trail of Slayers Leads to Texas: Posse Storms Home," *Springfield Daily News*, January 4, 1932. At the 1930 census, Judd was married to a woman thirty years younger than himself, with four children, ages five to fourteen, at home.

77. "Wounded Detective Tells Story of Fight in Which Six Officers Were Killed," St. Louis *Post-Dispatch,* January 4, 1932.

78. G. C. Pike's raid on Judd Haguewood's place in Bird Eye is reported in "Wounded Detective Tells Story of Fight In Which Six Officers Were Killed," *St. Louis Post-Dispatch,* January 4, 1932, and "Ex-Chief Pike Heads Search For Slayers," *Springfield Press,* January 4, 1932.

79. "Ex-Chief Pike Heads Search For Slayers," *Springfield Press*, January 4, 1932.

80. "Wounded Detective Tells Story of Fight in Which Six Officers Were Killed," St. Louis *Post-Dispatch,* January 4, 1932. Waiting for something to happen, Bilyeu talked with the reporter, complaining "bitterly" about the police department's deficient weaponry, "Half of the rifles are no good. There aren't any machine guns. Those boys yesterday were fighting high powered rifles with pistols and in broad daylight, too. It's a wonder any of them got away without being killed."

81. "Trail of Slayers Leads to Texas: Posse Storms Home," *Springfield Daily News*, January 4, 1932.

82. "Ex-Chief Pike Heads Search For Slayers," *Springfield Press*, January 4, 1932.

83. The Claude Pike/Bird Eye/Young hideout scheme is reported in the following: E.A. Greenshaw, "Believe Harry Young Planned Vast Criminal Ring Near Here," *Springfield Press,* January 5, 1932.

84. Just *which* Young brother Pike was negotiating with was not shared. As reported by Greenshaw in the *Press*, "The brother, according to Pike, wanted to pay only $500 down. The rest he would pay in monthly installments, he told Pike."

85. "Senator Patterson Knew All Involved in Wholesale Murder," *St. Louis Globe-Democrat,* January 4, 1932.

86. "Crosswhite Son Is Told of Death," *Springfield Daily News*, January 4, 1932.

87. "Vigilants Organize at Thayer to Help Officers Fight Crime," *Springfield Daily News*, January 5, 1932.

88. "Trail of Killers of Six Officers Leads to Texas," *St. Louis Post-Dispatch,* January 4, 1932. The *Springfield Press*, January 4 edition, intimates that, at one point, circa eight P.M. Saturday, Waddle did make a hurried trip to the farm ("Chief Waddle Is Kept Busy"), but if that indeed happened, it was not until the house had been "stormed" and the bodies removed. I would also note that, according to the *Daily News*, January 4 ("Curious Citizens Buzz Excitement At Headquarters"), the chief's wife likewise spent Sunday night in the office, answering phones, though she did break away to take a look at the crime scene.

Chapter 13

1. I FOUND A MILLION DOLLAR BABY (IN A FIVE AND TEN CENT STORE) / BY MORT DIXON, BILLY ROSE, HARRY WARREN / Copyright 1931 (renewed) WARNER BROS. INC. and OLDE CLOVER LEAF MUSIC. All Rights Reserved. Used by permission. Warner Bros. Publication U.S. Inc. Miami, Florida.

2. *The New Handbook of Texas,* Ron Tyler, editor in chief, the Texas State Historical Society, 1996.

3. The H. H. Carroll saga is told without much variation in all the papers we've been looking at. The best single source is probably the January 4, 1932, *Houston Chronicle* headlined, "Police Comb Houston For 'Mass Slayers,'" continued on the inside pages as "Manhunt."

4. "Police Comb Houston For Mass Slayers," *Houston Chronicle,* January 4, 1932.

5. According to the 1930 census, the only A. E. Gaddy in the two-county region was Ansel E. Gaddy. Listed as a "negro," Ansel E. Gaddy was born in 1884. In 1930, this A.E. Gaddy was living with a brother-in-law in Fairfield, south of Streetman in Freestone County. Also in the small town of Fairfield was one Lila Gaddy, likewise living with a brother-in-law.

Lila, three younger than A. E., is listed as "white." There were also "white" Gaddys in Navarro County.

6. "Bloody Suspects Are Seen in Texas," *Springfield Press*, January 4, 1932.

7. "Trail of Slayers Leads to Texas: A Clue From Texas," *Springfield Daily News*, January 4, 1932.

8. "Trail of Slayers Leads to Texas: Two Guns in Car," *Springfield Daily News*, January 4, 1932.

9. "Killers Elude Texas Raiders; Gun in Stolen Car Sold Here," *Springfield Leader,* January 4, 1932.

10. "Tells of Giving Youngs a Lift," *St. Louis Post-Dispatch,* January 5, 1932.

11. "Trail of Slayers Leads to Texas: Guard Girls' Cells," *Springfield Daily News*, January 4, 1932.

12. "Trail of Slayers Leads to Texas: Women Are Questioned," *Springfield Daily News*, January 4, 1932. In another article, "Guard Houston Highways," the paper carried an Associated Press report from Houston: "Captain of Detectives Roy Young ordered 15 picked men to stand guard on the highways in all railroad stations."

13. Newspaper accounts of the raids are inexact to the point of jumbled. Our account is cut-and-paste, but must surely be pretty close.

14. Mackey's employment is identified in "Killers Elude Texas Raiders; Gun In Stolen Car Sold Here," *Springfield Leader,* January 4, 1932. The Mackey residence is described in the *Houston Chronicle* of the same date, "Sister of Youngs Wishes Name Kept Out of Papers Because of Her Church."

15. "Texas Police Spur Search; Rangers Used," *Springfield Press*, January 4, 1932.

16. "Youngs Three Times Had Escaped Posses," *Springfield Press*, January 5, 1932.

17. "Police Comb Houston For 'Mass Slayers,'" *Houston Chronicle,* January 4, 1932.

18. Ibid.

19. "Youngs Three Times," *Springfield Press*, January 5, 1932.

20. "Killer Trail Leads to Texas; Search Centers At Houston: Bulletin," *Springfield Press*, January 4, 1932. According to the *Houston Chronicle* of the same date, police took Lily Shaw to the station for questioning.

21. "Search Ships At Sea For Desperado: Trace Hunted Man to Houston Docks Where Trail Ends," *Springfield Daily News*, January 5, 1932.

22. The January 4 editions of the *Springfield Leader* "Killers Elude

Texas Raiders; Guns In Stolen Car Sold Here," and *Houston Chronicle* "Police Comb Houston For 'Mass Slayers.'" Bacon grease detail from "Young Brothers End Own Lives as Cops Trap Them in East End House," *Chronicle,* January 5, 1932.

23. "Officers Gaze on Inert Faces of Men Who Killed Six of Their Fraternity," *Houston Chronicle,* January 6, 1932.

24. "Police Comb Houston For 'Mass Slayers,'" *Houston Chronicle,* January 4, 1932.

25. Census records tell the story. In 1910, William and Sarah Calvert are living in Houston County (Lovelady is in Houston County; the city of Houston is in the county of Harris), with ten children. Five-year-old Florence is listed as eighth born, "Lillie" fifth in line. In 1920, six children remain at home, Lillie/Lily having flown the coop. In 1930, Florence is listed is listed in Harris County Enumeration District No. 101-125, living with Lily and her husband, F. F. Shaw. A few lines up on the same page of 1930 census is one Claude Walker.

26. "Police Comb," *Houston Chronicle,* January 5, 1932.

27. Ibid.

28. Ibid.

29. "Sister of Youngs," *Houston Chronicle,* January 4, 1932. Florence Mackey seems to have been quite active in the congregation. On the 6th, the *Chronicle* reported Florence liked to take her Sunday School class to the bay for parties in the summer.

30. "Search Ships at Sea For Desperado: Seek Harry's Bride," *Springfield Daily News*, January 5, 1932.

31. "Police Comb," *Houston Chronicle,* January 5, 1932.

32. "Fort Worth Police Search For Youngs," *Springfield Press*, January 4, 1932; *Springfield Daily News*, January 4, 1932; and *Fort Worth Star-Telegram,* January 5, 1932.

33. Frank Farmer, "Shootout!" *Springfield News & Leader*, January 9, 1972.

34. "Police Scour Houston For Missouri Slayer," *Fort Worth Star-Telegram,* January 5, 1932.

35. "Tulsa Police Watch For Slayer There," *Houston Chronicle,* January 3, 1932. According to an article in the January 7, 1932, *Springfield Leader,* two young men from Muskogee, Harry Thurston and Fred Newell, claimed Tulsa officers had fired at them, mistaking them for the Youngs.

36. "Close Watch Being Kept in Tillman," *Frederick Leader,* January 4, 1932. Frederick's *Leader* was a daily paper. The *Frederick Press*, a weekly, reported Harry had once worked at Frederick's Carr & Pritchard Hardware Store, but had to wait until January 8 to report it.

37. "Harry Young Eludes Armed Cops Though Recognized in City," *Houston Post-Dispatch,* January 5, 1932.

38. *Springfield Leader,* January 5, 1932. This is from a short AP report, dateline Corpus Christi, appended to the headline story "Harry Young Eludes Armed Cops Though Recognized in City."

Chapter 14

1. *The Grapes of Wrath,* 121.

2. "Trail of Slayers Leads to Texas: Two Guns in Car," *Springfield Daily News*, January 4, 1932.

3. Woodside, *The Young Brother's Massacre,* 35.

4. The Coroner's report would include an accounting of items found on the respective bodies. The five dead at the farm each carried watches on a chain.

5. "Frank Pike Describes Bravery of Companions as They Fell," *Springfield Daily News,* January 4, 1932.

6. The account that has Virgil running off the road likely originated with Pike.

7. From *The W.P.A. Guide to Missouri,* 128-29: "Fox hunting is a popular sport in central and southwest Missouri. This is not, however, the English variety, with pink-coated hunters on horseback. The sport for Missourians is not a matter of social standing, nor is the object to catch the fox. The fun consists in gathering in the woods, listening to the belling of the dogs on the trail; there is not a hunter but can distinguish the voice of his dog and know when he is leading the pack." Reprinted by permission from *Missouri: A Guide to the "Show Me" State,* © 1998 by the Missiouri Historical Society Press, St. Louis, Missouri.

8. *Houston Post-Dispatch,* January 6. Information taken from a short AP report, dateline Springfield, beneath the headline story, "Harry Young Eludes Armed Cops Though Recognized in the City." While this and other initial reports attributed the sure shooting to Harry, Dan Nee made it clear that Jennings was the marksman.

9. According to Scott Curtis' testimony to the Coroner's Jury, when Curtis first went to the hardware store looking for guns, he was, in turn, referred to the Herrick brothers, "because the Police Department knows they have some good guns."

10. "Says He Heard Slayers Leave," *Springfield Press*, January 5, 1932.

11. Frank Farmer, "Shootout!" *Springfield News & Leader*, January 9, 1972.

12. Virgil Johnson statement to the Coroner's Jury, transcript, 10.

13. Woodside, *The Young Brother's Massacre,* 39.

14. "Frank Pike Describes Bravery," *Springfield Daily News,* January 4, 1932.

15. Ibid.

16. Unless otherwise noted, I have punctuated verbatim from the transcript kept at the Greene County Archives.

17. Woodside, *The Young Brother's Massacre,* 43.

18. *Springfield Press,* January 7, 1932. Photo captioned, "Where M'Bride Shot Harry Young."

19. "Killers Elude Texas Rangers; Gun in Stolen Car Sold Here," *Springfield Leader,* January 4, 1932.

20. Woodside, *The Young Brother's Massacre,* 52. While buying into the theory that Harry and Jennings did the actual killing, Woodside was by no means persuaded they were the only persons present in the house at the time.

21. "Youngs Seen In Oklahoma?" *Springfield Press,* January 4, 1932.

22. "Trail of Slayers Leads to Texas: Find Bed of Straw," *Springfield Daily News,* January 4, 1932.

23. "Young Believed to Have Stopped at Quapaw," *Joplin Globe,* January 4, 1932. "Officers Are Convinced Slayers Have Fled from State," *Springfield Leader,* January 4, 1932.

24. "Young Believed to Have Stopped at Quapaw," *Joplin Globe,* January 5, 1932.

25. "Tracing Young Gang South," *Frederick Leader,* January 4, 1932.

26. "Young Believed to Have Stopped at Quapaw," *Joplin Globe,* January 5, 1932.

27. "Killers Elude Texas Rangers; Gun in Stolen Car Sold Here," *Springfield Leader,* January 4, 1932.

28. Reports seem about evenly divided as to whether the wound was to Harry's right or left hand, but the January 7, 1932, *Springfield Press* offers a photograph that "plainly shows the bullet wound in Harry Young's right hand" (see note 18).

29. The Model A was produced from 1928-1931. Sales declined rapidly after "Black Thursday," October 24, 1929.

30. "Bloody Suspects Are Seen in Texas," *Springfield Press,* January 4, 1932.

31. Ibid.

32. "Tracing Young Gang South," *Frederick Leader,* January 4, 1932.

33. Ibid.

34. "Tells of Giving Youngs a Lift," *St. Louis Post-Dispatch,* January 5, 1932.

35. "Killers Elude Texas," *Springfield Leader,* January 4, 1932.

Chapter 15

1. Photo, *Springfield Leader,* January 4, 1932, captioned, "First Funeral of Massacre Victims." As related in the next morning's *Daily News* ("Three

Officers Are Buried With Solemn Funeral Rites"), from the mortuary, the hearse went north to the small village of Brighton, Crosswhite's old home town, where a second service was held in a rural white frame Methodist Church. Officer Crosswhite was laid to rest in the adjacent cemetery. The *Daily News* reported, "All the living members of a baseball team with which Mr. Crosswhite played when he was a boy were at the services."

2. "Into Every Clue," *Kansas City Star,* January 4, 1932.

3. "Sorrowing Throng Pays Tribute to Crosswhite," *Springfield Leader,* January 4, 1932.

4. "Agitated Congregations Join Ministers in Prayers For Officers' Families," *Daily News*, January 4. The officiating pastor, Thomas H. Wiles, had been a busy man. Maude Oliver was a member of his congregation, Grant Avenue Baptist, and Maude Hendrix attended Sunday school there. Wiles had visited in both homes on Saturday evening and again Sunday afternoon.

5. "Killian Is Ill," *Springfield Sunday News & Leader*, January 3, 1932. As soon as Killian recovered, he was planning on preaching for the Baptists of Prospect, Missouri.

6. Mashburn was also buried at Eastlawn, which offered free plots to all the slain. "Plan Impressive Funerals for Six Slain Officers," *Springfield Daily News, January 4, 1932.*

7. *"Hendrix's Widow to Be Appointed Until Election,"* Springfield Daily News, January 4, 1932.

8. "Curtis Will Contest With Mrs. Hendrix, Political Indication," *Springfield Leader,* January 7, 1932. If the Democrats did make a race of it, the Republicans were considering endorsing Maude's brother-in-law, Lillard, which would keep the office in the family and solve the potentially sticky issue of gender.

9. "Mrs. Hendrix Is Sheriff," *Springfield Press*, January 4, 1932.

10. "Mrs. Hendrix Will Accept," *Springfield Press*, January 7, 1932.

11. "Bloodstained Divorce Paper Back to Clerk," *Springfield Daily News*, January 5, 1932. The *Press*, reporting the same story on the January 4, added, "The summons was in the divorce suit of—Well, no matter who. There's been tragedy enough."

12. T. J. Stiles, *Jesse James: Last Rebel of the Civil War* (New York: Alfred A. Knoph, 2002), 304.

13. "Offer Rewards for Murderers or Their Bodies," *Springfield Press*, January 4, 1932.

14. "Rewards for Capture of Slayers to Total Between $2500 and $3000," *Springfield Daily News*, January 5, 1932.

15. Ibid.

16. The Greene County Archives retains expenditure statements from this period.

17. "Murder House Reveals Scene of Wild Disarray," *Springfield Leader,* January 4, 1932.

18. "Suspects Linked to Store Theft at Marshfield," *Springfield Daily News*, January 4, 1932.

19. "Young Sisters Laughingly Tell of Their Love for Sport and Sewing," *Springfield Daily News,* January 5, 1932.

20. Both the city and county jails offered meals of minimal quality, which could be supplemented by individual purchase.

21. "Vinita Popular Student," *Springfield Leader,* January 5, 1932. Her typewriting teacher, Ruth Williams, had written in the book, "Remember—Look well to this day for yesterday is already a dream. Tomorrow is only a vision. But today, well spent, makes every day a vision of happiness and tomorrow a dream of hope." The teacher thanked Vinita "for all the work you've done for me."

22. "Charges on Six Drawn by Nee," *Springfield Leader,* January 5, 1932. In a related article of the same day, "Capture Climaxes Greatest Manhunt Southwest Has Known for Years," the paper tracked the killing weapons. In June of 1923, the rifle had been shipped by the Remington Arms Company in New York to McGregor Hardware in Springfield, where it was sold off the retail shelf. The shotgun, also a Remington, had been sold to Simmons Hardware in St. Louis, "which company probably sent it into this territory in a wholesale shipment."

23. "Oscar Young, Brother of Killers, Confesses He Owned Guns Found in Texas," *Springfield Daily News*, January 5, 1932.

24. The papers, in turn, showed her considerable sympathy. This note, for instance, in Monday's *Springfield Press* ("Mother Feels Youngs Will Be Captured"): "The white hair and dejected manner of the older woman is winning for her much kindness and consideration from the other women who are kept with her in the close quarters."

25. "Mother Feels Youngs Will Be Captured," *Springfield Press*, January 4, 1932.

26. "Mother Pleads for Death, Urges Sons to Kill Selves," *Springfield Daily News*, January 5, 1932.

27. Ibid.

28. Ibid.

29. As reported in the *Houston Post-Dispatch,* January 5("Mother of Killers Hopes Hunted Sons Will End Own Lives"): "She declared she had not seen Paul, however, since the apple harvest last fall when he took a load of fruit to a daughter living in Frederick, Okla."

30. "Mother of Killers Hopes Hunted Sons Will End Own Lives," *Houston Post-Dispatch,* January 5, 1932.

31. "Mother Pleads," *Springfield Daily News*, January 5, 1932.

32. Ibid.

33. Willie Florence had good reason to fear that her sons, if arrested, wouldn't last long enough to face a legal execution. The United Press Wire Service reported Ed Waddle saying that if the brothers were taken alive, they faced "almost certain lynching at the hands of irate citizens." This was printed in the Frederick, Okla., *Leader,* January 4, 1932.

Chapter 16

1. Heard: "Chief Heard Is Veteran of Many Desperado Hunts; Once Had to Kill Bandit," *Houston Chronicle,* January 6, 1932. Beverly: "Young Brothers End Own Lives as Cops Trap Them in East End House: Killers of Six Cheat Capture, as Their Mother Had Wished," *Houston Chronicle,* January 6, 1932. Stinson: ""Young Brothers End," *Chronicle.* Singleton: "Painter, Who Was Knocking on Door of Hideout, Says Cops Used Him as Shield," *Chronicle,* January 5, 1932.

2. Tomlinson's story is found in "Boy Delivering Chronicle Began Moves that Ended in Deaths of Slayers,"*Houston Chronicle,* January 6, 1932.

3. Prompting this January 6 headline: "Boy Delivering Chronicle Began Moves that Ended in Deaths of Slayers."

4. "Mother of Killers Hopes Hunted Sons Will End Own Lives," *Houston Post-Dispatch,* January 5, 1932.

5. The "leads" in this section are all reported in "Young Brothers End Own Lives As Cops Trap Them In East End House," *Houston Chronicle,* January 5, 1932.

6. "Chief Heard Is Veteran of Many Desperado Hunts; Once Had to Kill Bandit," *Houston Chronicle,* January 6, 1932.

7. "Two Youngs Lie In Morgue Side by Side," *Houston Chronicle,* January 6, 1932.

8. "Chief Heard Is Veteran of Many Desperado Hunts; Once Had to Kill Bandit," *Houston Chronicle,* January 6, 1932. Mrs. Tomlinson had gone to the house of nephew E. A. Rech, who lived a few blocks away.

9. "Besieged Brothers Who Slew Six Kill Each Other," *Houston Post-Dispatch,* January 6, 1932.

10. "Youngs Die in Suicide Pact When Trapped by Officers," *Springfield Press*, January 5, 1932.

11. McCormick reports a barrage of gas had already been laid down, but this does not jive with other accounts.

12. The McCormick reporting is found in "Reporter Risks Life to Get

Eye-Witness Story of Climax in Young's Crime Career," *Springfield Press*, January 5, 1932.

13. "Officers Gaze On Inert Faces of Men Who Killed Six of Their Fraternity," *Houston Chronicle*, January 6, 1932. As he related previous adventures to reporters from his swivel chair at the Magnolia Park police station, Beverly was chewing gum and smoking a cigarette.

14. Beverly's account is printed in "Young Brothers End Own Lives as Cops Trap Them in East End House,"*Houston Chronicle*, January 5, 1932.

15. "Painter," *Houston Chronicle*, January 5, 1932. The paper definitely numbered the gas bombs at three.

16. "Young Brothers End Own Lives," *Houston Chronicle*, January 5, 1932.

17. "Painter," *Houston Chronicle*, January 5, 1932.

18. "Chief's Story of Walking in on the Youngs," *Springfield Leader,* January 5, 1932.

Chapter 17

1. "Chief Waddle Told by Texan How Youngs Shot Each Other," *Springfield Leader,* January 5, 1932.

2. Ibid.

3. "Officers Here Telegraph Thanks to Texas Possemen," *Springfield Leader,* January 5, 1932.

4. "Visitors Barred at Jail," *Springfield Press*, January 4, 1932.

5. The *Press* needed a victory. The Saturday evening, January 2, 1932, edition was on the street when news of the massacre reached Springfield. The paper did not publish on Sunday, putting the *Press* a full forty-eight hours behind the story.

6. Surely referencing a hangman's rope, rather than a latter-day prohibited substance.

7. Nancy Nance, "Excitement Prevails as News of Youngs' Death Is Spread," *Springfield Press*, January 5, 1932.

8. "Students Desert Classes to Read of Young Deaths," *Springfield Leader,* January 5, 1932.

9. This is a synthesis of reporting from the *Springfield Leader* and *Springfield Press*, January 5, 1932.

10. "Sisters Stoically Hear Brothers Dead," *Springfield Press*, January 5, 1932.

11. "'Why Should We Cry?' Sisters Cooly Ask, at Word of Capture," *Springfield Leader,* January 5, 1932.

12. "Breaks Her Teeth," *Springfield Press*, January 5, 1932.

13.Ginger Ruark, "Mother Glad Her Two Sons Killed Selves," *Springfield Press,* January 5, 1932.

14. Beth Campbell, "Mother Sobs, Loudly Prays as Youngs Die," *Springfield Leader,* January 5, 1932.

15. "'Oh God, Oh God!' Mother of Young Boys Cries, When Told They Were Slain Here," *Houston Chronicle,* January 5, 1932.

16. Ibid.

17. "That Doesn't Bring Marcell Back to Me, Sheriff Widow Sobs," *Springfield Leader,* January 5, 1932.

18. The J. W. Klingner and Co. Funeral Directors and Embalmers, 424 E. Commercial, billed a total of $495.50. In addition to the $350 casket, the Hendrix family paid $100 for a vault, $25 for embalming, $15 for the hearse, and $5.50 for various articles of clothing, including underwear, shirt, and hose.

19. "Hundreds Pay Slain Sheriff Final Tribute," *Springfield Leader,* January 5, 1932. Five were American flags. "Other flags were those of the Legion, the Veterans of Foreign War, the Disabled Veterans, Veterans of the Spanish American War and the flag of the Legion Auxiliary."

20. "Inquest into Six Killings Monday Night," *Springfield Press,* January 4, 1932.

21. "Hundreds Pay Slain Sheriff Final Tribute," *Springfield Leader,* January 5, 1932.

22. Ibid.

23. "Pay Tributes to Sheriff," *Springfield Leader,* January 5, 1932.

24. "'He Saved Others; Himself He Could Not Save,' Dr. Hale Says in Tribute to Hendrix,"*Springfield Press,* January 6, 1932. "City's Last Tribute to Sheriff Hendrix," *Springfield Daily News,* January 6, 1932.

25. "Bitterness Can't Bring Back Dead, Mrs. Oliver Says," *Springfield Leader,* January 5, 1932.

26. "Detective Is Laid at Rest," *Springfield Press,* January 6, 1932.

27. "City's Last," *Springfield Daily News,* January 6, 1932.

28. "Benefit Fund Put Over $2,000 by Quick Work," *Springfield Leader,* January 4, 1932. The Arch McGregor link is interesting. See note 22, chapter 15.

29. "Fund for Officers' Families Is Started With $100 Pledge," *Springfield Daily News,* January 4, 1932.

30. "Right Is Right," *Springfield Press,* January 5, 1932. The one-dollar donor is reported in "Relief Fund Here Grows."

31. In 1931, Missouri's county sheriffs were paid on a fee basis. For instance, per Section 11789 of *The Revised Statutes of Missouri, 1929,* "For summoning each witness, a sheriff was allowed a fee of fifty cents."

So, when Marcell Hendrix summoned twenty-five witnesses for the 1931 grand jury, he received $12.50. Two witnesses were "non-est" (he couldn't find them), but for trying, Hendrix was paid a quarter per. "For each mile actually traveled in serving any venue summons" the prescribed fee was ten cents; Hendrix reported 195 miles and received $19.50. Fees for the one transaction totaled $32.50. (Information gleaned from records kept in the Greene County Archives.) While no honest person was likely to get rich at that rate, the fees—including a per captia rate for boarding prisoners—must have added up to an attractive proposition, for there was certainly never any shortage of candidates for the office. We'll come back to this issue in Chapter 22, but suffice to say, Sheriff Marcell Hendrix earned every nickel—a nickel being the fee for several of the transactions in Section 11789.

32. "Relief Fund Here Grows," *Springfield Press*, January 5, 1932.

33. "Drake Urges Risk Policies for Officers," *Springfield Press*, January 8, 1932.

34. "Parsons Man Says Youngs Robbed Store," *Springfield Daily News*, January 5, 1932.

35. "Rewards to Be Paid by Missouri Court," *Houston Chronicle,* January 6, 1932.

36. "Identifies Loot at Youngs' Home," *Springfield Press*, January 7, 1932.

37. "Probe Youngs' Part in Auto Theft Gang," *Springfield Press*, January 8, 1932.

38. "City's Last," *Springfield Daily News*, January 6, 1932.

Chapter 18

1. "Officers Gaze on Inert Faces of Men Who Killed Six of Their Fraternity," *Houston Chronicle,* January 6, 1932. The detail about Tomlinson doing repairs himself is found in the same edition, "Boy Delivering Chronicle Began Moves that Ended in Deaths of Slayers."

2. Ibid.

3. "Souvenir Hunters Flock to Cottage," *Springfield Leader,* January 6, 1932.

4. "Officers Gaze," *Houston Chronicle,* January 6, 1932.

5. Ibid.

6. Ibid.

7. "Crimson Chapter of Youngs Is Ended," *Springfield Daily News*, January 6, 1932.

8. Woodside, *The Young Brother's Massacre,* 71.

9. "Officers Gaze," *Houston Chronicle,* January 6, 1932.

10. As reported in the January 5 *Springfield Leader* ("Chief Waddle Told by Texan How Youngs Shot Each Other"), this was thought unlikely, due to the absence of powder burns on the bodies.

11. "Officers Gaze," *Houston Chronicle,* January 6, 1932. The paper reported that in fact a blast from Beverly's shotgun had penetrated the bathroom door "and struck Jennings Young full in the chest."

12. "Youngs Die in Suicide Pact When Trapped by Officers," *Springfield Press,* January 5, 1932.

13. "Missouri Deputy's Own Gun Avenged His Death at Hands of Harry Young," *Houston Chronicle,* January 6, 1932.

14. The pistols are currently in the possession of the Ralph Foster Museum, "the Smithsonian of the Ozarks," on the campus of the College of the Ozarks, Hollister, Missouri. Hendrix's badge is part of the collection.

15. "Coroner Certain Only Two Gunmen in Massacre Here," *Springfield Daily News*, January 7, 1932.

16. "Officers Gaze," *Houston Chronicle,* January 6, 1932.

17. "Mayor Lauds Percy Heard and Beverly," *Houston Post-Dispatch,* January 6, 1932.

18. "Young Brothers End Own Lives as Cops Trap Them in East End House," *Houston Chronicle,* January 5, 1932.

19. Barrett and Barrett, *Young Brothers Massacre,* 32. This gets a little confusing, as Vinita indicates there was a second wife, who Harry had been living with at the time of the 1929 killing in Republic—which, if true, would make Florence Calvert wife number three, assuming there weren't still more Mrs. Harrys out there. But at the time of the Republic killing, Harry had only been divorced from Frances Lee O'Dell a few weeks, and as I find no other mention of an interim spouse, I wonder if Vinita, speaking fifty years after the fact, had her women confused.

20. "Harry Young Eludes Armed Cops Though Recognized in City," *Houston Post-Dispatch,* January 5, 1932.

21. *The Grapes of Wrath,* 58.

22. "Many Charges Face Youngs in Court Here," *Springfield Daily News*, January 6, 1932.

23. "Nee Will Continue Probe of Massacre," *Springfield Press*, January 6, 1932.

24. "Nee Charges Oscar Young in Massacre," *Springfield Press*, January 5, and *Springfield Daily News*, January 7, 1932.

25. "Gideon Urges High Powered Police Rifles," *Springfield Leader,* January 5, 1932. Gideon was quoted regarding his own role: "The chief and I held off about letting the men go out to the Young place and I cautioned

them as they left and said, 'Boys, you'll have to be careful or you'll all get killed.' I drew a plat of the country for I know it well and told them how they could get up to the house in the rear and not expose themselves. If Sheriff Hendrix had waited until the gas bombs took effect I believe they could have run the men out of the house."

26. "Gideon to Buy Riot Weapons," *Springfield Press*, January 7, 1932. Among items on Gideon's shopping list was an armored car.

27. Edward Eddy, "The Very Idea," *Springfield Leader,* January 13, 1932.

28. "Drake Urges Risk Policies For Officers," *Springfield Press*, January 8, 1932.

29. "Wishes Harry Had Given Up, Mother Tells," *Springfield Leader,* January 6, 1932.

30. "Down there" refers to Houston, I assume, rather than Hades. The Baptist mother was probably referring to a last-minute confession of sin and plea for divine forgiveness. She quoted Matthew 7:7, the "he" of course, being Jesus.

31. "May Retain Mrs. Hendrix," *Springfield Leader,* January 6, 1932. As reported in the *Springfield Press* of the same date, in order to spare the cost of a primary election, candidates for the special election would be nominated at party committee meetings.

32. "Last Honor Paid Charles Houser in Church Rites," *Springfield Daily News*, January 7, 1932. The hymn is "Others."

Chapter 19

1. "Picture Gideon And Bilyeu At Home Brew Festivities," *Springfield Leader,* April 26, 1932.

2. "Officer Oliver Failed to Pay On New Policy," *Springfield Daily News*, January 6, 1932. During the brief encounter with the insurance salesman, Oliver was inspecting the magazine of his revolver, making certain the gun was loaded.

3. The Fielder story is related by Paul and Mary Barrett, *Young Brothers Massacre,* 45.

4. Frank Farmer, "Shootout!" *Springfield News & Leader*, January 9, 1972.

5. Based on photographs published in various newspapers the first week of 1932 and the Woodside pamphlet.

6. Fort Street runs north and south. Perhaps Pike and Brown took Fort south to Sunshine, then Sunshine west to Brookline.

7. Personal conversations with Mick Brown in the years 1998-2002.

8. Renee Turner, "50 Years Later, Memory of Massacre Lives On," *Springfield Sunday News-Leader*, January 3, 1982.

9. In Johnson's chronology, Oliver, Houser and Bilyeu were just now arriving "through the field from the back," an estimated five minutes having elapsed since Hendrix's car drove up the farm lane. Assuming Johnson is correct on this detail, Pike and Brown must have arrived about the time Oliver did.

10. Advertisement in the Woodside pamphlet, 21.

11. Pike puts himself at the back door with Hendrix and Mashburn. This is not how J. R. Woodside reconstructs it. Woodside has Pike in the front yard all along, positioned behind a tree when the shooting starts; his wounds suffered in the course of running away. And that's how the *Press* reported it on January 4, 1932. Did Frank betray his own story in testifying, "there was a back door around on the south-west side of the house *the way I get it*"?

12. According to "Cruel Butchery of 6 Is Pictured as Inquest Is Held, *"Springfield Daily News*, January 5, 1932, the "indication" was two quick snaps of his fingers.

13. John F. Jones, interview with the author, Springfield, May 17, 2002.

14. "Six Officers Slain by Fugitives Who Escape Trap at Mother's Home," *Springfield Sunday News & Leader*, January 3, 1932.

15. "Where Three Trapped Fugitives Killed Six Officers of The Law," *St. Louis Post-Dispatch,* January 4, 1932.

16. "Officers Here Recall Tragic Day Decade Ago When Desperate Young Brothers Killed 6 Men," *Springfield Leader and Press*, January 2, 1942.

17. "Barker Named in Young Gang, Surprising Crowd at Inquest," *Springfield Press*, January 5, 1932.

18. "Where Three Trapped Fugitives Killed Six Officers of the Law," *St. Louis Post-Dispatch,* January 4, 1932.

19. "Oren Brown Tells Story," *Springfield Press*, January 4.

20. Farmer, "Shootout!" *Springfield News & Leader*, January 9, 1972.

21. The Woodside pamphlet, 35.

22. Farmer, "Shootout!" *Springfield News & Leader*, January 9, 1972.

Chapter 20

1. "What's Wrong in the Ozarks?" *St. Louis Post-Dispatch,* January 6, 1932.

2. "Urges Reelection of Sheriffs to Curb Spreading Outlawry," *Springfield Sunday News & Leader*, January 10, 1932.

3. This is hard to figure: Whereas the Ash Grove chicken thief was sentenced to two years in the state pen, the Ash Grove bootleggers, objects of the intense January 2 dawn raid, were sentenced to just ninety days each

in the Greene County Jail! Of course, this may factor in: some of the key witnesses against the bootleggers were dead.

4. Toward this end, the Springfield PD was in the process of installing "a Police Radio Broadcasting Station to not only serve Springfield, but all towns within a radius of 75 miles." Kansas City had recently adopted the new technology with gratifying results.

5. "Lack of Zeal Cost 6 Lives?" *Springfield Press*, January 14, 1932.

6. "Learned Harry Young in Houston Months Ago," *Springfield Press*, January 8, 1932.

7. Woodside, 27. At the time of the 1932 massacre, Woodside was reporting for the *Springfield Press*. Twenty years later, he was the proprietor of Mac's Trading Post. This is gleaned from an introduction, probably written by George Olds, to a December 26, 1951, article titled, "The Farmhouse Slaughter of Six Brave Men," by Duane Yarnell, in the regional periodical *Bias*.

8. Gary Ponder, interview with the author, Ralph Foster Museum, College of the Ozarks, Hollister, Mo., April 11, 2002.

9. Woodside, *The Young Brother's Massacre,* 74.

Chapter 21

1. "Man Who Turned in Young Boys Receives Death Threat, Report," *Houston Chronicle,* January 7, 1932.

2. The telephone conversation between Willie Florence and daughter Florence Mackey is reported in "Grant Desperadoes' Wish, Prepare Graves in Texas," *Springfield Daily News,* January 7, 1932, and the evening *Leader.* The phone call was arranged by the Houston mortuary. The presence of Gladys and Mary Ellen was reported in the January 7 *Springfield Press* article, "Must Return Bodies if Young Reward Paid."

3. "Must Return Bodies if Young Reward Paid," *Springfield Press* and *Springfield Daily News*, January 7, 1932. In the *Press* version, Jan. 7, the announcement is made by Judge Sam Moore of the county court. The *Daily News* source is Presiding Judge R. A. Young.

4. "Grant Desperadoes' Wish, Prepare Graves in Texas," *Springfield Daily News*, January 7, 1932.

5. Ibid.

6. Maybe it went like this: The court, assuming the bodies would be buried in Houston, saw a way out of paying the thousand-dollar reward. In the meantime, Starne had secured Willie Florence's signature on the release form, and the daughters and daughters-in-law decided not to fight it. It seems that in Willie Florence's Wednesday afternoon long-distance telephone conversation with her daughter Florence, in which mother had

finally agreed with daughter that the burial should indeed be in Houston, Willie Florence neglected to mention Starne had already left for Texas.

7. According to the one article, Starne and the hearse had left Springfield circa 6 P.M. Tuesday, pulling into Houston at 1:30 Thursday morning. "Man Who Turned in Young Boys Receives Death Threat," *Houston Chronicle,* January 7, 1932.

8. It is interesting to peruse mortuary advertisements in the April 1931 Springfield telephone directory—part of the Bell System. In a full-page ad at the front of the directory, Herman Lohmeyer Funeral Home and Ambulance Service, Phone 33, educated would-be consumers: "Many factors must be considered before one can properly decide upon the comparative desirability of the funeral directing organizations in his community. Certainly, price alone is not enough. One should consider as well as the age of the firm, the type of equipment used, the establishment itself and the reputation of the firm in the community." Floyd Fox Funeral Home and Ambulance Service (Call 106) purchased a half-page, touting ten years of experience. J. W. Klingner & Co. also bought a half-page, boasting a chapel seating capacity of three hundred and "Pipe Organ Services Free." Alma Lohmeyer had a nice half-page ad featuring a photograph of the stately home at 534 St. Louis. The operators were Mrs. Alma Lohmeyer herself and Jewell E. Windle, Sr., who had been defeated by Murray Stone in the most recent race for the coroner's office. Thieme Funeral Home bought only a quarter-page, offering Dignity and Simplicity as the "Keynotes of Our Services." In addition to reasonable charges, Thieme offered a "Lady Assistant." But W. L. Starne had no advertisement, beyond the single line on page 36 of the "Where To Buy It Pages," the information limited to the address, 430 W. Walnut, and phone number, 752.

9. Woodside, *The Young Brother's Massacre,* 65.

10. "Desperadoes' Bodies to Be Brought Here for Private Funerals," *Springfield Leader,* January 5, 1932.

11. "Gideon Keeps Office by Majority of 887," *Springfield Daily News,* October 19, 1929. Furthermore, the January 7 *Leader* ("Continue Fight to Get Bodies of Murderers") reported Starne had gone to Texas carrying "a deputy sheriff's commission from Greene County."

12. Barrett and Barrett, *Young Brothers Massacre,* 119.

13. "Young Denies Sending Threat of Death or Killing Officers," *Houston Chronicle,* January 8, 1932. The "Young" in this headline is Paul.

14. "That Doesn't Bring Marcell Back to Me, Sheriff Widow Sobs," *Springfield Leader,* January 5, 1932.

15. E. A. Greenshaw, "Sisters Don't Want Burial Beside Dad," *Springfield Press,* January 8, 1932.

16. Willie Florence's "strange blending of grief and elation" and funeral plans are reported in "Plans Funeral of Sons," *Springfield Leader,* January 6, 1932.

17. Ibid.

18. But you want more? "There were many letters too from 'Tom,' (an) apparently slightly jealous friend of 'Brudders' in Houston, and from 'Pinkey,' a young Kansas City hotel clerk who wrote of visits and parties with Vinita in Kansas City. There were letters from traveling salesmen stopping briefly at the Kentwood Arms hotel and asking for dates or referring casually to earlier meetings. There were letters from young Springfield fraternity men whom she had known ever since her days in high school." A salesman at the Kentwood Arms wrote: "Thanks Baby for a wonderful evening and believe me when I say I'm sorry I must leave so quickly."

19. Barrett and Barrett, *Young Brothers Massacre,* 57.

20. "Youngs Plan to Sell Farm; Prefer It Be Kept as Curio," *Springfield Press*, January 7, 1932.

21. The Greenshaw interviews with Vinita and Lorena appeared in "Sisters Don't Want Burial Beside 'Dad,'" *Springfield Press*, January 8, 1932.

22. "Continue Fight to Get Bodies of Murderers," *Springfield Leader,* January 7, 1932.

23. "Oscar's Wife Released on $5,000 Bond," *Springfield Press*, January 7, 1932.

24. The allegation of intoxication and description of the Ford are from "Paul Young Is Being Trailed by Policemen," *Springfield Press,* January 6, 1932. The *Daily News*, January 7, 1932 ("Coroner Certain Only Two Gunmen in Massacre Here"), suggested "the report originated when two sisters and a brotherinlaw of the Young brothers, from Frederick, Okla., stopped at the farm to view the ravages of the massacre on their mother's home and then drove into Springfield to visit the aged mother."

25. "Bodies of Youngs Will Arrive Here by Hearse Today," *Springfield Daily News*, January 9, 1932.

26. "Seek Paul Young at Houston," *Springfield Press*, January 7, 1932.

27. The Paul Young surrender is reported in the January 8, 1932, *Houston Chronicle* ("Young Denies Sending Threat of Death Or Killing Officers"), with this interesting note, "Young was arrested 10 days ago by officers working out of the West End police station and was charged at that time with carrying a pistol and with driving an automobile with wrong license plates."

28. Woodside, *The Young Brothers Massacre,* 16.

29. "Nee asks Houston to Hold Paul Young," *Springfield Press*, January 8, 1932.

30. "Young Burial Plans Balked," *Houston Post-Dispatch,* January 10, 1932.

31. "Bodies of Youngs Will Arrive Here by Hearse Today," *Springfield Daily News*, January 9, 1932. According to the January 8 *Leader* ("No Violence, Six Widows Plead, When Slayers' Bodies Arrive"), Starne had apparently tried to deceive reporters by announcing a return route via Shreveport, Louisiana.

32. "Hearse Carrying Bodies of Slain Desperadoes Passes Through Here, Headed North," *Denison Daily Herald,* January 8, 1932.

33. "Bodies of Youngs," *Springfield Daily News*, January 9, 1932.

34. "Halt Return of Young Bodies," *Springfield Press*, January 9, 1932.

35. "Keep Young Bodies Hidden; Relatives to Other Jails," *Springfield Leader,* January 9, 1932. In an attempt to confuse would-be troublemakers, Starne had taken the company name plate off the hearse. According to Paul and Mary Barrett (*Young Brothers Massacre,* 119), Starne was quoted as saying the wives of the deceased, also en route from Houston to Springfield, had caught up with the hearse and signed off on the delay.

36. "Curious Crowd Vainly Waits at Empty Grave for Youngs," *Springfield Daily News*, January 11, 1932.

37. "No Violence, Six Widows Plead, When Slayers' Bodies Arrive," *Springfield Leader*, January 8, 1932.

38. Ibid.

39. "Bodies of Youngs Will Arrive Here by Hearse Today," *Springfield Daily News*, January 9, 1932.

40. "Curious Crowd Vainly Waits at Empty Grave for Youngs," *Springfield Daily News*, January 11, 1932.

41. The January 13 edition of the *Leader* includes a photograph of "relatives of the Young brothers" digging the grave, under the caption, "Grave Diggers' Work at Ozark Proves Needless."

42. "Young Burial Plans Still Are Mystery," *Springfield Press,* January 11, 1932.

43. "Curious Crowd," *Springfield Daily News*, January 11, 1932.

44. "Young Burial Plans," *Springfield Press,* January 11, 1932

45. E. A. Greenshaw, "Weird Funeral For Youngs," *Springfield Press*, January 13, 1932.

46. Beth Campbell, "Mother Sobs Only Requiem for Two Men," *Springfield Leader,* January 13, 1932.

47. "Keep Young Bodies Hidden; Relatives to Other Jails," *Springfield Leader,* January 9, 1932.

48. "Curious Crowd," *Springfield Daily News*, January 11, 1932.

49. "Young Burial Plans," *Springfield Press*, January 11, 1932.

50. "Guard Maintained Over Young Graves," *Springfield Press*, January 14, 1932.

51. The community memorial service is described at length in "City, County. State Join in Memorial to Officers," *Daily News,* January 11, 1932. Governor Caulfield took what sounds like a swipe at prohibition, bemoaning "petty violations" of laws "not made for normal men and women," diverting the attention and resources of police. The governor was, in fact, a proponent of repeal. As reported in the *Springfield Daily News*, April 20, 1932, Caulfield told a gathering of the New England Society of St. Louis that prohibition was "fundamentally wrong—not wrong in purpose, but wrong governmentally."

52. "Lone Guard Watches Youngs' Graves/Little Fear of Desecration Is Held," *Joplin Globe,* January 14, 1932.

53. "Grim incidents as Bodies Are Fleetingly Displayed," *Springfield Leader,* January 13, 1932.

54. Greenshaw, "Weird Funeral," *Springfield Press*, January 13, 1932.

55. "Officers Guard as Desperados Buried at Joplin," *Springfield Daily News*, January 14, 1932. The *Daily News* termed the proceeding "doleful."

56. "Lone Guard Watches Youngs' Graves/Little Fear of Desecration Is Held," *Joplin Globe,* January 14, 1932.

57. Whereas other members of the Bixby team, male and female, wrote under pseudonyms, Beth Campbell seems to have in fact been Beth Campbell. She would later edit the paper's religion page. In a 1951 master's thesis, Dean Frank Rea would tell this story: "In one of her columns she stated that the sermons preached in Springfield churches were not too inspiring, and that she could preach a better sermon herself. A preacher challenged her, and a large crowd turned out one Sunday morning to hear her reply from the pulpit."

58. "Youngs Are Buried at Joplin!" *Springfield Leader,* January 13, 1932.

59. Ibid.

60. Greenshaw, "Weird Funeral," *Springfield Press*, January 13, 1932. "Harry Boy" quote from *Springfield Daily News,* January 14, 1932.

61. Ibid. While it appears the other living brothers and sisters were in attendance, the papers make no mention of Jarrett's presence. According to the January 5 *Houston Post-Dispatch,* the eldest of the Young brothers was married and living in Stuttgart, Arkansas. A fascination with automobiles must have run in this family; Jarrett was reported making his living as a car salesman.

62. Beth Campbell, "Mother Sobs Only Requiem for Two Men," *Springfield Leader,* January 13, 1932.

63. "Lone Guard," *Joplin Globe,* January 14, 1932.

64. Ibid.

65. Campbell, "Mother Sobs," *Springfield Leader,* January 13, 1932.

66. Ibid.

67. Greenshaw, "Weird Funeral," *Springfield Press*, January 13, 1932.

68. "Lone Guard," *Joplin Globe,* January 14, 1932.

69. "Police Benefit Show Pleases Large Crowd," *Springfield Press*, January 14, 1932.

70. "'Pretty Boy' Floyd Named as Raider in Bank Robbery," *Springfield Press,* January 14, 1932.

Chapter 22

1. I cannot help but wonder where Lewis M. Hale was in all of this. At the Houser funeral, Hale had reminded mourners, "There are those who will live their loss over every day—they have made the greatest sacrifice, they have paid the dearest price." Augusta clearly fit into this category. Yet, in her time of crisis, there seems to have been no one to publicly defend her, including Reverend Hale. One exception was Mrs. Ed Waddle. According to the *Leader,* the chief's wife "happened to view the marriage certificate a few months ago when she was at Mrs. Houser's home."

2. "Curtis Names New Deputies," *Springfield Press*, January 30, 1932. Jailer Willey would also be ousted.

3. Ibid.

4. "That Funeral Scene," *Springfield Press*, January 14, 1932.

5. "'I'll Never Go Back to Wife,' Starne Says After Divorce Denied," *Springfield Press*, January 28, 1932.

6. "Starne Seeks Young Reward," *Springfield Press*, January 15, 1932.

7. Ibid.

8. "Young Reward Claims Filed for 4 Texans," *Springfield Press*, January 21, 1932.

9. "Continue Fight to Get Bodies of Murderers," *Springfield Leader,* January 7, 1932.

10. "Rewards to Be Paid by Missouri Court," *Houston Chronicle,* January 6, 1932.

11. In a letter dated August 18, 1985, Paul Barrett refers to his vain attempt to find any record of the distribution of reward funds.

12. "Probe Big Car Theft Rings," *Springfield Press*, January 28, 1932.

13. Transcript of Criminal Procedure, State of Missouri, #97187.

14. "Oscar Young Held to Trial," *Springfield Press*, January 27, 1932.

15. "Great Crowd Jams Hearing of Mrs. Young," *Springfield Leader,* February 3, 1932.

16. Ibid.

17. "Police Told Killer Seen on Square," *Springfield Press*, February 9, 1932. On this date in history, Will Rogers returned from a world cruise, famously remarking he was the only American to ever visit Cairo without seeing the Sphinx: "I thought it was unnecessary. I've seen Coolidge."

18. Frank Farmer, "Shootout!" *Springfield Sunday News & Leader*, January 9, 1972.

19. "Seek Paul Young and Mother on Car Theft Charges," *Springfield Press*, February 18, 1932.

20. "Paul Young Held by U.S. Officers for Auto Thefts," *Springfield Daily News*, February 20, 1932.

21. "Distributes Relief Fund to Families," *Springfield Press*, February 20, 1932. "Mrs. Houser Gets Nothing as Fund Paid," *Springfield Leader,* February 20, 1932.

22. "Few Remember Massacre Date," *Springfield Leader & Press*, January 2, 1936.

23. "Life in Prison to Crosswhite and Pal Seen," *Springfield Leader,* February 19, 1932. "Just think of it," said his mother, "he's only 19."

24. "Rev. Hale Criticizes Editorial; Views of Jenkins Follow It," *Springfield Daily News*, March 7, 1932.

25. "Waddle Says Cops Responsible in Gideon Defeat, They Blame Him," *Springfield Daily News*, March 23, 1932. According to information included in his obituary (January 15, 1945, *Springfield Leader and Press*), Waddle relocated to Kansas City. Despite suffering three strokes in his last three years of his life, Ed Waddle was on the roster of the Kansas City Police Department at the time of his passing.

26. "Paul Young Gets Four Year Term, Mother Is Freed," *Springfield Daily News*, April 6, 1932.

27. "Further Police Squad Changes Is Frey's Plans," *Springfield Daily News*, April 19, 1932. In a classic case of "What have you done for us lately," the paper added that Johnson was said to be "unpopular in the department." Like Frank Pike, Virgil would eventually rotate back on to the Springfield PD. In a January 25, 1999 *News-Leader* article, veteran reporter Hank Billings recalled Johnson coming to Boyd School "to talk to the schoolboy patrolmen about pedestrian crossing safety." This would have been some six years after the massacre. Billings remembered that Johnson "drove a white safety car with a loudspeaker. He used it to exhort all drivers to 'watch out for the li'l children' and to single out embarrassed offenders for all to see."

28. "She Knew Gideon as 'Jack Wilson' on Brew Parties," *Springfield Daily News*, April 26, 1932.

29. "Bilyeu Draws 2-Year Term in U.S. Prison," *Springfield Press*, April 26, 1932.

30. "Gideon Trial Is Postponed Until April," *Springfield Press*, January 14, 1932.

31. "Gideon Jury Fails to Agree," *Springfield Daily News*, April 21, 1932.

32. Ethel Strainchamps, "Citizen of the Week," *Bias,* April 6, 1951.

33. "Death to Colorful Thomas H. Gideon," *Springfield Leader-Press*, February 13, 1959.

34. Circuit Court, Greene County, Criminal Record, Book 29, 318.

35. Orville Young, telephone interview with the author, March 28, 2002.

36. As previously mentioned in Chapter 17, note 29, county law enforcement was largely an entrepreneurial enterprise. Steinbeck addressed the issue in *The Grapes of Wrath:* "Sheriff gets seventy-five cents a day for each prisoner, an' he feeds 'em for a quarter. If he ain't got prisoners, he don't make no profit." In Hendrix's case, the specific issue seems to have been the definition of a court appearance. Was he to receive a fee for every day the county court was in session, or only those days when he himself was actually in court?

37. "Give Ruling On Salaries," *Springfield Press*, January 5, 1932.

38. "Payment of $1033 Settles $9372 Hendrix Estate Bill," *Springfield Leader,* June 5, 1933.

39. "Joining of Leader And Press to Make a Better Newspaper," *Springfield Leader-Press*, May 15, 1933.

Chapter 23

1. The January 10, 1932, *Sunday News & Leader* offered half a page of such odes under the heading, "Slain Officers' Heroism inspires Poems of Praise," including one written by young Elmo Ingenthron, whose books *Baldnobbers* and *Border Rebellion* have served as resources for this manuscript.

2. Maxine Hendrix McIntyre, interview with the author, April 12, 2002. It didn't help that the Frisco tracks passed within yards of her bedroom. Friends coming to visit had a tough time sleeping.

3. Ibid. Maude was buried beside Marcell, near Sidney Meadows and Wiley Mashburn, in Eastlawn Cemetery's Section 3, otherwise knows as the "Garden of Tranquility."

4. Some of the Parker material is from an article by Brian C. Hammer in *The Handbook of Texas Online,* the Texas State Historical Association, 1997-2002.

Bibliography

Bande, William L., and Harry T. Brundidge. *The Inside Story of the Kidnapping and Murder of Baby Lloyd Keet.* Springfield, Mo.: Webster Publishing Company, 1918.

Barrett, Paul W., and Mary H. Barrett. *Young Brothers Massacre.* Columbia and London: University of Missouri Press, 1988.

Bartee, Wayne C. *A History of the First Baptist Church, Springfield, Missouri, 1852-1977.* Self-published.

Brinkley, Douglas. *Wheels for the World: Henry Ford, His Company, and a Century of Progress.* New York: Viking Penguin, 2003.

Christian County, Mo. History and Families. Paducah, Ky.: Turner Publishing Company, 1998.

Christian County: Its First 100 Years. Ozark, Mo: The Christian County Centennial Inc., 1959.

Clark, Norman C. *The Dry Years: Prohibition and Social Change in Washington.* Seattle: University of Washington Press, 1965.

Cravens, Chris. *Streetman, Texas: The New Handbook of Texas.* Ron Tyler, ed. Streetman: The Texas State Historical Society, 1996.

Daniels, Jonathan. *The Time Between the Wars.* New York: Doubleday and Company, 1966.

A Diamond Jubilee History of Tillman County, 1901-1976. Tillman County Historical Society, 1976.

Fairbanks, Jonathan, and Clyde Edwin Tuck. *Past and Present of Greene County, Missouri.* Indianapolis: A. W. Bowen & Company, 1915.

Faulkner, William. *Light In August.* New York: The Modern Library, 1950.

Flanders, Robert. "The Haseltine Orchards Historic Area." *OzarksWatch* 9, no. 1 (1996).

Garton, Shirley Walker. *The Brookline Shoot-Out: America's Bloodiest Massacre by Shirley Walker Garton as told to Bradley Allen Garton.* Nixa, Mo.: A. & J. Printing, 1996.

Gordon, Ernest. *The Wrecking of the 18th Amendment.* Francestown, N.H.: The Alcohol Information Press, 1943.

Hammer, Brian C. *Quanah Parker.* The Handbook of Texas Online. The Texas State Historical Association, 1997-2002.

Hartman, Mary, and Elmo Ingenthron. *Bald Knobbers: Vigilantes on the Ozarks Frontier.* Gretna, La: Pelican Publishing Company, 1996.

Holcombe, R. I., ed. *History of Greene County, Missouri.* Clinton, Mo.: Printery, 1969. Originally published by the Western Historical Society in 1883.

Honor Roll of Greene County, Missouri: An illustrated historical biography compiled from private and public authentic records. Chicago: Faithorn Company, G. R. Collins, 1919.

Hultsch, E. *Authentic Story of Claud Piersol, the Kidnapper.* Springfield, Mo.: Hultsch Publishing, 1918.

Ingenthron, Elmo. *Borderland Rebellion.* Branson, Mo.: The Ozarks Mountaineer, 1980.

King, Jeffrey S. *The Life and Death of Pretty Boy Floyd.* Kent, Ohio: The Kent State University Press, 1998.

Larson, Edward J. *Summer for the Gods: The Scopes Trial and America's Continuing Debate Over Science and Religion.* Cambridge and London: Harvard University Press, 1997.

Lederer, Katherine. "Indian Annie." *OzarksWatch* 11, no. 3-4 (1998).

Missouri: A Guide to the 'Show Me' State. Compiled by Workers of the Writers' Program of the Work Projects Administration in the State of Missouri. Sponsored by the Missouri State Highway Department. New York: Duell, Sloan, and Pearce, 1941.

Moser, Arthur Paul. *A Directory of Towns, Villages and Hamlets of Missouri.* Point Lookout, Mo.: Lyons Memorial Library, 1979.

O'Connor, Richard. *Wild Bill Hickok.* Stamford: Longmeadow Press, 1987.

Oklahoma: A Guide to the Sooner State. Compiled by the Workers of the Writers' Program of the Works Project Administration in the State of Oklahoma. Norman: University of Oklahoma Press, 1941.

Pictorial and Genealogical Record of Greene County, Missouri: together with biographies of prominent men of other portions of the state, both living and dead. Chicago: Goodspeed Brothers, 1893.

Pike, Frank. "I Survived Missouri's Posse Massacre." *Startling Detective Adventures Magazine.* Robbinsdale, Minn.: Fawcett Publications, undated.

Piston, William Garrett, and Richard W. Hatcher, III. *Wilson's Creek: The Second Battle of the Civil War and the Men Who Fought It.* Chapel Hill and London: The Univeristy of North Carolina Press, 2000.

Rea, Dean Frank. *A History of the*Springfield (Mo.) Leader and Press,*1867-1950.* Unpublished master's thesis, 1951.

Redding, William M. *Tom's Town.* Columbia: University of Missouri Press, 1986.

Reiner, G. K. "Prohibition Comes To Missouri, 1910-1919." *Missouri Historical Review* 62, no. 4 (1968).

Republic, Missouri: Home of 3,000 Good Neighbors. Republic Historical Society, 1971. Reprinted by Greene County Archives and Records Center, 2001.

Schulz, Darrell. "Springfield's Crime of the Century." *Gateway Heritage* 23, no. 4 (2003).

Shannon, David. *The Great Depression.* Englewood Cliffs, N.J.: Prentice-Hall, Inc., 1960.

Sibley, Marilyn M. *Houston Ship Channel.* The Handbook of Texas Online. The Texas State Historical Association, 1997-2002.

Skousen, Mark. *Did the Gold Standard Cause the Great Depression?* www.libertyhaven.com. Copyright 2000-2001 by the LibertyHaven Foundation.

Souvenir Review of the Department of Police, City of Springfield, Missouri, 1932. Springfield, Mo.: Allied Printing, 1932.

Stevens, Walter. *Missouri, the Center State, 1821-1915.* Vol. 3. Chicago and St. Louis: The S. J. Clarke Publishing Company, 1915.

Stiles, T. J. *Jesse James: Last Rebel of the Civil War.* New York: Alfred A. Knoph, 2002.

Strainchamps, Ethel. "Citizen of the Week." *Bias* 1, no. 47 (1951).

Timberlake, James H. *Prohibition and the Progressive Movement, 1900-1920.* New York: Atheneum, 1970. Copyright 1963 by the president and fellows of Harvard College.

Wallis, Michael. *Route 66: The Mother Road.* New York: St. Martin's Press, 1990.

Wilson, Charles Morrow. *The Commoner: William Jennings Bryan.* Garden City: Doubleday & Co., 1970.

Winter, Robert. *Mean Men: The Sons of Ma Barker.* Danbury, Ct.: Rutledge Books, 2000.

Woodside, John R. *The Young Brothers Massacre.* Springfield, Mo.: Springfield Publishing Company, 1932.

Yarnell, Duane. "The Farmhouse Slaughter of Six Brave Men." *Bias* 2, no. 33 (1951).

——. "At the End of the Massacre Trail." *Bias* 2, no. 34 (1952).

Newspapers

Ash Grove Commonwealth, 7 January 1932.

Christian County Republican, 17 December 1918.

Dallas Times-Herald, 3 January 1932.

Denison Daily Herald, 8 January 1932.
Fort Worth Star-Telegram, 3 January 1932.
Frederick Leader, 4 January 1932.
Frederick Press, 8 January 1932.
Houston Chronicle, 3 January-8 January 1932.
Houston Post-Dispatch, 5 January-10 January 1932.
Joplin Globe, 5 and 14 January 1932.
Kansas City Star, 4 January 1932
Missouri Weekly Patriot, 10 August 1865.
Republic Monitor, 6 June 1929.
St. Louis Globe-Democrat, 4 January 1932.
St. Louis Post-Dispatch, 3 January-5 January 1932.
Springfield Daily News, 17 April-18 April 1928; 19 June 1928; 18 July-31
    July 1928;
1 January-2 January 1929; 10 September-19 October 1929; 21 September-
    18 October 1930; 29 January 1931; 4 January-14 January 1932; 20
    February 1932; 7 March 1932; 23 March 1932; 6 April-26 April 1932.
Springfield Leader, 14 April 1924; 7 February 1927; 8 April 1928; 2
    November-9 November 1928; 31 December 1928; 3 June-6 June 1929;
    14 October 1929; 21 November 1929; *19 December 1929; 11 April
    1930; 11 October-17 October 1930; 20 December 1930; 28 January
    1931; 2 April 1931; 1 January 1932-3 February 1932; 26 April 1932;
    5 January 1933; 5 June 1933.*
Springfield Sunday News & Leader, 21 March 1928; 11 November 1928;
    3 January 1932; 10 January 1932.
Springfield Leader & Press, 15 May 1933; 2 January 1936; 2 January
    1942; 20 August 1958; 13 February 1959.
Springfield News-Leader, 27 September 1959; 9 January 1972.
Springfield Press, 3 June 1929; 12 October-19 October 1929; 16 April
    1930; 7 June 1930; 28 January 1931; 21 May 1931; 11 February 1931;
    24 February 1931; 26 December 1931-18 February 1932.
Springfield Republican, 4 February-8 February 1917, 15 April 1924.

Archives

Anderson History Room, Christian County Library, Ozark, Missouri.
Christian County Recorder's Office, Ozark, Missouri.
Greene County Archives, Springfield, Missouri.
Greene County Recorder's Office, Springfield, Missouri.
History Museum for Springfield-Greene County, Springfield, Missouri.
Lawrence County Recorder's Office, Mt. Vernon, Missouri.
Missouri State Archives, Jefferson City, Missouri.
Ralph Foster Museum, College of the Ozarks, Hollister, Missouri.

Springfield Police Dept. Museum, "The Calaboose," Springfield Missouri.

State Historical Society of Missouri, Columbia, Missouri.

Shepard Room, Springfield-Greene County Library, Springfield, Missouri.

Texas and Local History Collection, Houston Public Library, Houston, Texas.

Republic Museum, Republic, Missouri.

Tillman County Historical Museum, Frederick, Oklahoma.

Tillman County Recorder's Office, Frederick, Oklahoma.

Web sites

www.ci.springfield.mo.us/spd/history.html. "A History of the Springfield Police Department." Springfield Police Department, 2001.

www.rootsweb.com/~oktillma/history.html. County Information for Tillman County. Oklahoma Department of Commerce. Revised May 2000.

www.paperlessarchives.com. FBI FILES/Ma Barker/Karpis Gang.

http://goodies.freeservers.com/quanah.html. "Quanah Parker."

www.blackmaskmagazine.com/bm_13.html. "The 17 Detective Magazines." From *Writer's Digest,* April 1930. *Black Mask Magazine.* Entire Web site %c Keith Alan Deutsch 2000, 2002.

www.tsha.utexas.edu/handbook/online/. The Handbook of Texas Online.